P9-DWE-058

FIRE
IN MY
BELLY

FIRE
REAL COOKING
IN MY
KEVIN GILLESPIE
WITH DAVID JOACHIM   **PHOTOGRAPHY BY ANGIE MOSIER**
BELLY

Andrews McMeel
Publishing, LLC

Kansas City · Sydney · London

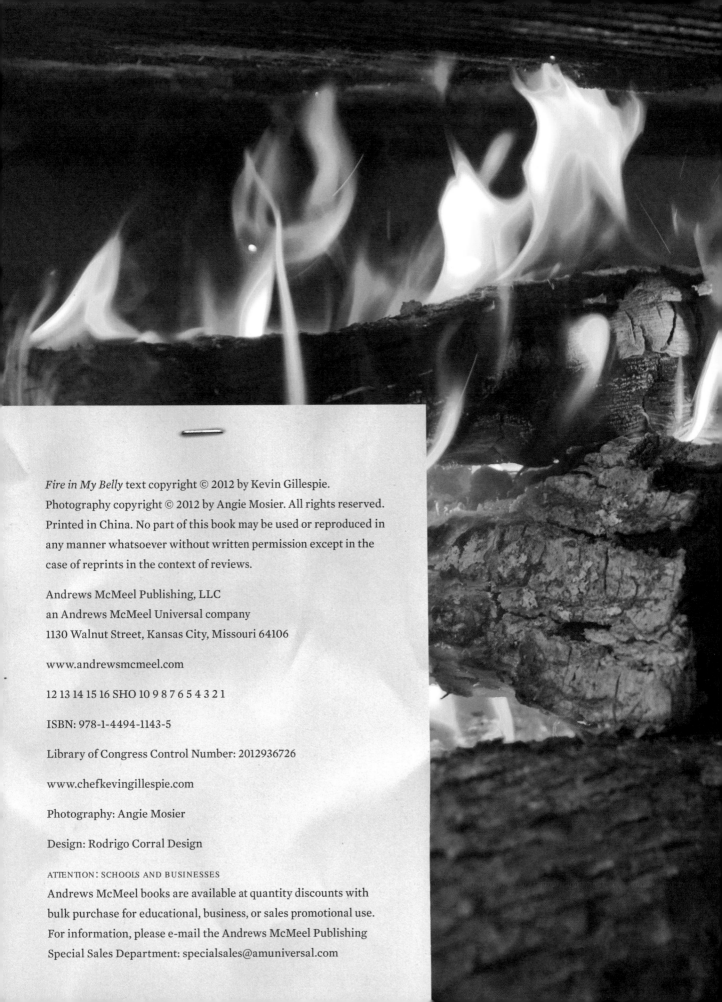

Andrews McMeel Publishing, LLC
an Andrews McMeel Universal company
1130 Walnut Street, Kansas City, Missouri 64106

www.andrewsmcmeel.com

12 13 14 15 16 SHO 10 9 8 7 6 5 4 3 2 1

ISBN: 978-1-4494-1143-5

Library of Congress Control Number: 2012936726

www.chefkevingillespie.com

Photography: Angie Mosier

Design: Rodrigo Corral Design

ATTENTION: SCHOOLS AND BUSINESSES
Andrews McMeel books are available at quantity discounts with
bulk purchase for educational, business, or sales promotional use.
For information, please e-mail the Andrews McMeel Publishing
Special Sales Department: specialsales@amuniversal.com

I dedicate this book to all the amazing women in my life. For those who are here today and those who live on in my memories, it's your strength that reminds me of what true greatness looks like.

CONTENTS

INTRO-DUCTION
page ix

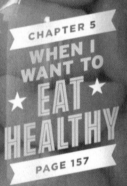

I caught the chef bug at a young age, and my family got behind me 100 percent.

WHAT DRIVES ME TO COOK

OPPOSITE TOP:
Sunshine Circle,
Locust Grove,
Georgia—
home to lots of
Gillespies.

OPPOSITE BOTTOM:
Mom, Dad, and
Granny.

My aunt Lynn named our street Sunshine Circle. Before that, it was just a dirt road in Locust Grove, Georgia. My granny moved there in the 1970s from the mountains near Walhalla, South Carolina. She tried to re-create what her generation had in the mountains—an extended but close-knit family all living together on a big stretch of land. My uncle Clint and his wife, Lynn, bought the lot next door; my aunt Debbie and her husband settled across the road; and my mom and dad bought the piece of land at the end of the road.

I grew up with nine cousins, all within five years of age and 500 yards of each other. Our parents worked in and around Atlanta. Granny took care of the kids. My mom cooked as much as she could, but like most working parents, she didn't have a lot of time. Granny woke up at the crack of dawn to cook one meal, clean it up, and then start cooking the next. She made it possible for the whole family to sit down and share meals together every day.

Sometime in the fifth grade, I decided someone else in the family should know how to cook. I caught the chef bug at a young age, and my family got behind me 100 percent. Granny let me help out in the kitchen, and she turned on PBS cooking shows. My grandmother on my mother's side bought me cookbooks from TV chefs like Emeril Lagasse and encouraged me to step outside my comfort zone instead of just cooking the food I grew up with. Uncle Richard took me to fancy restaurants. He has a cable company with job sites all over the country. We went to Emeril's in New Orleans; ate Mexican food in Phoenix and Tucson; had fresh fish in Oregon; and dined in Atlanta's best restaurants, like Bacchanalia and Pano's and Paul's. Uncle Richard thought nothing of buying me a whole rib eye to cook with. He ate all of my cooking experiments.

Eventually, I had to tell my parents that I didn't want to be an engineer. I was terrified to talk to them about it. But my mom didn't bat an eyelash. "I'm so glad you know now who you want to become," she said. "You could waste a lot of your life trying to figure that out."

Instead of going to MIT, I went to culinary school.

OPPOSITE: Sautéing with the "washing machine method" at Woodfire Grill.

I got a scholarship to the Massachusetts Institute of Technology (MIT). Instead of going to MIT, I went to culinary school at the Art Institute of Atlanta and helped pay for it with a scholarship I won in a national cooking competition. After a few years of working in Atlanta's top restaurants, I needed a change of scenery and moved to Portland, Oregon. Portlanders are militantly seasonal in their cooking. That was how Granny always cooked, and I was immediately drawn to it. Out there, my appreciation for fresh, high-quality ingredients grew deeper. When I moved back to Atlanta, I took over the kitchen at Woodfire Grill, one of the city's leading farm-to-table restaurants. Since then, my main focus has been on cooking with ingredients available in and around Georgia at any given time of the year. When the seasons change, the dishes change. I cooked the same way when I competed on Bravo TV's *Top Chef*. I created dishes on the spot based on what was available to us at that time of year. I firmly believe that good cooking starts with good ingredients. I would even argue that cooking is, at its root, figuring out the great qualities of any food and then making those qualities shine.

That's the philosophy behind the recipes in this book. I created most of them from scratch. This is not a chef's book crammed with difficult dishes; there are only a handful of recipes from Woodfire Grill, like the sage-battered mushrooms with cheddar fonduta and candied garlic syrup (page 32). That dish might sound fancy, but the ingredients are available everywhere, and it's not hard to make. Tomate frito (page 312) is another one from the restaurant. It's my single most-requested recipe, and I finally wrote it down.

Just about everything else here was developed specifically for home cooks. There's a huge range of recipes—everything from World Classics Revisited (page 109) to Junk Food (page 255). I eat all kinds of food. When creating the recipes, I let my taste buds guide me. Sometimes I folded in a flavor memory from a dish I tasted somewhere at some point. But mostly, I tried to amplify and balance the taste of the ingredients themselves. In writing the recipes, my goal was to get you to do the same thing on your own, to encourage you to really start cooking instead of just following a recipe.

REAL COOKING

I firmly believe
that good cooking starts
with good ingredients.

Real cooking is flying by the seat of your pants. It's finding some inspiration among the ingredients in front of you or your favorite techniques and putting them together to make something good to eat.

That's why I did away with some of the old ways of writing a recipe. Instead of writing "1 cup chopped onions," I wrote things like "Onion—1 baseball-size, chopped." That simple switch puts the ingredient first and the measurement second—the right order of things, if you ask me. It gets you to think more like a chef. Likewise, I didn't just write a list of cooking instructions. I tried to explain here and there why you do things a certain way. These little explanations help you become a better cook.

But maybe you don't care about cooking better. Maybe you just want something completely delicious to eat. You'll find that here too. These recipes—and the whole book, for that matter—are a direct result of my dreaming up delicious things that I couldn't help but share with my family and friends, and now with you. That's what drives me to cook. That's the fire in my belly.

Spargeltoast mit Schinken

500 g gekochter/frischer Spargel

Für den Kräuterquark:
250 g Quark
4 el Sahne
Salz
Zucker

1/4 gemahl. weißer Pfeffer
je 1 El gehackter Schnittlauch
und Petersilie

Den Quark mit der Sahne den Salz
Zucker, Pfeffer, Schnittlauch und
Petersilie verrühren.
Für den toast: 4 Scheiben toastbrot
aus butter, 4 Salatblätter,
4 Scheiben gekochter Schinken

My old recipe book.
This is a recipe for a
white asparagus dish
written in German

1

WHAT I MEAN WHEN I SAY . . .

A couple years ago at Woodfire Grill, we were serving a carrot dish that was made at the cold station in the restaurant kitchen. At that time, a cook named John was at the station, and he was responsible for making the dish. It was an exploration of carrot with four different components: a cold carrot broth, a carrot gelée, baby carrots, and a carrot sauce. This was a technical dish that was difficult to execute. The components needed to be served on the same plate but at slightly different temperatures so the flavors would come across properly. This was right after *Top Chef* Season 6 had aired, so the restaurant was getting busy, and I was fielding a lot of calls. I quickly summed up for John why he needed to constantly move the sauce from the oven to the cold station to maintain the correct temperature of the sauce. I remember saying, "It needs to be just above 'below room temperature.'" That's a crazy-ass way of putting it, but the phrase made perfect sense to me.

It was getting colder in the kitchen because winter was coming on, and even with the burners and fryers cranked up, the room temperature was somewhat cold. Below room temperature would have been too cold, but at just a few degrees higher than below room temperature, the sauce was perfect. After hearing me speak that phrase, John looked at me like I had three heads. I was too busy to explain it further. I walked away to let him figure it out.

Throughout my career, one thing that's made me successful is my ability to clearly communicate. I have, however, come to the realization that some phrases I think are perfectly clear may not be so clear to others. I have a million thoughts running through my head, and sometimes when I speak, I'm only saying the twelfth sentence of what was actually a complete articulated thought in my head. But sentences one through eleven, the ones that really help to explain what I mean, never get spoken. As a result, I've become known for a kind of shorthand "Kevin-speak" in the kitchen.

My chef de cuisine, E.J. Hodgkinson, has gotten pretty good at understanding Kevin-speak and reading my mind. But I realize that the terminology I use may not be familiar to everyone. Here's a thorough explanation of what I mean when I say things like *balance, buried, cut like a whole vegetable, GBD, pitch, plucky,* and *washing machine method.* I organized this glossary of Kevin-speak alphabetically by Ingredients, Techniques, and Equipment, so you can easily find out just what the hell I'm trying to say in the recipes.

I realize that the terminology I use may not be familiar to everyone, so here's a thorough explanation of what I mean when I say things like *balance, buried, cut like a whole vegetable, GBD, pitch, plucky,* and *washing machine method.*

Ingredients

Black pepper: I always grind it fresh. Like any other spice, black pepper starts to lose its aroma as soon as you grind, crack, or crush it. Fill a pepper grinder with Tellicherry peppercorns and keep it on your kitchen counter. A single grind usually measures out to a "pinch," and 6 grinds should be about ¼ teaspoon.

Browned butter: One of my favorite flavors with fish and vegetables. I give instructions for making it with the recipes, but you owe it to yourself to make this on a whim. It's dead easy. Heat a heavy skillet over medium heat; add some butter and let it melt and foam up. When the foam fades, the milk solids will sink to the bottom of the pan and start to turn brown. Give the butter a stir so it browns evenly. The color will go from light brown *(beurre noisette)* to dark brown *(beurre noir)* and the aroma will become increasingly intense and nutty. To cool it quickly so the milk solids don't burn, I pull the pan from the heat and dip the bottom of it into a big bowl of ice water.

Butter: Unsalted, always. The fresher the better, but regular grocery store butter will do.

Clarified butter: Another kitchen staple. You strain out the milk solids from melted butter so that the butter can withstand higher temperatures for sautéing and such. It's made like browned butter but without the browning. Put a pound of butter in a small heavy-bottomed saucepan and melt it over medium heat. The milk solids will drop to the bottom of the pan and the liquid on top will look clear. Pull the pan from the heat and skim off any foam and water from the top. Strain the butter through a fine-mesh strainer lined with cheesecloth or a clean coffee filter, leaving the milk solids behind in the pan. You should be left with only golden, clarified butter. Pour it into a container, cover, and refrigerate for up to 2 months. Use it whenever you're cooking with high heat. Ghee is clarified butter that's allowed to brown

and is then strained to remove the browned milk solids. It has an even higher smoke point than clarified butter.

Espelette pepper: This is my go-to "mild" ground red chile pepper. It's a little hotter than paprika, a little milder than cayenne, and more aromatic than both. Espelette comes from the Basque region of France, and the genuine article tastes best. You want to buy authentic *piment d'Espelette* that carries an AOC *(Appellation d'Origine Contrôlée)* label, which guarantees that the product actually comes from the town of Espelette in France. Upscale spice sections will carry Espelette pepper, or you can find it online (see Sources, page 327).

Lemons and limes: I always call for whole fresh citrus in the recipes, so you can zest it or squeeze it on the spot. Don't use the lemon or lime juice stored in those citrus-shaped plastic bottles. It's crap. Lemons and limes keep in the fridge for at least 2 weeks, and you should be using them all up in that time anyway. Plus, they're cheap.

On a shopping spree at Morningside Farmers' Market.

Oil: When I'm sautéing or cooking with high heat, I use grapeseed oil. It has a high smoke point (about 445°F) and a clean, mild flavor. But I probably use more olive oil than anything else. My day-to-day olive oil for cooking is made in Chile from Arbequina olives (see Sources, page 327). It's reasonably priced and has a softer, less intense, and more balanced flavor than most of the Arbequina oils from Spain and Italy. That's my cooking olive oil. For raw preparations or drizzling onto the plate, I use the best olive oil I can. When I call for "best-quality" or "finishing-quality" olive oil, what I mean is that you should pull out your top-shelf, teeny-tiny bottle of the good stuff. Mine is an Italian oil from Liguria. It's DOC (*Denominazione di Origine Controllata*); that is, the Italian government guarantees that this oil is made in Liguria from Ligurian olives the way it has been for centuries. We have an importer in Atlanta named Franco Boeri, and I use his family's oil. Franco can usually be found on Saturday mornings selling his goods at the Sandy Springs Farmers Market just outside of Interstate 285 up Roswell Road in Atlanta. Or you can buy Franco's stuff online (see Sources, page 327). A quick note about lemon olive oil: This is a very specific ingredient called for throughout the book. Crushing lemon peels in with the olives makes it intensely lemony. This oil is not made by steeping lemon peels in olive oil, so I'm pretty adamant about using the right thing here. I use Gianni Calogiuri "Le Spezie" extra-virgin olive oil with lemon, made in Italy. Franco's family also makes a pretty good one called Frantoio di Caprafico. I use some other oils throughout the book, like pumpkin seed oil. You can find these at most gourmet retailers (see Sources, page 327).

Panko dust: Japanese panko bread crumbs produce a lighter, crispier crust on breaded foods. For an even crispier crust, I like to grind the panko to dust in a food processor, then shake it through a sieve to filter out any large pieces.

Parsley: I keep fresh flat-leaf parsley in the fridge at all times. Yes, it will eventually go bad, but usually it's used up by then. To make fresh parsley last longer, trim the stems when you get it home from the market; rinse it, shake out the water, and then wrap it in a dry paper towel. Stuff the towel-wrapped bundle in a plastic bag and store it in the vegetable bin.

Piquillo peppers: These are small, mild red chiles from Spain, where they're usually roasted whole over embers and then peeled and served as tapas. The chiles are also available jarred or canned. Piquillo peppers are like roasted red bell peppers but a little smokier. The smaller jarred roasted red peppers on the grocery store shelves are most likely piquillo peppers.

Salt: I always say, "What grows together goes together." So I use sea salts with seafood and mined or earth salts with land-based foods. My basic salt for pinching up is Diamond Crystal kosher salt. That's what I mean when I call for salt in the recipes. When I say *finishing salt,* I mean Maldon salt, a delicate, crispy-textured flake salt from Essex, England. As for the exact measurement of a "pinch of salt," see the description of a "Kevin pinch" on page 11.

> I remember saying, "It needs to be just above 'below room temperature.'" That's a crazy-ass way of putting it, but the phrase made perfect sense to me.

Bigger shrimp are better for grilling and smaller ones are better for ceviche and salads.

Shrimp: Georgia white shrimp are my all-time favorite. They're sweet, firm, and better tasting than your garden-variety brown Gulf shrimp. You can order them from Georgia Seafood (see Sources, page 326). Shrimp are sold by count, meaning how many shrimp come in a pound. The lower the count, the bigger the shrimp. I use various sizes depending on the recipe. Bigger shrimp are better for grilling and smaller ones are better for ceviche and salads. Retail names like "jumbo shrimp" aren't too reliable, so go by the count. *U10* means under 10 shrimp per pound; *16/20* means 16 to 20 shrimp per pound; *31/35* is 31 to 35 per pound . . . you get the idea.

Simple syrup: Just like the name says, this is simply sugar dissolved in water to make a syrup. Combine one part sugar to one part water in a saucepan and bring to a boil. Simmer until the sugar dissolves, then cool, cover, and store it in the fridge for up to 6 months. There's no better way to sweeten cocktails without adding other flavors—although sometimes I will use a little agave nectar instead.

Sweet herb mix: My basic fresh herb combo. Gather together equal parts fresh celery leaves, parsley leaves, tarragon, and thyme (stems removed). Mince and go.

Toasted nuts: What a simple way to amplify flavor. Toasting nuts brings their oils to the surface and browns them so the nuts taste, well, nuttier! Toast the nuts in whatever pan you'll be using later in the recipe to capture those oils in the pan, too. On the stovetop, toast nuts in a skillet or saucepan over medium heat, shaking the pan a few times until the nuts start to brown and smell fragrant. Or you can do the same thing on a baking sheet in a 350°F oven.

Warm spice blend: This is sort of like pumpkin pie spice or apple pie spice but without the cinnamon. Grind 2 tablespoons whole cloves and 2 tablespoons whole allspice in a spice grinder, a clean coffee grinder, or a mortar and pestle. The spices should be ground to a fine powder, so pass them through a fine-mesh strainer and discard any big pieces. Grate 4 whole nutmeg seeds on a Microplane zester to make about 2 packed tablespoons. Mix the nutmeg with the cloves and allspice and store the warm spice blend in an airtight container. It should make about ½ cup and last about 6 months. You can also mix equal parts of preground spices, but it's not nearly as good as fresh.

Techniques

3-step fry prep: I was taught Escoffier's method of breading food on day eleven of culinary school, and I don't remember it exactly. The 3-step fry prep is the standard breading and frying method I use. Basically, you pat dry your food, dust it with a little flour to make it really dry, and then dip it in some liquid with a little fat in it (egg, buttermilk, or batter). Finally, you dip it in your breading that will form the outer crust (cornmeal, bread crumbs, or panko). I usually set up the flour, liquid, and breading in three separate shallow bowls or dishes. To keep from breading yourself, it helps to use one hand for dredging in dry ingredients and the other for dredging in wet ingredients. Better yet, use tongs. To help the crust set up, let the breaded food rest on a wire rack for 10 to 15 minutes before cooking it.

Acidity: Foods that don't have acidity taste boring after a while. Think of braised short ribs. They're really rich and, in my opinion, one-dimensional. You can change that just by adding some acidity, some ingredient with sharpness to it, like lemon juice. Although the ribs will taste just as rich as before, the acidity helps prevent your palate from becoming completely overwhelmed by richness. See also Plucky (page 11).

Balance: This is what I strive for on the plate. A balance of color, texture, temperature, and flavor. Mostly when I talk about balance, I'm talking about balancing the flavors. The primary flavors we taste are sweet, sour, salty, bitter, and savory (umami). Foods tend to taste primarily like one or another of these flavors. For instance, sugar is sweet. Vinegar is sour. Salt is salty. Coffee is bitter. Cheese is savory (umami). When I'm building a dish, I think about what flavor each ingredient brings to the plate. If the ingredient tastes one-dimensional or only has one dominant flavor, I'll add other ingredients with other dominant flavors to balance out the overall taste. Generally, if you can get all five primary mouth flavors into a dish, the dish will taste fuller and more delicious. Balance is hitting all or most of the flavors in the same dish without one flavor dominating.

Some chefs will try to achieve balance in every bite you get. But I take a different approach. I like each component on the plate to represent just one or two flavors (a component being one part of the entire plate). Rather than balancing each component so it has every flavor in it, I push the singular flavor of each component to the nth degree. That way, each bite tastes incredibly dynamic, and when you taste all the components together, you taste balance. For instance, in the cast-iron skillet chicken with farro and Brussels sprouts (page 89), the farro has a lot of lemon juice, so it tastes acidic and sharp. The chicken tastes umami or savory. The tahini tastes bitter. The Brussels sprouts bring the sweetness. On their own, these components would taste somewhat one-dimensional, but together they create a well-balanced dish.

Blanch and shock: Chefs use this term to describe a first-step preparation for vegetables. You submerge a vegetable in boiling water for 30 seconds or up to 3 minutes (if it's tougher), then immediately plunge the vegetable into ice water to stop the cooking. It's the same technique used to "shock" whole tomatoes and peaches to make them easier to peel. I don't salt my blanching water.

Browning: Here's where cooking really changes the flavor of ingredients. Browning means literally turning food brown by applying heat to it. As food cooks and goes from light brown to golden brown to dark brown, it becomes increasingly less sweet and more savory and caramel-like. When you create color, you create flavor. Want to taste the difference that browning makes? Cut two thin slices off a room-temperature raw beef tenderloin steak (filet mignon) and put the slices on a plate (carpaccio). Heat up a heavy pan until it's smokin' hot. Pat dry the remaining steak and sear it in the pan until it's deep brown on both sides and medium-rare in the center. Taste the carpaccio and seared steak side by side. It's the same beef. But browning makes the meat taste more savory, roasty, and delicious.

The flavor of browning is so important in cooking that it's worth paying attention to getting the best browned flavors you possibly can. There are four keys to doing so:

1. Get the pan, grill grate, or other cooking surface smokin' hot. The higher the heat, the deeper the browning and the better the flavor—just don't go overboard and incinerate the food.

2. Bring the food to room temperature before cooking. Browning doesn't occur until about 250ºF, so give the food a head start by taking the chill off it first. The food will brown better and more quickly.

3. Create an even surface. This is especially important for food browned in a pan. If the food isn't directly touching the hot pan, it won't brown well. Cut foods so they are evenly flat or spread chopped foods into a single layer in the pan. That way, you'll get the most surface area and the best browning.

4. Dry the food. Again, browning can't happen below 250ºF, and moisture doesn't evaporate until 212ºF. Translation: If the food is wet, it won't have a chance to brown before being cooked. Pat dry beef, chicken, pork, or anything else you want to get a good sear on before it sees the heat. Dry food browns faster and better. Don't be afraid to deeply brown your onions or other vegetables when you're looking for a deep, roasty flavor in a dish. Light browned means light flavor. Deeply browned means deep flavor.

Buried: Something is buried when you need to read an ingredient list to understand what you're eating. Sometimes I'll taste a dish and say, "This tastes good, but I'm not getting the tarragon; it's buried by the grapefruit." In my recipes, every ingredient

has a reason for being there and should be tasted. If a dish is supposed to have tarragon and lemon and crab and garlic, you should be able to identify the flavors of all those ingredients. Of course, that doesn't mean that everything has to be at the same pitch (see page 11).

Chiffonade: A classic French knife cut where you cut ingredients with a single slice into very thin, thread-like strips. For leaves like basil, it's easiest to stack three or four leaves, roll the stack like a cigar, then cut crosswise at ⅛-inch intervals to make thin strips.

Component: It may sound like electronics, but this is a useful way to think about building a dish. Every recipe has different components or basic parts, each with its own flavors, textures, and colors. For instance, on a pizza, the crust is one component, the sauce is another component, and the cheese and toppings are additional components. By themselves, the components would taste pretty boring, but together they taste delicious.

Confit: French for "preserved." Like many French things, that means "in fat." You "confit" an ingredient by slowly poaching it in fat and then storing it under a layer of that fat. It often refers to duck or goose poached and preserved in its own fat, but I confit everything from pork belly in pork fat to fennel in olive oil. This classic method makes food taste rich and succulent for weeks.

Cut like a whole vegetable: Sometimes I will say, "Cut this vegetable down, but when you cut it, I want it to look like a whole vegetable." With a radish, for instance, what I mean is to slice it from stem to tip so when you hold up each individual slice, it's still recognizable as a radish because it retains the basic shape.

Dice: The classic knife cuts are still around because they're useful. Saying "cut into a ½-inch dice" is easier than saying "Get out your ruler and cut this into perfect squares or cubes that measure an equilateral ½ inch on each side." Generally, *dice* means

perfect squares for thin ingredients like bell peppers or perfect cubes for thick ingredients like potatoes. Most other classic knife cuts, like brunoise and julienne, I explain in each recipe, with the exception of chiffonade (see page 8).

Emulsion: This is a mixture of two ingredients that don't normally mix—typically some kind of fat and some kind of liquid because oil and water don't mix. To blend them, start with the watery ingredients and add the oil, butter, or other fat. You want to whisk or blend like hell while very slowly trickling in the fat to avoid overwhelming the water with fat. Once it starts to thicken up, you can add the fat a little

faster but still whisk or blend like hell. Without some kind of emulsifier, all emulsions will eventually separate back out into fat and water. To keep the emulsion from separating, you beat in an emulsifier like egg yolk, mustard, honey, or another ingredient that will keep the fat and water blended together. Mayonnaise, hollandaise, and vinaigrettes are common emulsion sauces. They get their rich mouthfeel from millions of tiny droplets of fat suspended in the liquid part of the emulsion.

GBD: Golden brown and delicious. This is similar to browning (see page 7), but I use it exclusively for fried food. It's a broad description for how something should look on the surface when it comes out of a fryer. Generally speaking, you should trust your intuition on this one. When you put food in hot oil, it's usually ready when it looks like what you hope it would look like—golden brown and delicious.

Grilling and smoking: I absolutely love the flavor of fire and smoke. There are plenty of ways to cook over fire and generate smoke, but there are only a few basic things you need to know. First, grilling and smoking are not the same thing. Grilling is cooking food directly over relatively high heat in a fairly

short amount of time. Grilled food bears the flavor of fire. Smoking, on the other hand, is cooking food *indirectly* or away from the heat, using lower heat, and with the added element of more smoke. It's basically barbecuing. Barbecued food tastes more like smoke than fire.

To grill, you set up a gas, charcoal, or wood grill and put a grate over the fire. Then let the grate get good and hot, scrape it clean, and add the food. If I'm grilling something that might stick, like fish, vegetables, or bread, I like to oil the grill grate before adding the food. Just wad up a paper towel, dip it in grapeseed oil or another vegetable oil, and use tongs to rub the oily paper towel over the hot grill grate. That gets the grate superclean and lubricates it to help prevent sticking. To smoke food, you can set up a gas, charcoal, or wood grill the same way, but you need a lid to trap the heat and smoke. You also need enough space to move the food far enough away from the heat so that it doesn't burn on the outside before cooking all the way through.

For some barbecue, food will smoke for as long as 48 hours. In that case, you want the food at least a couple feet away from the heat source. To set up a wood or charcoal grill for this kind of cooking, pile all the coals on one side of the cooking chamber and leave a big open space on the other side. On a gas grill, turn on the burners on one side of the grill but leave the other burners off. Then you put the food over the unheated side of the grill. A wood grill will produce plenty of smoke; charcoal will produce a little; and gas barely any. To get more smoke, use wood chips. On a charcoal grill, just toss the chips onto the hot coals and close the lid. On a gas grill, wrap the chips in foil and put them directly over one of the lit burners underneath the grill grate. When they start smoking, close the lid. Replace the chips whenever they burn out and stop smoking. As for heat level, I usually hold my hand a few inches above the grill grate directly over the fire and start counting "one Mississippi, two Mississippi . . . " until it gets so hot I have to pull my hand away. High heat is about two Mississippi. Medium is about six Mississippi. Low heat is about ten Mississippi.

Kevin pinch: This is literally how I measure salt when I grab it from the open bin on my kitchen counter. My fingers are pretty chunky, so a Kevin pinch is a big pinch. It measures about 1 teaspoon. One Kevin pinch is more of an all-fingers-and-thumb pinch than a single-finger-and-thumb pinch. It is not a tiny amount. A teeny pinch is more like ⅛ or ¹/₁₆ teaspoon, which is why I specify a "Kevin pinch" in the recipes when necessary.

Pitch: This is the "loudness" of an ingredient relative to other ingredients in a dish. In music, if you want everything to sound cacophonous, you play all the instruments at the same volume. But if you want subtlety, some instruments are loud, some are soft. Just know that there's a fine line between things being subtle and things being lost. You want to adjust the amounts of various flavors in your cooking so they have the right pitch. This means you have to taste as you go and pay attention to what you're tasting. In my recipes, I make it clear when something is meant to be a background flavor or a primary flavor, like the backing vocals or the lead vocals in a song.

When cooking my recipes, read the description of the dish, so that if you know you're supposed to taste crab, lemon, tarragon, and garlic in that order, you can adjust the amounts to achieve the right end result. If the recipe calls for 1 lemon, but the dish tastes like it needs more lemon to achieve the right pitch, don't be a slave to the recipe: Add more lemon! This is what it means to be a cook instead of someone who just follows recipes.

Plucky: I use this term to describe a flavor quality I'm trying to achieve with acidic ingredients like lemon juice or vinegar. When something has a very bright acidity, you get a little twinge in the back of your throat. That's plucky. It tastes sharp. Piercing. Think of a glass of lemonade. It's the difference between packets of Country Time lemonade mixed with water and actual lemons squeezed for their juice and mixed with sugar. Homemade lemonade tastes pluckier. It's this kind of stabbing sensation on your tongue that turns out to be a very pleasant sensation when it's balanced with other tastes like sweetness and richness. Adjust the pluckiness of a dish by adding more or less of an acidic ingredient like lemon juice or vinegar. See also Acidity (page 7).

Presentation side: You always want the most beautiful side of the food to be face up on the plate. So, for instance, when grilling, I put the food "presentation side down" first, because you get the best sear when the food first hits the grill grate. A skin-on trout fillet is a good example. I grill it flesh-side down first, then flip it so it's skin-side down. That way, the best-looking side (the flesh side) will go face up on the plate. As you're cutting and cooking food, you always want to keep the presentation side in mind.

Quick marinating: This is how I quickly infuse flavors into thin foods. You stretch plastic wrap over the top of a rimmed baking sheet to form a flat, stretchable surface that is nonreactive. Then arrange thinly sliced foods like salmon or cucumber on top of the plastic wrap in a single layer. Spoon marinade over the ingredients, and then stretch another

It usually happens in a sauté pan. You agitate the pan forward and backward over the burner while vigorously stirring the center of the pan with a spoon, fork, whisk, or other utensil. The utensil acts like the center agitator in a washing machine. It's a particularly helpful technique for creating a more stable emulsion sauce. It's also how most chefs scramble the eggs in a pan when making an omelet.

Equipment

Most of the equipment I recommend can be purchased at The Cook's Warehouse or online (see Sources, page 327). It's a locally owned business in Atlanta just around the corner from my restaurant. Give them a ring. The sales staff can tell you what's what.

sheet of plastic wrap over the top of the food. The plastic wrap will cause the liquid marinade to travel across the food and keep marinade and food in direct contact with each other. It also eliminates air and creates a light vacuum effect for faster marinating. Just be sure to stretch the plastic wrap fairly tight to create light pressure on the food.

Render: This just means to cook the fat out of food.

Sear: When food hits a smokin' hot pan or grill grate, it sears and turns brown and delicious. This process doesn't "seal" in the juices, but it does create amazing flavor and a great browned crust. See also Browning (page 7).

Smokin' hot: I use this term to describe how hot a pan should be before searing food in it. To get a good sear on any food, the cooking surface has to be so hot that it starts to send up wisps of smoke. If the pan isn't hot enough, you won't get a good sear and you won't develop deep, flavorful browning (see page 7). That hot pan is one of the keys to creating great flavor in foods that will be seared and browned.

Sweat: To sauté without browning. I use this technique to soften vegetables with gentle heat in a pan but without letting them change color. Sometimes you don't want browning. In some dishes, you want the clean flavor of the food itself.

Washing machine method: This is a method of stirring that mixes ingredients quickly and evenly.

Dutch oven: This is just a big, sturdy, even-heating pot with a tight-fitting lid. It's what I use for most braised dishes, so it needs to be ovenproof. This type of dish shows up in a lot of my recipes. Most often, I use a 5½-quart Le Creuset enamel-coated cast-iron pot with a heavy, tight-fitting lid. Steady, even heating is the goal here.

Mandoline: You don't need to drop $200 on a stainless-steel mandoline. A $25 handheld Benriner Japanese Mandoline Slicer comes with three julienne blades and will suffice for all the slicing done in this book. Just don't try to get paper-thin slices with a knife. It's not worth the trouble. An inexpensive handheld mandoline does a better job and does it much faster than a knife.

Microplane zester: This handy gadget creates fine shards of cheese, citrus zest, and nutmeg.

Mixer: You can use an old-fashioned handheld mixer for most of the recipes here, but I recommend getting a stand mixer. It makes mixing so much easier. They last longer and you can leave the mixer running while you do other things. If you get a KitchenAid, you can also buy all sorts of attachments that allow you to roll pasta, grind meat, stuff sausage, and make ice cream. A stand mixer is a worthwhile investment.

Oven: I use a convection oven, which has fans that blow the hot air all around the food. The hot air currents deliver more heat to the surface of food, helping it cook about 25 percent faster. Convection helps crisp up the surface of roasted chicken and blister the top of pizza crust. But in the recipes here, I've written the oven times and temperatures for an oven with no convection, since that is what most people have at home. If you do happen to have convection, by all means turn it on, and lower the temperatures stated in the recipes by about 25°F and reduce the cooking time by about 25 percent. The only time I wouldn't recommend convection is when you don't want deep surface browning or if the food is delicate and might get blown around too much by the air currents, such as the meringue topping on a banana cream pie.

Saucepans: These are used a lot throughout the book. All-Clad is pretty much the gold standard for a heavy bottom with even cooking and no hot spots. Pots and pans should last a lifetime, so invest in good equipment. Trust me, it's worth it. You'll want one small saucepan for low-quantity jobs like toasting nuts or making browned butter. Beyond that, a 2-quart, 4-quart, and 6-quart should handle everything you'll ever make.

Sauté pan: Similar to a skillet (see page 13) but with straight sides instead of sloped sides. Either way, you want a heavy bottom and a tight-fitting lid. All-Clad makes a good set. An 8-inch, 10-inch, and 12-inch sauté pan will handle all the jobs in this book. Sauté pans are used primarily for lower-heat jobs like sautéing and sweating (see page 12), while skillets are used for browning and frying.

Sieve: Chefs typically use a cone-shaped chinois or China cap for straining ingredients. Keep at least one midsize fine-mesh strainer in your kitchen. One of the secrets to cooking like a professional chef is straining everything under the sun a million times to get a supersmooth and silky texture. In addition to a large fine-mesh strainer or chinois, it's handy to have a small (3- or 4-inch) fine-mesh strainer for little things like straining out lemon seeds or sieving spices.

Sizzle plate: This is an aluminum or stainless-steel hot server. You can cook on it and serve on it. Nordic Ware makes a good one (and again, The Cook's Warehouse stocks these). You'll want one that's about 11 inches in diameter for the recipes in this book. It's an indispensable tool for taking food from the stovetop to the oven to finish cooking. It also has a little bit of a dip, so you can use it on top of an open grill as a makeshift lid.

Skillet: I believe that every kitchen needs a set of seasoned cast-iron skillets. You'll need at least a large one (12 inches by 2 inches deep) and a small one (8 inches by 1½ inches deep). Preferably, you'll have inherited these from your granny; but if not, for the real deal, buy original cast iron from Lodge Manufacturing (see Sources, page 327). Lodge cast-iron skillets come preseasoned, so they're pretty much nonstick.

Vitamix: The Lamborghini of blenders. A Vitamix will puree vegetables to a smooth, velvety consistency in a flash. In fact, the blades go so fast that if you leave something mixing in the blender for too long, it will actually heat up and start cooking. I use this machine for grinding pepper and spices in quantity. Again, The Cook's Warehouse is a great source for this piece of equipment. If you have a standard upright blender, let it go a little longer to get the kind of smoothness you'd get from a Vitamix.

Y-peeler: Forget the old-fashioned straight vegetable peelers. These work better! I buy Kuhn Rikon brand in the three-pack. Cheap and good!

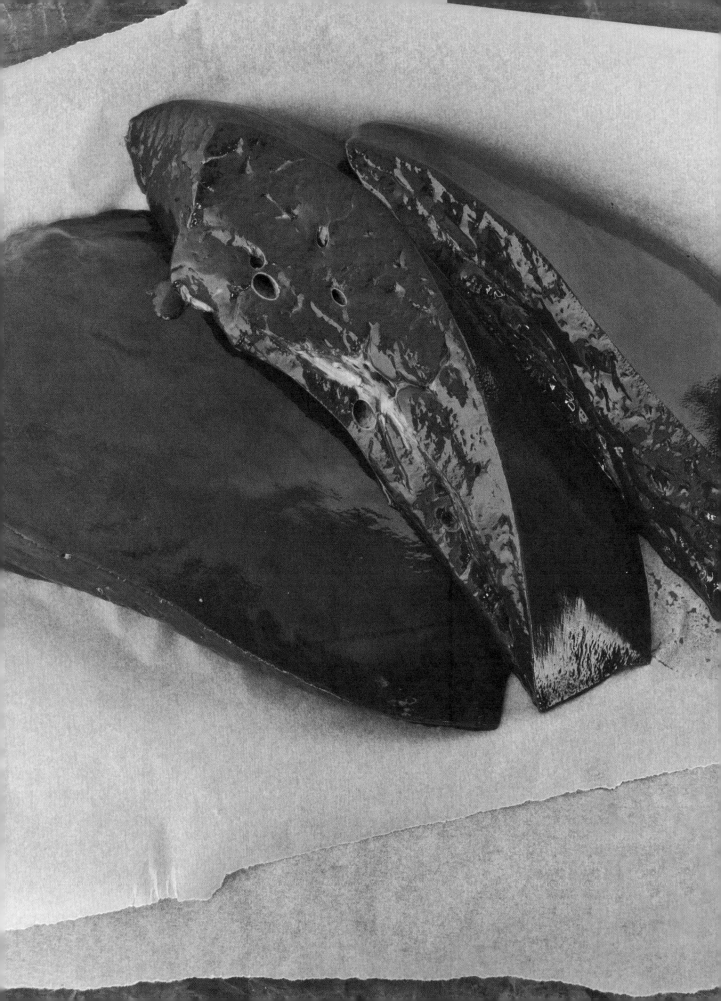

IT WAS 1995. I was thirteen. In middle school. I woke up way too early

one Saturday morning. Lying in bed in a fog, I thought, "Why am I awake?" I really wanted to sleep until noon. Was it cinnamon rolls? Did I smell cinnamon rolls? They were my dad's Saturday morning favorite. I sat up and took a whiff. My nostrils filled with the foulest odor of canned fish frying in overused cooking oil. It was salmon croquettes. Immediately, I threw up in my lap. A complete gut reaction. Sitting up on my bed, disoriented, weak, disgusted, I decided to get up. I stumbled to the kitchen, the sun blinding my squinted eyes, and asked, "Why are you doing this, Mom?" She looked up from the stove and said, "I wanted salmon croquettes." I'm not usually at a loss for words. But I was so repulsed that I couldn't even speak. Rather than tell my mom I just threw up in bed because of her craving for fried cat food, I turned and staggered back to bed. Broken. Sick. At that moment, I preferred to smell vomit than salmon croquettes.

Only when I tried the real thing did I realize why people loved salmon so much.

You have to understand: Salmon croquettes are a common breakfast food in the South. My mom made them all the time. You take canned pink (chum) salmon and mix in some chopped onions, a heavy roux (flour cooked with fat), a little milk to thin it out, and maybe some bread crumbs. Then you form the mixture into patties and pan-fry them. I couldn't stomach them. Later that Saturday, my mom found out that I'd actually thrown up. It was the last day I ever personally witnessed her make salmon croquettes at our house.

Those croquettes explain why I hated salmon for the first fifteen years of my life. Then, once I decided to be a chef, I gave salmon a second chance. I tried some poached farm-raised salmon. It was okay—completely different than canned salmon—but farm-raised salmon was a food I just could not get behind. Knowing how it was raised—in those crowded, unsanitary ocean feedlots and being fed pellets of ground-up dead fish—I just couldn't enjoy eating it.

Later, when I was twenty, I started cooking professionally as an intern at The Ritz-Carlton, Atlanta. We got in these big, wild Alaskan salmon with the heads still on. The chef filleted the whole salmon and offered me some of it. Raw. He said, "You have to try it. You'll never be a chef if you don't try everything." Of course, I tried it. And loved it! Right then, I changed my mind about that fish. Only when I tasted the real thing did I understand why people love salmon so much.

Years later, in the spring of 2007, I was cooking at Fife restaurant in Portland, Oregon. Salmon season was in full blast, and we got in all this gorgeous, fresh wild salmon. I had just butchered them and had buckets of scraps. My hatred for salmon was long gone, but I still hated salmon croquettes. I'd been in Oregon for almost a year, so I was probably a little homesick. A switch flipped in me and I decided to grow up and face my fear. I would tackle my childhood nemesis and make salmon croquettes for staff meal. "Southerners eat salmon croquettes for breakfast, lunch, and dinner," I thought to myself. "There has to be something good about them."

So I started with a béchamel (white sauce), which is how I'd learned to make croquettes with my French training. I added nutmeg, flour, onion, milk, lemon zest, and herbs. I folded in the salmon scraps. I chilled it so it would set up. Then I scooped it out and breaded it in a classic breading of flour, egg, and bread crumbs. I couldn't believe I was actually making this. My stomach turned a little at the memory of that rude awakening so many Saturdays ago. With total skepticism, I fried up the little logs. The ingredients were impeccable, the oil was fresh, and the croquettes were browning up beautifully. Still, I hesitated to take a bite. I let one cool, closed my eyes, and lifted the fork to my mouth. I tasted the browned, fried breading. Then the creamy béchamel. And then something clean, minerally, and unbelievably rich.

Salmon! A door opened. A weight was lifted! I had carried around this weight for years. This salmon croquette tasted delicious! Twenty-five years of hatred and disgust suddenly gave way to love. It was a breakthrough in my development as a chef and as an eater.

I'm not a food evangelist, but this is the kind of moment that I live for. I absolutely love tasting food, and I love turning other people on to food. If I can get you to say "yum" about a food you thought you hated, I've done my job. Just think of all the joy and pleasure you could be missing out on because you have closed off an entire food group.

The point here is to trust me. I am a professional chef and I know what I'm doing. If you think you hate Brussels sprouts, try my Brussels sprouts gratin (page 34). Think you don't like broccoli? Or spinach? Try my spinach pie (page 36). If your stomach turns just looking at the recipes in this chapter, step back and take a leap of faith.

It's not that there is something inherently wrong with Brussels sprouts. There is just something wrong with the way that they have been cooked for you. I would argue that that's what cooking is: It's figuring out the great quality of any food and making that quality shine. The recipes in this chapter do just that. Before you turn to the next chapter, give them a shot. You may discover a whole new world of delicious food.

25 years of hatred and disgust suddenly gave way to love.

ASPARAGUS SALAD

My father really likes canned asparagus for some reason. He's a sick man. We ate it a lot when I was growing up, and I couldn't stand it. At one meal, we had canned asparagus and salmon croquettes together on the plate. I thought the gates of hell would open up. I never had fresh asparagus until junior high, and then I thought, "Hey, this is actually really good if you don't cook the piss out of it." When it's fresh and in season, asparagus has a clean, grassy flavor. Do yourself a favor and don't make this dish in the dead of winter. The only asparagus you can get then will be flown in from Peru, and it will never taste above subpar. This dish has to start with fresh spring asparagus or it loses its luster. The asparagus is blanched and shocked (see page 7), so it's cooked but not cooked for very long. Early in my career, the French guys I worked for hammered it into my head that asparagus should always be crisp and tender. A knife pierced through the asparagus should go all way through, but not without a little resistance. If you pinch it and it squishes flat, it's overdone. The exact cooking time will vary depending on the freshness and density of your asparagus. When in doubt, undercook it. The asparagus marinates in olive oil with lemon, basil, and garlic and is served cold with a crumble of feta cheese. It's supersimple. And completely delicious.

1. Bring a large pot of water to a boil. Pour the oil into a loaf pan or 1-quart casserole dish. Add the basil leaves to the oil along with the garlic. Using a Microplane zester, zest half the lemon directly into the oil. Using a vegetable peeler, strip 2 large pieces of the peel into the oil; make sure you leave a little peel on the lemon.

2. Drop the asparagus in the boiling water for 1 minute. Use tongs to pull the asparagus from the water and tap the tongs on the side of the pot to shake off any excess water. Lay the asparagus in the dish with the oil. The asparagus should be completely submerged; add a little more oil if you need to. Wrap the pan with plastic wrap and refrigerate until cold, about 4 hours.

3. Pull the asparagus from the oil and arrange in a single layer on a serving platter. Sprinkle with salt and a tiny squeeze of lemon juice. Grate or crumble the feta over the asparagus and garnish with a few basil leaves and a grating of lemon zest.

ENOUGH FOR 8 AS A SIDE DISH

Olive oil
about 2 cups

Fresh basil
2 tablespoons small leaves + a few for garnish

Garlic
2 cloves, thinly sliced

Lemon
1 fat one

Asparagus
1 pound, trimmed of woody ends

Salt
preferably coarse

Feta cheese
4-ounce block, about ½ cup crumbled

PICKLED BEET AND CHARRED BROCCOLI SALAD

I never loved broccoli as a kid. Once again, it was always boiled or steamed to oblivion. Often, it was frozen broccoli with a little water drizzled on it, covered and nuked in the microwave. Not my favorite thing in the world—the broccoli didn't stand a chance! And I never got on board with the cheese sauce idea. Then I had a revelation when my friend Rachel's mom served me a dish of fresh cold broccoli with lemon, garlic, and Turkish olive oil. It was awesome. I had a similar revelation with beets. I'd only ever had them canned, and they were terrible. But the truth is, beets are incredibly sweet and earthy and delicious. This salad plays up the best of both ingredients: The earthy sweetness of the beets tempers the sulfury funkiness of the broccoli. If you hate beets and you hate broccoli, wipe the slate clean and start over.

1. Peel the beets, slice off the tops and roots, and cut the beets into 1-inch wedges.

2. In a medium nonreactive saucepan, combine the red wine vinegar, sugar, pickling spice, cinnamon, and star anise. Bring to a boil and stir until the sugar dissolves, about 2 minutes. Pull the pan from the heat and let the spices steep for about 10 minutes. Strain and reserve the liquid, discarding the spices. Return the liquid to the pot, add the beets, and bring to a boil over high heat. Cut the heat down so that the liquid simmers, and cook for 10 minutes. Pull the pan from the heat and let the beets cool in the liquid; they will finish cooking as they cool.

3. Heat a medium cast-iron skillet over high heat until smokin' hot. Drop half of the broccoli florets into the dry skillet, being careful not to crowd the pan. After about 30 seconds, toss the florets, and continue tossing as they char and cook, about 2 ½ minutes total. The tender florets will char easily, which is good; you want that smoky flavor. Transfer the first batch to a plate and repeat with the remaining broccoli. Refrigerate the charred broccoli until ready to serve.

4. In a small bowl, whisk the goat cheese, lemon juice, water, and a large pinch of salt until smooth. In a separate bowl, toss the frisée with 2 teaspoons of the olive oil and ⅛ teaspoon salt. Drain the beets and discard the pickling liquid. Place the beets in a third bowl and toss with 2 tablespoons of the olive oil, ¼ teaspoon salt, and 3 grinds of black pepper. In a fourth bowl, toss the chilled charred broccoli with the remaining 1 teaspoon olive oil, ⅛ teaspoon salt, and 2 grinds of black pepper. Yes, I realize you've got four separate bowls; it's imperative that the components stay separate until they are plated. You don't want the ingredients to mingle because each item brings a specific flavor, texture, and color to the final dish.

5. Divide the beets evenly among four plates. Top with the broccoli, the frisée, and the crumbled feta cheese. Drizzle on the goat cheese mixture, and finish with a few drops of pumpkin seed oil around the outside of the plate.

Beets
4 baseball-size, about 2 pounds

Red wine vinegar
1 ½ cups

Sugar
1 ½ cups

Pickling spice
⅓ cup

Cinnamon stick
4 inches, broken into a few pieces

Star anise
1 pod

Broccoli
*1 fist-size crown,
cut into small florets*

Fresh goat cheese
¼ cup, 2 ounces

Lemon juice
1 tablespoon

Water
1 ½ teaspoons

Salt
about 2 teaspoons

Frisée
*1 cup trimmed and torn into
bite-size pieces*

Olive oil
3 tablespoons

Black pepper
5 fresh grinds

Feta cheese
¼ cup crumbled, 2 ounces

Pumpkin seed oil
⅛ teaspoon

PREP TIP / **Look for pickling spice in the spice aisle of your grocery store. It usually includes bay leaves, dill seeds, mustard seeds, peppercorns, whole allspice, and whole cloves.**

CHARRED OKRA WITH TOMATO-COCONUT CHUTNEY

I'm probably the one Southern kid who didn't grow up absolutely loving fried okra. I hated the texture of okra. In true fat-kid fashion, I would just eat the fried breading and not eat the okra. Jump forward twenty years, and I ate dinner a few times at an Indian restaurant called Bombay Cricket Club in Portland, Oregon, that had a shitload of okra on its menu. They had a braised okra dish, a curry, a few other things; I filed that away in my memory bank because I liked the way the okra tasted. Later, in August 2008, I was in my first year of owning Woodfire Grill, and I had okra coming out of my ears. If it's a hot year in Georgia, we get tons of okra. So I tasked myself with finding a way to use it. I'd heard that high heat and quick cooking is the key to cutting the slime factor in okra. I took it one step further and cauterized the okra in a hot pan. It worked—no slime! I served the charred okra with a tomato-coconut chutney based on various Southern Indian chutneys I'd had over the years. It completely sold me. I thought that if I enjoyed okra this way, other people would too. Be forewarned: This dish is not for those who don't like spicy food. The chutney has ghost pepper hot sauce in it, and ghost peppers are balls-to-the-wall hot. But without the sauce, the chutney loses its backbone. It needs the heat to wake up the coconut and tomato.

1. Trim the stem ends from the okra, then split the pods in half lengthwise and sprinkle with salt. Heat a large cast-iron skillet over high heat. Add the okra, cut side down, in a single layer, and sear until the cut side is charred and the outer skin turns bright green and starts glistening, about 2 minutes. By *charred* I mean more than golden brown; you want a good dark char to seal in the slime in the okra. When charred, turn the pods and cook for another 30 seconds. Pull the pan from the heat and stir in 2 tablespoons of the warm chutney. Toss to mix, and serve warm with the remaining chutney on the side.

ENOUGH FOR 4 AS A SIDE DISH

Okra
12 pods, each about 3 inches long

Salt

Tomato-coconut chutney
(recipe follows)
¼ cup, warm

CONTINUED →

TOMATO-COCONUT CHUTNEY

MAKES 2 CUPS

Unsweetened flaked coconut
⅓ cup

Canola oil
1 teaspoon

Jalapeño chile peppers
3, seeds and ribs removed,
finely diced, about ⅓ cup

Vidalia onion
¼ cup finely diced

Fresh ginger
2 tablespoons peeled and
finely diced

Garlic
1 clove, thinly sliced

Madras curry powder
1 tablespoon

Ripe tomato
1 large, diced, about 2 cups

Tomato paste
1½ teaspoons

Lime juice
1 tablespoon

Indian green chile pickles
2 teaspoons minced

Turmeric pickles
2 teaspoons minced

Jaggery
(a.k.a gur or date palm sugar)
2 teaspoons

Salt
¼ teaspoon

Ghost pepper sauce
(or other excruciatingly
hot pepper sauce)
a dash

1. Toast the coconut in a 10-inch skillet over medium-high heat just until light golden, about 3 minutes. Put the toasted coconut in a large mixing bowl and let cool. Return the pan to the heat and crank up your stove as high as it will go (seriously). Add the oil, and swirl to coat the bottom of the pan. Add the jalapeños, onion, ginger, garlic, and curry powder (stand back; the curry powder can be pungent). Toss and cook for 30 seconds. Stir in the tomatoes and tomato paste and cook just until the tomatoes start releasing their liquid, another 30 seconds. Add the tomato mixture to the coconut, and then add the lime juice, chile pickles, turmeric pickles, jaggery, salt, and hot sauce. Cool, cover, and refrigerate for up to 2 weeks.

PREP TIP / The chutney tastes better after it chills for a day, so make it ahead. Use the extra chutney with grilled fish or lamb or mixed with crab for a cold crab salad. A good Indian grocer should have the green chile pickles, turmeric pickles, and jaggery (in a pinch, you can substitute dark brown sugar). Or buy online from the Sources on page 326. You can get ghost pepper hot sauce online too, or use another hot sauce.

SKILLET-ROASTED CABBAGE

While I now have a fondness for stewed cabbage, I certainly did not have that as a child. Whenever my mom made it, the whole house smelled like cabbage for three days. What I like best about cabbage is that, unlike most leafy things, cabbage has structure to it. It retains its shape. Most cooked leaves get slimy and wimpy. Cabbage doesn't. The original idea here was to make glazed cabbage in a wood-burning oven. We thought we'd put some oil in a pan with the cabbage, let it cook down in the wood oven, and then sauté it. But the fire was so hot that we could have used it to smelt pig iron. The cabbage roasted, browned, and got deeply caramelized. Okay, then, let's keep going in that direction: We added a little stock to slow down the cooking and seasoned it with spices you would normally see on pastrami, like coriander, black pepper, and caraway. It made sense that those spices would work on cabbage. The heavy caramelization actually increased the spiciness of the spices and intensified the sugar in the cabbage. The whole dish took on this incredible flavor and a texture you wouldn't expect with cooked cabbage. The texture is more like cole slaw or chow mein—soft yet crisp. Plus, the cabbage cooks so fast that those nasty sulfur compounds never get a chance to go airborne. The cabbage stays nice and sweet. It goes great with grilled duck breast (page 203) or grilled scallops (page 196). Be sure to use fresh cabbage here, preferably from a farmer's market. It's better and cheaper than the shredded stuff in bags. Remove the large outer green leaves and save those for another use, such as cabbage dumplings (page 92).

1. Preheat the oven to 500°F.

2. Using a spice grinder or mortar and pestle, grind the peppercorns, caraway seeds, and coriander seeds to a fine powder.

3. Heat a large cast-iron skillet over high heat. Add the grapeseed oil and swirl to coat the bottom of the pan. When the oil starts smoking, add the cabbage and spread evenly in the pan; it will be very full. Place the pan in the oven until the cabbage turns a brighter, greener color on top, about 2 minutes. Wearing an oven mitt (the handle will be HOT!), pull the pan from the oven, then use tongs to toss the spice blend into the cabbage, taking care to mix the browned, caramelized bottom layer into the middle and top layers. Carefully slide the pan back into the oven for another 5 minutes. Again with the mitt, pull the pan from the oven and add the butter, chicken stock, and a pinch of salt. Toss all of the ingredients until the butter is completely melted. Finish the dish with a brief squeeze of lemon juice and toss once more before serving.

ENOUGH FOR 4 AS A SIDE DISH

Black peppercorns
¼ teaspoon

Caraway seeds
¼ teaspoon

Coriander seeds
¼ teaspoon

Grapeseed oil
2 teaspoons

Green cabbage
4 cups shredded, from ½ head

Butter
2 tablespoons

Chicken stock
¼ cup

Salt

Lemon juice
a tiny squeeze

Here's a laundry list of foods that I've changed my mind about over the years. First I hated them. Then, at some point in my life, I tasted the real McCoy or had the food prepared properly, and suddenly I loved it.

x **FISH** *4th grade*

I hated all fish until the fourth grade. That year, when my family was out to dinner one night, my cousin ordered halibut—"for the hell of it," as he said. He thought it was funny. Then he gave me a bite. I loved fish for the first time in my life.

x **ASPARAGUS** *12 yrs. old*

The only asparagus my mother ever served was canned. Barf. Then when I was 12, we got our first real grocery store in town, a Kroger. They had fresh asparagus, and my grandmother bought it on one of her health kicks. I thought, "Why would you pay more for something that's going to suck as bad—or worse—than that awful canned crap?" She ended up overcooking it, but that asparagus still had texture, it had flavor, it had a pleasant grassy taste. Not that tinny, metallic, mushy, awful taste of canned asparagus. After tasting it fresh, I was a convert. I look forward to fresh asparagus every spring.

x **BROCCOLI** *17 yrs. old.*

In high school, everybody knew I wanted to be a chef. Whenever I went to my best friend Rachel's house, her mom would cook for me. She was from Turkey. Rachel spent her whole life eating Turkish-American food and never wanted to eat it again. Rachel craved pizza, hamburgers, and real American food. But I loved eating at Rachel's. Turkish food was completely new to me. I gobbled up everything they put on the table. One day, Rachel's mom, Asuman, put a big plate of broccoli in front of me. "You have to taste it, Kevin," she said. I grabbed the dish. It was ice-cold. I hated broccoli. I always associated it with a bland, mushy, slightly rank taste, like soggy socks. And the plate was heaped with it. I usually make a point of cleaning my plate to avoid being rude, but how was I going to eat all this soggy-sock broccoli? I swallowed my pride and took a bite. It was crunchy, not soggy. Cold, not hot. Super-acidic and not sock-like at all. It was more puckery, like a Lemonhead or Cry Baby candy but without the sugar. The sharp taste of garlic came through. So did the spicy aroma and rich, full taste of Turkish olive oil. I ate the whole plate. And then the whole platter. Rachel's mom beamed with pleasure. That marinated Turkish broccoli opened the door to a vegetable I'd hated all my life up to that point. I just wanted not to be rude, but I ended up discovering a whole new food.

x OYSTERS *16 yrs. old*

I was in Panama City Beach, Florida—the Redneck Riviera, as I like to call it (not the classiest place in the world). I was on spring break with my neighbors at their condo down there. We went out for fresh seafood, and they ordered three dozen raw oysters. All I could conjure was the stench of oyster stew that my dad stunk up the house with during my childhood. When I saw the raw oysters in front of me on the table, my neighbors begged me to eat just one little white blob. Fine, I'll try one. A raw oyster on a saltine cracker with lemon juice and horseradish. In my imagination, it was going to taste like mud or guts. I put it in my mouth. It had this clean flavor. The texture was soft, the temperature was cold, the horseradish gave it punch. It rearranged my mind.

x LIVER *21 yrs. old*

I was working as an intern at The Ritz-Carlton, Atlanta. I hated liver. Beef liver, chicken liver—you name it, I wanted none of it. I figured all liver would have that god-awful mealy texture and iron-y taste. "You have to eat it," said Jean-Luc Mongodin, the chef I worked for, "or you'll never be a chef." He gave me a bite of seared foie gras. I remember the deep caramel browned taste and then the long, slow sensation of something rich, creamy, and savory melting and disappearing in my mouth. It was completely delicious. I was a changed man.

x MUSHROOMS *Sept. 2006*

I had just moved to Portland, Oregon. I was 24 years old. On my third day there, I went to a little neighborhood restaurant and saw trout with pan-roasted morels on the menu. My position on mushrooms at that time was that they are fungus. Mushrooms grow out of shit. How could they taste like anything but shit? I took a bite, and those pan-roasted morels tasted incredible. They blew my mind.

SAGE-BATTERED MUSHROOMS WITH CHEDDAR FONDUTA

This book doesn't have many dishes from the Woodfire Grill menu. But here's an exception. When we first made it, the dish got amazing feedback from our guests. We ran it on the menu for longer than we run most dishes—about a month. Then we took it off the menu and six months later, my chef de cuisine and I decided to put it back on. That's rare. The restaurant was founded on the idea of changing the menu and constantly pushing our creativity in the kitchen. But this dish is simply one of our best. It just works. Oyster mushrooms are great fried because they stay nice and firm. To keep the mushrooms from getting greasy, we use a thin, tempura-style batter that fries up fast and super-crisp. For something creamy, the fonduta acts like a classier version of ranch dip (it's always good to have something creamy with fried food). The combination is so popular that these mushrooms go back on the menu every six months or so. The exact time coincides with whenever we get a new intern who has to work the line. "You want experience?" I say to them. "Okay. Let me put you on this dish so you can see what it feels like to have your ass handed to you during service—because you'll be making it a million times over." It's ordered so often that you feel like you're frying all the mushrooms in the world.

ENOUGH FOR 4 SMALL PLATES

Oyster mushrooms
10 ounces of large clusters

Sharp white cheddar cheese
8 ounces

Heavy cream
1½ cups

White pepper
a couple grinds

Salt

Canola oil for frying

Cornstarch
½ cup

All-purpose flour
½ cup

Fresh sage leaves
1 tablespoon chiffonade

Rubbed sage
1 teaspoon

Club soda or seltzer water
1 cup cold

**Candied garlic syrup
(page 321)**
about ⅓ cup

1. Trim the tough root end from the mushrooms, leaving the clusters as intact as possible. Set aside.

2. Cut the cheese into ½-inch chunks and place in a microwave-safe bowl. Loosely cover with wax paper or parchment paper and microwave on 50 percent power until the cheese softens but doesn't completely melt, about 30 seconds.

3. In a 2-quart saucepan, bring the cream to a boil over medium-high heat. Stir in the cheese, a couple of grinds of white pepper, and a small pinch of salt until everything looks smooth. Keep the fonduta warm until you're ready to serve it. If you need to hold it for more than an hour, it keeps warm best in a double boiler.

4. Heat the oil in a deep fryer to 350°F. Place a cooling rack over a baking sheet.

5. In a large bowl, whisk together the cornstarch, flour, fresh sage, and dried sage. Add a few ice cubes to the club soda and swirl to chill. Remove the ice cubes and whisk the club soda into the cornstarch mixture to form a smooth batter. Working with

one mushroom cluster at a time, dip and swirl the cluster in the batter
to completely coat the mushrooms. Let excess batter drip away, then
drop the clusters, one by one, into the fryer and fry until crispy, about 2
minutes. The mushrooms won't brown but will have a very crispy coating. Using a spider strainer or tongs, transfer the fried mushrooms to
the rack and immediately sprinkle with salt.

6. For each plate, spoon one-quarter of the fonduta in the center, drizzle
with the garlic syrup, then mound one-quarter of the fried mushrooms
on top.

BRUSSELS SPROUTS GRATIN

My mom always hated Brussels sprouts. They were taboo in our family. Every once in a blue moon, my grandmother made them. But she usually boiled them, and they got that nasty sulfur smell that just made you want to retch. I hated them, too, until I learned how to cook them. Now I absolutely love Brussels sprouts. I shave them really thin and stir-fry them. I separate the leaves and serve them raw in salads. And I roast them every which way. That's my go-to method for turning people on to Brussels sprouts. Of course, I was determined to convert my mom. So I came up with this gratin for our family Thanksgiving in 2009. I couldn't roast the sprouts because it was a covered dish situation. I had to make something that could be baked in a crowded oven. One taste of this gratin and the whole family loved it. Now, it's a requested dish at almost every family function. My mom and dad even ask me to make it for potlucks they're going to, and they pass it off as their own. I hope that upon publishing this book, my parents will start making it. The secret is slicing the sprouts super-thin and barely cooking them.

SHOULD BE ENOUGH FOR 12 PEOPLE

Butter
11 tablespoons + some for greasing the pan

Vidalia onion
1 baseball-size, cut into ¼-inch dice, about 2 ½ cups

Garlic
⅓ cup chopped, about 8 big cloves

Salt

Heavy cream
4 cups

Brussels sprouts
2 pounds

All-purpose flour
3 tablespoons

Colman's mustard powder
1 tablespoon

Freshly grated nutmeg
¼ teaspoon

Panko bread crumbs
1 cup

Parmesan cheese
1 ½ ounces, about 1 cup freshly grated

Lemon
1 fat one

1. Preheat the oven to 375°F. Rub the inside of a 2-quart casserole with butter.

2. Melt 3 tablespoons of the butter in a 4-quart Dutch oven over medium heat. Add the onions, garlic, and a pinch of salt and cook until very soft and translucent, about 15 minutes. Add the cream and bring the mixture to a simmer. Cut the heat down to low and cook until the cream is slightly thickened, about 5 minutes.

3. Meanwhile, thinly slice the Brussels sprouts crosswise on a mandoline, slicing just until you get to the hard core; reserve the rest of the sprouts for another use. Or, if you have a 2mm slicing disk for your food processor, you can carve out the hard core of the Brussels sprouts and then process the sprouts through the feed tube. You should end up with about 14 cups of thin, coleslaw-like rounds.

4. Melt another 2 tablespoons of the butter in a small skillet over medium heat. Stir in the flour and cook, stirring constantly, just until the mixture begins to smell toasty, about 2 minutes.

5. Mix the mustard with 1 tablespoon of water to make a thin paste. Whisk 2 tablespoons of the flour-butter mixture into the onions along with the mustard paste, nutmeg, and 2 teaspoons salt; crank the heat up to medium and continue whisking until the mixture comes to a simmer and begins to thicken, about 2 minutes. Cut the heat to low and cook until the sauce loses any floury taste or grainy texture, about 10 minutes.

6. Fit a food processor with the metal blade, and add the panko, Parmesan, 1 teaspoon salt, ½ teaspoon lemon zest, and the remaining 6 tablespoons butter. Process to a crumbly paste. Spread the crumb mixture on a sheet of parchment paper or plastic wrap, top with another sheet, and, using a rolling pin, roll the crust to fit the top of the casserole.

7. Carefully pour the onion sauce into a blender and blend until smooth. Add the remaining zest from the lemon, all of the lemon's juice, and 1 teaspoon salt. Blend again until smooth. Pour the sauce back into the pot and fold in the sliced Brussels sprouts. Bring the mixture to a gentle simmer and cook until the sprouts are wilted, about 5 minutes.

8. Spoon the mixture into the prepared casserole. Remove the top sheet from the panko crust and invert over the Brussels sprouts. Remove the other sheet and bake until golden brown and bubbly, about 40 minutes. Serve hot.

PREP AHEAD / **You can make and puree the sauce, slice the Brussels sprouts, and make and roll out the topping ahead of time and refrigerate them. Then just reheat the sauce, fold in the Brussels sprouts, assemble, and bake. Once you assemble the dish, it should be baked right away. If the Brussels sprouts sit in the sauce for too long before baking, they will lose their delicate flavor and texture.**

SPINACH PIE

I don't know why people don't like spinach. It's pretty easy in my mind to get on board with this vegetable. I'm sure it's because they've only had it overcooked, like so many other vegetables that people now hate. Just remember that spinach is a leaf; there isn't much in it except air pockets and water, so it can't take a lot of heat. If you're going to cook spinach at all, you have to look for grown-up spinach, not baby spinach. Baby spinach is great for a salad or another raw preparation, but the second it meets any heat, it turns slimy and has absolutely no substance. Mature spinach has a much fuller flavor and texture; it softens when it cooks but doesn't turn to complete mush. This dish wins over spinach haters by playing up the things that most people like. The raw spinach gets folded into a cream sauce and baked inside a rich pastry shell. You could hate spinach—absolutely detest it—and I'll bet you end up liking this dish.

FEEDS ABOUT 4 FOLKS

Butter
2 tablespoons

Vidalia onion
1, halved and thinly sliced into strips

Bacon
2/3 cup diced

Salt
1 1/4 teaspoons

Garlic
2 cloves, thinly sliced

Heavy cream
1 cup

Mascarpone cheese
1/4 cup

Colman's mustard powder
1/2 teaspoon

Sugar
1/4 teaspoon

Warm spice blend (page 6)
1/8 teaspoon

Spinach
2 bunches, about 12 ounces total, tough stems removed

All-purpose flour
about 1/4 cup

Puff pastry
1 sheet, thawed but still cold

Egg white
1, beaten to a froth

Parmesan cheese
2-ounce block

1. Melt the butter in a Dutch oven over medium heat and swirl until the butter melts. Add the onion, bacon, and 1/4 teaspoon of the salt. Cook until the onion starts to brown and caramelize, about 10 minutes, stirring now and then. Cover the pot and cut the heat down to medium-low; this helps the onion to sweat and get very soft. Cook, covered, until creamy and dark brown, about 30 minutes more, stirring every 10 minutes. Add the garlic and crank the heat up to medium-high. Cook for 1 minute, and then stir in the cream, scraping up all the browned bits. Bring the mixture to a boil, then cut the heat down to medium and cook for 3 minutes. The mixture will look a bit curdled at first, but as the cream heats, it will blend with the butter and thicken into a velvety sauce.

2. Pull the pan from the heat and stir in the mascarpone cheese until melted. In a small bowl, combine the mustard with 1 teaspoon water and stir to form a paste. Stir the mustard paste, sugar, the remaining 1 teaspoon salt, and the warm spice blend into the sauce. Fold in the spinach a couple of handfuls at a time until it is all incorporated; the warm sauce will wilt and cook the spinach.

3. Preheat the oven to 375°F. Dust a flat work surface with flour and gently spread the pastry on the floured surface, sprinkling a little flour on top of the pastry. Roll the pastry sheet to a 15 by 10-inch rectangle. Cut in half to make two rectangles, each 10 by 7 1/2 inches. Line a baking sheet with parchment paper and place one pastry sheet in the center of the pan. Using a fork, poke holes evenly throughout the top of the pastry (called docking) to prevent it from puffing up. Brush a 1-inch-wide area around the edges with the egg white. Place the

second piece of puff pastry on the floured work surface and use the fork to perforate a "frame" in the pastry that is 1½ inches wide. Make sure you completely pierce the framing all the way through the pastry so the middle rectangle can be easily taken out. Brush the second sheet with the egg white and place directly on top of the first, lining up the edges. Press around the edges to seal the two pastry sheets.

4. Bake until puffed and golden brown, about 30 minutes. Pull the pan from the oven; carefully "punch" through the perforated frame of the top layer of pastry and pull out the center rectangle of pastry. Basically, you'll have a crust with a thick top edge, kind of like an entire casserole dish made from pastry. Return the pan to the oven and continue baking to crisp the center crust, about 4 minutes.

5. Using a slotted spoon, spoon the spinach from the sauce to fill the crust. Spread the spinach into the crust, filling all the corners. Grate the Parmesan cheese over the top of the pie; it will be thick, like it is covered in snow. Return the pie to the oven and bake until the cheese is melted and the edges are lightly browned, 8 to 10 minutes.

6. Bring the remaining sauce from the spinach to a boil over medium-high heat. Cut the heat down to medium and cook until slightly thickened, about 1 minute.

7. Pull the pie from the oven and spoon the sauce over the top. Cut into quarters and serve.

PREP TIP / It's important to use mature spinach here—the kind that's dark green with lots of folds in the large leaves. You'll find it in bunches at the grocery store. You can even find it prepped with all the big stems removed. The light green baby spinach leaves won't hold up when cooked and won't contribute much flavor to this pie (maturity does have its advantages). If you can't find mature spinach, use chard leaves instead and remove the tough stems.

SAVORY FIG TART

In California, people love figs. Californians may think I'm bat-shit crazy for putting this dish in the category of "foods you thought you hated." But not all of us are fortunate enough to have grown up in California where sweet Black Mission figs flow like lava from the trees. In Georgia, most kids have some story about the green fig, the ugly stepsister of the fig world. Green figs look like regular figs; they have the same shape, the same seed content, the same texture . . . but they are not sweet. They are mostly white, milky, and gross. Just the thought of eating them turns my stomach. As a kid, I ate a bunch of those figs and shit myself. I did the same thing with crabapples. Ate too many and shit myself. I pretty much grew up assuming that I didn't like figs and never would. Even sweet Black Mission figs sometimes taste one-dimensional to me. This dish changes all that. It takes figs out of the dessert category and plays up their savory qualities instead. Paired with rich fromage blanc, piney fresh rosemary, and peppery arugula, figs show a completely different side of themselves. Sometimes I put a little prosciutto on this tart for salty punch. The key here is seasoning the figs so their natural sweetness isn't the death of them. Brown Turkey figs are my favorite to use here. But you can also use fresh Black Mission figs.

**ENOUGH FOR
6 APPETIZERS OR
20 HORS D'OEUVRES**

Onion
1 softball-size

Butter
2 tablespoons

Salt

Puff pastry
1 sheet, thawed but still cold

Brown Turkey figs
12, a little more than 1 pint

Sugar
2 tablespoons

Fresh rosemary
½ teaspoon minced

Fromage blanc
¾ cup, about 6 ounces

Arugula
2 cups loosely packed

Olive oil
about 2 teaspoons

Black pepper
a grind or two

Prosciutto
6 slices (optional)

LET'S GET STARTED →

SAVORY FIG TART

1. Preheat the oven to 400°F.

2. Peel the onion and cut in half lengthwise through the root and stem ends. Trim and discard the stem and roots. Slice the onion lengthwise into thin strips. Heat a 10-inch sauté pan over medium heat, add the butter, and swirl until it melts and starts to foam. Drop in the onions, sprinkle with a Kevin pinch of salt, and shake to spread out the onions. Cut the heat down to medium-low and cook until the onions are golden brown, about 40 minutes, stirring now and then. Line a plate with a double layer of paper towels and drain the onions on the towels.

3. Roll the pastry sheet to a 17 by 11-inch rectangle. Line a baking sheet with parchment paper and lay the pastry on the parchment. Using a fork, poke holes evenly throughout the top of the pastry (called docking) to prevent it from puffing up. Top the dough with a sheet of parchment paper and top that with an empty baking sheet, which will weigh it down and further ensure that the pastry doesn't puff; it also helps the pastry to brown evenly. Place in the oven and bake for 10 minutes. Remove the baking sheet and parchment paper from the top of the pastry and return to the oven until golden brown and crispy, another 8 to 10 minutes.

4. Trim the stems from the figs and discard. Slice the figs into ¼-inch rounds and place in a medium saucepan. Add the sugar and cook over low heat, stirring now and then, until the figs begin to release their juices and the sugar starts to caramelize, about 15 minutes. Stir in the rosemary and a pinch of salt and pull from the heat.

5. Just before serving, spread the cheese in an even layer on the puff pastry, spread the onions on the cheese, and top with the figs. In a small bowl, toss a handful of arugula with just a little olive oil and a pinch of salt. Spread the arugula over the figs and crack a nice grind of black pepper over the top. Cut into larger rectangles or bite-size squares.

6. To bump this up a bit, thinly shred the prosciutto, crisp it in a hot skillet, and sprinkle over the top.

———

PREP TIPS / **Look for all-butter puff pastry from brands like Dufour in the freezer section of your supermarket.**

If you can't find fromage blanc at your market, mix together 3 ounces goat cheese and 3 tablespoons sour cream. Or mix together 3 ounces cream cheese (1 small block) and ⅓ cup plain Greek-style yogurt. You're looking for tanginess in the fromage blanc.

LOW-COUNTRY OYSTER ROAST

Palmetto Bluff, South Carolina, sits about 20 miles northeast of Savannah, Georgia. It's one of the largest waterfront properties on the East Coast, full of nature preserves and walking trails, and with a swanky inn and spa that overlooks the May River. It's a classy place, and every year they celebrate the region's food and culture at the Music to Your Mouth culinary festival. After the event is done on Saturday, the organizers put on this supercool party for the visiting chefs as a sort of thank-you. They swing these massive cast-iron griddles out over a giant bonfire on the riverbank. They load up the griddles with May River oysters and roast 'em until they pop open. They dump the roasted oysters on a picnic table and you stand elbow to elbow with other guests, squeezing lemon juice or hot sauce onto the juiciest, sweetest, saltiest roasted oysters you've ever tasted. I love it. Every year, I spend the entire party time standing at the table. I feel like I'm knocking back a grotesque amount of oysters. One year, I came back from the event and apparently hadn't gotten my fill because I developed this recipe to satisfy a need. I made a spicy emulsified butter sauce to spoon into the warm oysters. At first, I worried about serving this dish. People never have two minds about oysters: They either love them or hate them. I've since served these oysters hundreds of times, and all of six people have refused to try them. That's a pretty good percentage. I should also mention that an exponentially large number of people ate this dish simply because it was put in front of them. And they ended up loving it!

FEEDS ABOUT A DOZEN FOLKS

Oysters
1 bushel (12 dozen)

Lemon juice
¼ cup

Worcestershire sauce
¼ cup

Prepared horseradish (not raw)
2 teaspoons

Tabasco sauce
2 teaspoons

Salt
1 teaspoon

Butter
½ cup, cut into 8 chunks

PREP TIP / Use the freshest warm water oysters you can find. My favorite types are Atlantic Bull's Bay oysters from Charleston, South Carolina, and Apalachicola Bay oysters from Florida.

1. Heat a grill for direct medium-high heat.

2. Spread the oysters in a single layer directly on the grill grate and cover with a wet towel. Close the lid of the grill or, if cooking on an open grill, cover with a large metal bowl or roasting pan (to capture the steam). Steam the oysters until they start to pop open, about 5 minutes. Using tongs, transfer the oysters to baking sheets.

3. In a small saucepan, combine the lemon juice, Worcestershire, horseradish, Tabasco, and salt. Bring the mixture to a boil over medium-high heat, then pull from the heat and whisk in the butter, 1 chunk at a time, until melted. The sauce will separate as it sits, but that is not a problem; gently warm and stir it just before serving.

4. To shuck the oysters, cover your hand with a thick glove or towel, cradle the oyster in your gloved hand, and gently pry open the hinged end with an oyster knife. Remove and discard the top shell and, using the knife, separate the oyster from the bottom shell. Spoon a small amount of the warm sauce onto each oyster and slurp it right out of the shell.

SALMON CROQUETTES

For half my life, I hated salmon croquettes. Everybody in the South makes salmon croquettes, but cheap ingredients like canned chum salmon make them utterly unpalatable. When I moved to Portland, Oregon, and started working at Fife restaurant, I made this recipe as an answer to those bad childhood memories. It takes a totally different approach. I based it on a fantastic braised chicken croquette that I had as a snack at an otherwise unmemorable Spanish restaurant. I wasn't sure if it would work with fresh Pacific salmon because it's so fatty. But I made a béchamel and flavored it with onion, garlic, chives, lemon zest, and nutmeg. Then I folded in fresh, diced salmon, chilled it, and shaped it. Southern croquettes are usually shaped into patties, but I like small football shapes (called quenelles) better. A quick dredge in flour, egg, and panko bread crumbs, and the quenelles were ready for frying. To my absolute surprise, the staff at Fife loved them. And so did I! Try them with a sauce gribiche (page 298) or béarnaise (page 305).

SERVES 4

Butter
2 tablespoons

Flour
about 1 cup

Heavy cream
1 cup

Nutmeg
2 grates on Microplane

Onion
½ cup, finely diced

Garlic
2 cloves, minced

Chives
2 tablespoons, minced

Lemon zest
½ teaspoon

Cayenne pepper
pinch

Fresh salmon
12 ounces, finely diced

Salt

Eggs
2

Panko bread crumbs
about 2 cups, finely ground

Canola oil for frying

1. Melt 1 tablespoon of the butter in a small saucepan over medium heat. Stir in 1 tablespoon of the flour and cook, stirring constantly, until the flour is dissolved, about 1 minute. Whisk in the cream and the nutmeg and increase the temperature to medium high. When the mixture starts to boil, reduce the heat to medium and, stirring frequently, cook the sauce until it is very thick, about 3 minutes. Transfer the sauce to a small metal bowl, press plastic wrap directly onto the top of the sauce and refrigerate until cold, about 45 minutes. The plastic wrap will prevent a skin from forming on the sauce.

2. Rinse and dry the saucepan and heat over medium-low heat. Add the remaining tablespoon of butter, the onions and garlic and cook until the onions are translucent, about 3 minutes. Line a plate with a paper towel and spoon the onion mixture onto the towel to drain. Refrigerate until cold.

3. In a bowl, combine the sauce, the onion mixture, chives, lemon zest and cayenne until thoroughly blended. Using a large rubber spatula, gently fold in the salmon.

4. Shape the mixture into 12 quenelles or cylinders (a small ice cream scoop is perfect for portioning out pieces, a little larger than a golf ball). The shape is important for even cooking and maintaining a creamy center. Spread the croquettes on a sheet pan and refrigerate until very cold, about 1 hour.

5. Preheat the deep fryer to 350°F or, if you prefer to pan-fry, heat 1 inch of oil in a skillet over medium high heat to 350°F.

6. Spread the remaining flour in a shallow dish and whisk together with a Kevin pinch of salt. Crack the eggs in another shallow dish and whisk together with another Kevin pinch of salt. In a third shallow dish, whisk the panko and a Kevin pinch of salt. Using the 3-step fry prep (see page 7) deep fry the croquettes until GBD, about 4 minutes. If pan frying, cook 2 minutes, turn and cook another 2 minutes. Remove to a paper towel to drain.

CRISPY SWEETBREADS WITH CELERY RELISH

Everyone hates sweetbreads for the same reason. They think all internal organs taste like liver. But the reality is that only liver has that strong, metallic, iron-y intenseness. Sweetbreads taste completely mild and creamy. If you've never had them, this dish is a good introduction. Frying something is almost guaranteed to make it taste good. Sweetbreads come in a few different varieties. They are either the pancreas or thymus gland of either lamb or veal. Lamb is a little stronger. I don't recommend starting with that. Veal sweetbreads are nice and mild, and the thymus is smaller and sweeter than the pancreas. Go for veal thymus if it's your first time. When in doubt, pick the smaller ones. Lemon and celery in the relish cut through the fattiness that comes from frying and give the dish a breath of fresh air. It's also pretty awesome on top of the Southern revival potato salad, as in the photo on the opposite page. The potato salad is spiked with a ton of mustard that sharpens and brightens all the flavors on the plate.

---

1. Preheat the oven to 325°F.

2. Rinse the sweetbreads under very cold water, then trim off all the connective tissue and excess fat. Cut the entire head of garlic in half crosswise to expose the cloves. Put both halves of the garlic, the thyme, and shallot in the bottom of a small baking dish and top with the sweetbreads. Cover with enough grapeseed oil to fully submerge everything. Bake, uncovered, for 45 minutes. Pull the baking dish from the oven and turn the sweetbreads over, making sure they are still fully submerged in oil. Return the dish to the oven and bake until the sweetbreads are tender and spongy, another 45 minutes or so. Pull the dish from the oven and cool the sweetbreads in the oil to room temperature. When completely cool, drain the sweetbreads and discard the oil.

3. Place the sweetbreads on a baking sheet, cover with another baking sheet, and weigh down with a brick or heavy skillet to compact the sweetbreads. Refrigerate until cold, about an hour. Trim off and discard any coagulated membrane or skin from the compacted sweetbreads, and then cut into four equal portions and pat dry with a paper towel.

4. Heat the oil in a deep fryer to 325°F.

5. Bread the sweetbreads using the 3-step fry prep with the flour, eggs, and panko (see page 7). Fry the sweetbreads until GBD, 5 to 6 minutes. Set on a rack over paper towels to drain and sprinkle with salt.

6. Divide the sweetbreads among serving plates and top with the celery relish.

*ENOUGH FOR
4 SMALL PLATES*

Veal sweetbreads
1 pound

Garlic
1 whole head

Thyme
3 sprigs

Shallot
1, peeled and thickly sliced

Grapeseed oil
about 4 cups

Canola oil for frying

All-purpose flour
about 1 cup

Eggs
2 large, beaten

Panko bread crumbs
about 1 cup finely ground

Salt

Celery relish
½ cup (recipe follows)

CELERY RELISH

MAKES ABOUT ½ CUP

Shallots
3 tablespoons finely diced

Celery
3 tablespoons finely diced

Scallions
3 tablespoons finely chopped

Lemon
1 fat one

Salt
1 teaspoon

Ground black pepper
¼ teaspoon

1. Toss the shallots, celery, scallions, ½ teaspoon lemon zest, 2 tablespoons lemon juice, salt, and pepper until combined. Let the relish rest for at least 1 hour; stir to redistribute the flavors before serving.

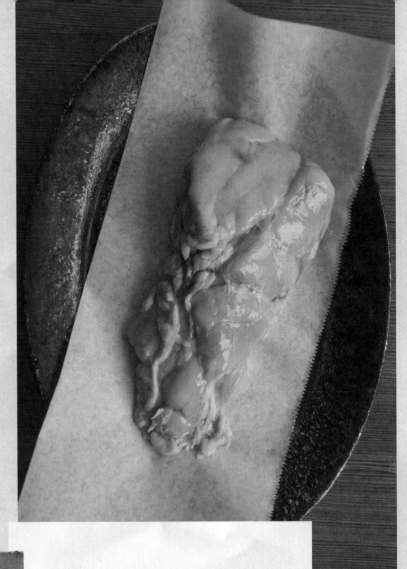

What the Hell's a Sweetbread, Anyway?

Sweetbreads are the pancreas or thymus glands of either veal or lamb. I prefer the softer thymus glands to the harder pancreas. I also prefer veal here because lamb sweetbreads would be too strong tasting. Look for veal sweetbreads at better farmer's markets and butcher shops. I fry them at a somewhat low temperature to make sure they heat all the way through without overbrowning the breading.

NEW AND IMPROVED LIVER AND ONIONS

It doesn't get much more classic than this. Or much more reviled the world over. Liver and onions is abhorred and detested by thousands of people. Yet it's also cherished and devoured by an equal number of liver fans. If this combo has been around for such a long time and drawn so many fans, there has to be something good about it. It's true that the sulfuric, almost antiseptic, taste of onions cleans up the metallic taste of liver. But even so, the downfall of most liver dishes is that people often bypass the necessary steps to cleaning up the liver before it's cooked. If you soak calf's liver in milk before cooking, the milk gets rid of that muddy, iron-y taste. It's also important not to overcook it. Overcooked liver has a nasty, garbage-can aroma that's completely absent when liver is cooked just until it's firm. I wanted to add some nontraditional flavors here, so I season the liver with warm chai spices including cardamom, anise, and ginger. Some gently simmered pears add a little sweetness, which amplifies the sweetness of the sautéed onions. As a whole, the dish is a well-thought-out and finessed approach to organ meat. If you're on the cusp of liking liver, try it. You might become a convert. Just make sure your liver is very fresh and then marinate it in milk for the better part of a day.

ENOUGH FOR 6 FOLKS

Calf's liver
2 slices, each about
4 ounces and ½ inch thick

Milk
1 cup

Bacon
2 extra-thick slices cut into
½-inch dice

**Tea masala
(recipe follows)**
2 teaspoons

Onion
1 cup cut into ½-inch dice

D'Anjou pears
2 peeled, cored, and
cut into ½-inch dice,
about 2 cups

Garlic
1 clove, minced

Fresh ginger
1-inch piece, peeled
and minced

Chicken stock
½ cup

Apple cider vinegar
1 teaspoon

Butter
¼ cup + 1 tablespoon

Honey
2 teaspoons

Salt

All-purpose flour
about ¼ cup

Fresh chives
1 tablespoon thinly sliced

**Ground black
pepper**

Coarse finishing salt

LET'S GET STARTED →

1. If you bought sliced liver, drop the liver into a gallon-size zip-top bag, pour in the milk, and zip the top closed. Refrigerate for at least 8 hours or overnight. If you have whole liver, lay it on a cutting board and place your hand on top of the liver. Firmly and evenly press the liver down and, holding a very sharp knife parallel to the board, slice the liver into ½-inch-thick slices. Drop the slices into a gallon-size zip-top bag, pour in the milk, and zip the top closed. Refrigerate for at least 8 hours or overnight.

2. Heat a 10-inch sauté pan over medium heat and cook the bacon until lightly browned, about 8 minutes. Add the tea masala and stir for 30 seconds. Heating the spices will bring out their natural oils and release more flavor into the dish. Add the onions and cook until they are soft and beginning to brown, about 5 minutes. Add the pears, garlic, and ginger and cook until the edges of the pears start to soften, another 3 to 4 minutes. Add the chicken stock and vinegar to the pan and cook until almost all of the liquid is gone, 4 to 5 minutes. Using the washing machine method (see page 12), emulsify 1 tablespoon of the butter, the honey, and a Kevin pinch of salt into the mixture. Transfer to a bowl until serving time. Rinse and dry the skillet.

3. Line a plate with a double layer of paper towels.

4. Remove the liver from the milk and pat dry. Using sharp kitchen scissors, cut the liver into 6 equal strips and lightly dust both sides of each piece with flour, shaking off any excess. Heat the sauté pan over medium-high heat and add the remaining ¼ cup butter to the pan. When the butter starts to foam, add the liver in a single layer. Don't crowd the liver or it won't cook evenly; you may need to work in two batches. Tilt the pan and spoon the juices over the liver to baste it. Cook, tilting and basting nonstop, until the surface of the liver is nicely caramelized, about 2 minutes. Return the pan flat to the heat, flip each slice of liver over, and repeat the spooning and basting process until the liver is lightly browned and just firm, another 2 minutes. Transfer the liver to the paper towels and reserve the pan juices.

5. For each plate, set a 3-inch ring mold in the center. Spoon one-quarter of the pear mixture into the mold and press with the back of the spoon to compact and fill the mold. Carefully remove the mold and sprinkle some of the chives over the pear mixture. Top with 1 slice of liver and a drizzle of pan juices. Sprinkle a few more chives over the liver and finish with 2 grinds of pepper and a pinch of finishing salt.

TEA **MASALA**

MAKES 2 ½ TEASPOONS

Ground cardamom
1 teaspoon

Ground anise seed
¼ teaspoon

Ground allspice
¼ teaspoon

Ground cinnamon
¼ teaspoon

Ground ginger
¼ teaspoon

Ground nutmeg
¼ teaspoon

Ground black pepper
¼ teaspoon

1. Mix the cardamom, aniseed, allspice, cinnamon, ginger, nutmeg, and pepper together and store in an airtight container for up to 1 month.

TEA MASALA / Typically used to flavor chai tea, this warm spice blend has a ton of other uses. Rub it on strongly flavored meats like venison and bison. Infuse it into cream to make chai ice cream. Or of course, you can steep some tea masala with black tea to make a rich and aromatic cup of chai.

HAGGIS
WITH CARAMELIZED TURNIP
AND POTATO PUREE

If it's not blatantly apparent from my photographs, I am of Scottish descent, unadulterated on both sides. Proud Southerners like to embrace their Scottish heritage, but they also cherry-pick the things they like best, such as getting blackout drunk and holidays that encourage you to get blackout drunk. Burns Night is such a holiday. My family celebrates Burns Night every January. Ever since I proclaimed my desire to be a chef back in high school, the task of making haggis for Burns Night was doled out to me. Robert Burns is the only notable poet from Scotland. To celebrate his life, what you do is read a bunch of his poetry out loud on January 25, clink glasses, and drink Scotch. You also read his poem "Address to a Haggis." With that reading, you then serve a traditional dinner of haggis, neeps, and tatties (turnips and potatoes). Now, haggis is notoriously nasty stuff. It often starts with funky bits and pieces like lungs, kidneys, heart, and liver from sheep. The organ meats are bound up with Scottish oatmeal and then stuffed into a sheep's bladder or stomach for cooking. The Scotch are utilitarian folks and not very wealthy.

But haggis doesn't have to be gross. I adapted the traditional preparation to use milder-tasting calf's liver, meaty lamb's tongue for oomph, and some ground lamb to temper the intensity of the organ meats. I also jettisoned the sheep's stomach and used a terrine mold instead. The stomach was always just a cooking vessel anyway (you don't eat it), so why not? If a terrine will get more people to enjoy the dish, I'm all for it. I chill the cooked terrine, slice it thick, brush it with mustard, roll it in bread crumbs, and pan-fry it on one side in clarified butter. The texture of the finished haggis is a little like pâté with one crunchy fried side. With the turnips and potatoes caramelized in cream and pureed until velvety smooth, this is a haggis dinner like you've never had it before. For years, my family has been choking down haggis on Burns Night. I wanted to make a dish that everyone would really look forward to eating year after year. I think this country-style terrine does the trick.

LET'S GET STARTED →

Scottish oats
1 cup

Lamb's tongue
8 ounces, about 6

Calf's liver
8 ounces (can substitute lamb liver)

Salt and ground black pepper

Butter
1 teaspoon

Onion
1 softball-size, finely chopped, about 2 cups

Garlic
2 cloves, minced, about 1 tablespoon

Rubbed sage
2 tablespoons

Dried thyme
2 teaspoons

Ground allspice
½ teaspoon

Ground cinnamon
½ teaspoon

Ground cloves
½ teaspoon

Ground mace
½ teaspoon

Lamb
1 pound ground

Gelatin
0.25-ounce packet powdered, about 1 tablespoon, or 4 sheets

Beef stock
1 cup, cold (mushroom stock also works)

Dijon mustard
about 2 tablespoons

Panko bread crumbs
about 1 cup finely ground

Clarified butter
about 2 tablespoons

Caramelized turnip and potato puree (page 303)
1 cup, warm

Pickled shallots, turnips, or other vegetables (page 321)
1½ cups

Celery leaves or young micro herbs
about ½ cup

Flake salt, such as Maldon

HAGGIS WITH CARAMELIZED TURNIP AND POTATO PUREE

1. Toast the oats in a 10-inch skillet over medium heat, shaking occasionally, until they smell a little nutty and turn light golden brown, about 5 minutes. Transfer to a plate and set aside to cool.

2. Remove the outer membrane from the tongue and discard. Coarsely chop the tongue and liver into 1-inch cubes, pat dry, and season with salt and pepper. Heat the skillet over high heat, add the butter, and swirl the pan until the butter is melted. Add the tongue and liver and cook for 1 minute. Add the onions and garlic and toss to combine. Cook just until the onions start to brown on the edges, about 2 minutes. Spread the mixture on a baking sheet and cool to room temperature.

3. In a food processor fitted with a metal blade, blend the tongue and liver mixture until it starts to cream up, about 40 seconds. Blend in the sage, thyme, allspice, cinnamon, cloves, mace, and 1 teaspoon black pepper. The mixture should have a little texture but no large chunks. Transfer to a large bowl and, using a large spoon or spatula, mix in the toasted oats and ground lamb until thoroughly blended. Refrigerate until cold, about 30 minutes.

4. In a small bowl, soften the gelatin powder in ¼ cup of the cold stock. Place the remaining ¾ cup stock in a small pan and bring to a boil over high heat. Pull the pan from the heat and whisk in the gelatin mixture until completely dissolved. Stir in 2 tablespoons salt until dissolved. Transfer the gelatin mixture to a metal bowl, stir in 4 ice cubes, and continue stirring until the temperature of the mixture drops to room temperature.

5. Preheat the oven to 275°F.

6. Pull the meat mixture from the refrigerator and stir in the gelatin mixture until well blended. Line a 12 inch by 4 inch by 4-inch terrine mold with plastic wrap, leaving extra wrap overhanging the edges. Spread the meat mixture in the mold and firmly tap the mold on the counter to get rid of any air bubbles. Fold the extra plastic wrap over the top and, using a separate sheet of wrap, tightly cover the mold. Wrap a piece of aluminum foil over the plastic wrap and secure around the edges of the mold. Place the lid on the mold and place in a baking dish or roasting pan with sides at least 1 inch higher than the mold. Fill a pitcher with warm water. Slide the pan partially into the oven and pour the water into the pan, filling it almost to the top of the mold. Carefully slide the dish into the center of the oven, close the door, and bake for 3 hours.

7. Partially slide the baking dish out of the oven and carefully remove the terrine from the pan. Leave the water-filled pan in the oven to cool, so you can safely pull it out later. Pull off the lid, foil, and plastic wrap from the terrine. The terrine should be cooked through and a thermometer should register at least 185°F when inserted into the center. If it isn't, bake longer. Set the terrine on a rack and cool to room temperature, then cover it tightly and refrigerate until completely set—overnight is best. Or you can keep the chilled haggis in the refrigerator for up to 1 week.

8. Before serving, preheat the oven to 350°F.

9. Using a wet serrated knife, cut the chilled haggis into slices about 1-inch thick. Brush one side with Dijon mustard and dip into the panko. Heat a 10-inch sauté pan over medium-high heat, add about 2 teaspoons of the clarified butter, and heat for 30 seconds. Gently slide 4 slices of haggis, panko side down, into the hot butter. Cook until lightly browned, about 2 minutes. Don't crowd the pan; a 10-inch pan will comfortably hold 4 slices. Place the skillet in the oven to take the chill off the top side, about 2 minutes but not much longer. Remember, this is still a terrine and it can melt! Pull the pan from the oven and, using a thin spatula, transfer the slices to paper towels to drain. Repeat with the other slices of haggis, or use three 10-inch sauté pans to do all the slices at once.

10. For each serving, swirl about 2 tablespoons of the turnip and potato puree in the center of a serving plate. Place the haggis, browned side up, on the puree, and garnish with pickled goods (shallots, turnips, or other pickled vegetables), celery leaves, and a sprinkle of flake salt.

KNOW YOUR OATS / Scottish oats are simply oat groats ground into small pieces with coarse stones. Irish or steel-cut oats are very similar but cut by steel instead of stone. Rolled oats are completely different because they are rolled flat. Rolled oats (old-fashioned, quick-cooking, or instant) will not work well in this recipe, but Irish, steel-cut, or pinhead oats will work fine.

MY VERSION OF SOUTHERN FOOD

I don't like the term *modern Southern cuisine.* It seems hollow. In 2003, I started working at the Atlanta Grill at The Ritz-Carlton, Atlanta. I had just graduated from culinary school at the Art Institute of Atlanta, and I was talking with the chef de cuisine. It was my second day, and he said, "The Atlanta Grill is supposed to be a modern Southern restaurant." Casually, I asked him, "Where are you from, Julian?" "Brooklyn," he replied. "Where is the head chef from?" "France." There were two other guys and a girl from New York, a guy from Haiti, and a guy from California. It seemed odd that we were trying to make modern Southern food, and I was the only person there from the South.

Atlanta Grill served fried chicken, but it was only a breast and didn't have any bones. We served watermelon but used three different colors of watermelon and cut it up into little cubes. This was my introduction to sophistication. It was a crock of shit.

Like every regional food in every country, Southern American food is extremely specific. It has well-defined traditions. There is no modernizing. From that moment forward, I looked down upon the idea of cooking "modern Southern food." It seemed too clichéd to build a career on.

Over the next few years, I cooked various styles of food. My Ritz-Carlton experience built on my classical French training. When I moved to Portland, Oregon, in 2006, I got schooled in local farm-to-table cuisine. When I moved back to Atlanta in 2008, the ingredient-focused theme was driven home by Michael Tuohy's ultra-simple California cuisine at Woodfire Grill.

Later that year, Michael moved on and I became executive chef of Woodfire. At first, my food was a combination of techniques I'd learned at the Ritz, ingredient combinations picked up from Michael, and a few twists from my time in the Pacific Northwest. But I grew tired of doing subtle spins on the food I had been emulating. I felt deep down that I should be able to cook whatever flew into my mind.

When I climbed out of the copycat rut, my identity as a chef began to emerge. It dawned on me that I did know another cuisine—the Southern cuisine I grew up with. This was not a skill set I had acquired professionally. But if I wanted to cook from deep inside, I had to fold that whole bank of Southern food knowledge into the mix.

It was a liberating realization. Then I read a review of my cooking that described it as "modern Southern food." I nearly had a heart attack. "Oh well," I thought, "my career is over." It's true that I was

We care about the history of the food in our region. We buy ingredients from small-scale farmers and ranchers who grow high-quality foods in the South.

cooking sophisticated food with a distinctly Southern feel. But in my mind, I was just exploring the food that I really cared about. I wasn't "modernizing." My dishes were springing from food memories, often from my childhood.

One-pot hog supper (page 83) is a good example. When I was growing up, Granny cooked this dish a lot. She came up with it as a teenager when it was her night to cook for the family and she had nothing but a hodgepodge of ingredients on hand. She rendered some fatback in a pot, then layered in potatoes, cabbage, and tomatoes and slow-braised the whole thing on the stovetop. No stirring. No heavy seasoning. Just vegetables, fatback, salt, and pepper. Her brothers teased her, saying, "What's this? Some slop you feed the hogs?" Granny thought that was funny, and one-pot hog supper became a family tradition.

In 2010, I served this dish to the founder of Slow Food International, Carlo Petrini, at a benefit dinner held at Watershed restaurant in Decatur, Georgia. The chefs were all Southerners, and each of us served a dish that embodied the region we grew up in. One-pot hog supper was the perfect representation of my roots. But I didn't take this hearty, family-style dish and update it. I made only two changes: I served it in individual cast-iron pots instead of one large pot, and I garnished it with a mixed herb salad for contrast.

After the course was served, the president of the local Slow Foods chapter said Carlo Petrini wanted to talk to me. Carlo asked me where I was from. I told him I was from Atlanta. I explained that the dish was my grandmother's and she was from the mountains north of the city. He didn't speak much English. I didn't speak any Italian. But he could taste that there was a story and a history to the food. He talked about generations past and generations to come. He said that one-pot hog supper is what Slow Food is all about. It is part of a traditional way of life. He encouraged me to keep cooking this kind of food.

That dish made me realize that I've always embraced Southern food. Not modern Southern food. Not strictly conventional Southern food. Just Southern food. I cook a style of Southern food from two specific regions, the mountains and the plantations. My father's family comes from the Appalachian Mountains in north Georgia, South Carolina, and North Carolina. They emigrated from Scotland to a remote region of the South that mirrored their mountainous homeland. Multiple families relocated as a group, and they brought with them a strong sense of community and an extremely resourceful, utilitarian approach to food. They sat down and enjoyed meals together every day. That communal quality of mountain food is enormously important to me.

My mother's side of the family grew up in the traditions of Southern plantation cooking. They were Atlanta people. Plantation owners were wealthier and their food was served with more presentation, pomp, and circumstance. It wasn't just eaten for sustenance but also for pleasure. The dishes were a little richer, included more meat and heavy cream, and used spices from all over the world. But the food still had a strong communal backbone.

My Southern food combines both styles. I follow the utilitarian traditions of the mountains as well as

> I explained that the dish was my grandmother's and she was from the mountains north of the city. He didn't speak much English. I didn't speak any Italian. But he could taste that there was a story and a history to the food. He talked about generations past and generations to come.

the celebratory enjoyment of the plantations. That doesn't mean I modernize the classics by frying chicken without the bones or dicing watermelon into perfect cubes. I approach a dish by coming to grips with why Southerners first made that dish the way they did.

I'm proud to be able to carry the Slow Food logo on Woodfire Grill's menus. You don't see that very often. It's not a sign that everything we do reverts back to some antiquated way of cooking. It means that our values as cooks are strongly aligned with the values of Slow Food International. We care about the history of the food in our region. We buy ingredients from small-scale farmers and ranchers who grow high-quality foods in the South. We support what they do because they are responsible stewards of the land and take exceptional care with our region's plants, animals, and soil. We try to strengthen those fragile links between agriculture, community, and the sheer pleasure of eating good food.

My version of Southern food is not just about preserving traditional dishes of the South. The truth is that Southerners have always accepted the foods and traditions of others—from India's curry in the now-classic Southern dish called country captain to sesame seeds from Africa folded into Charleston benne wafers to farro grains transplanted from Europe and immortalized in old Southern recipe books. In the past decade alone, the South has seen an unprecedented influx of immigrants from other states and countries. The area's population grew by 14 percent from 2000 to 2010, making it the fastest-growing region in the United States. These demographic changes expose the South to new influences that expand Southern food culture, which I think is a good thing.

When I pair charred okra with tomato-coconut chutney (page 27) or fried green tomatoes with Indian raita (page 74), I know that the okra is Southern by way of West Africa, the coconut is Southern via India, and the green tomatoes are Southern by way of South America. Are these dishes traditionally Southern? Modern Southern? I don't know and don't care. They are dishes built from the ingredients and people in this region. When I make boiled peanuts, braised pole beans, and banana pudding, I recognize how deeply ingrained these foods are in the minds of Southerners. It would be arrogant of me to recklessly "modernize" them. I prepare them with care and an understanding of why these dishes were created in the first place. My primary job as a Southern chef is to apply a skilled, intelligent approach to food grown, eaten, and enjoyed by people in the South. But the dishes themselves tell a story of Southern food that has been hundreds of years in the making. Southern food history is an open-ended book. It's still being written. The important thing is that the story stays true to its roots.

BUTTERMILK BISCUITS

Biscuits are a fine art—one that I am capable of saying I have not mastered. My biscuits usually come out good, sometimes great. But my chef de cuisine at Woodfire Grill, E.J. Hodgkinson, has mastered biscuit making. It's difficult to admit this because E.J. is not from the South; he's from California. This is his recipe, and it comes out the same every single time. The recipe is based on weight, not volume, though I have included both measurements here. Biscuits are often erratic because people measure by ingredient volume, which changes with the weather. When it's humid, flour absorbs moisture from the air and increases in volume. For consistency, it helps to measure by weight whenever you're baking. But what really makes this recipe unique is how the fat is incorporated into the flour. In any biscuit, the fat needs to be mixed into the dry ingredients as quickly as possible so that the butter doesn't melt. Most recipes call for cutting the butter into small pieces, then cutting them into even smaller pieces in the flour with a handheld pastry blender. To simplify the process, E.J. freezes the butter hard as a brick, then grates it like cheese on a box grater directly into the dry ingredients. This method quickly incorporates the butter without overworking the gluten in the dough, which is what toughens biscuits. His recipe makes a sturdy, layered, fluffy biscuit. It's not the softest biscuit on the planet. But the method is bulletproof and not finicky at all. As soon as the biscuits rest for a couple minutes out of the oven, I like to split them in half and spread them with peach butter (page 317).

MAKES ABOUT 24

All-purpose flour
4 cups (20 ounces) + additional for dusting the board

Baking powder
3 tablespoons (1¼ ounces)

Sugar
2 tablespoons (¾ ounce)

Salt
1 tablespoon + 2 teaspoons (½ ounce)

Butter
14 tablespoons (7 ounces), frozen

Buttermilk
about 2 cups (14 ounces)

1. Preheat the oven to 400°F.

2. In a large bowl, whisk together the flour, baking powder, sugar, and salt. Using a box grater, grate the frozen butter into the flour mixture, tossing after each quarter stick of butter is added to coat the butter shards with flour. Toss to combine. Stir in 1¾ cups of the buttermilk and, using large strokes and stirring from the bottom up, stir just enough to combine the mixture into a crumbly mass, 20 to 25 strokes. If the dough doesn't come together, stir in more buttermilk a tablespoon at a time, just until the mixture barely holds together.

3. Dust a clean, flat work surface with flour. Scrape the dough onto the floured surface, gather into a ball and gently knead with the palms of your hands about 10 times, just enough to form a cohesive dough ball (if you want to get fanatical, it helps to chill your hands in ice water to keep the warmth of your hands from melting the butter). Sprinkle a little more flour onto the dough and gently roll or pat to an even ¾-inch thickness.

4. Dip a 2½-inch round biscuit cutter in flour and, punching straight down without twisting, punch out the biscuits. Punch the rounds as close together as possible to use up as much dough as possible in the first roll (re-rolled dough is always chewier). Gather any remaining

dough, knead a few times to form a cohesive ball and, again, roll or pat the dough to an even ¾-inch thickness. Punch out the remaining biscuits and gather the last remnants of dough into a rough ball, which some people call "the cat head" because of its size and shape. Place the biscuits on a baking sheet, close enough so the edges just touch. Add the cat head to the sheet and bake until the biscuits start to brown; they should be more than just a touch of golden here and there. It will take about 20 minutes. The biscuits are pretty thick, so you need to bake them long enough to cook the dough all the way through. Let the biscuits rest for 5 minutes before serving. The resting time allows the steam inside the biscuit to finish cooking the center.

Anson Mills

Sometime in 2000, I was driving around the mountains of South Carolina and came across a roadside store that sold odds and ends like wicker furniture and apple cobbler. I picked up a white paper bag stamped "Anson Mills Antebellum Grits." The bag looked supercool. But when I got the grits home and onto the stove, I had to keep adding water and they never seemed to soften up. I did some digging and found that these were stone-ground, old-school grits that needed more time and more liquid than modern grits. So I put another pot on the stove—this time with a little more patience—and they turned out awesome. They were really creamy yet had an identifiable coarseness. I was so impressed with them that I starting using Anson Mills grits at The Ritz-Carlton, Atlanta, where I worked. When I moved to Oregon, I had them shipped out to Fife restaurant. And I had them shipped to Washington when I moved there.

Glenn Roberts started Anson Mills in South Carolina in 1998 to help protect and revive heirloom grains. He tracked down a pre–Civil War era variety of milling corn known as Carolina Gourdseed White. This variety of corn has huge

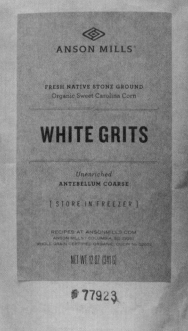

kernels and a creamy starch that makes incredible grits. Within a couple of years, Glenn was growing nearly a dozen varieties of heirloom mill corn plus other heirloom grains like Carolina Gold rice. If you care about good ingredients, try Anson Mills heirloom grains instead of your run-of-the-mill commodity grains (see Sources, page 326). I will warn you, though: Old-school grits take a tragically long time to cook—at least 4 hours—and if you take them off the heat sooner, you'll get tough bits of corn stuck in your teeth like popcorn. But trust me. That long, slow cooking time is well worth the wait.

OVERNIGHT GRITS
WITH TOMATO-BRAISED GREENS

Two quick stories about this recipe: In 2009, I was making grits for 1,000 people for a Slow Food dinner in Decatur, Georgia. One of the cooks at Woodfire Grill was helping to finish up the grits the day before the event. He put the grits in our hotbox to keep them warm and forgot about them. The next morning, I opened it up and 5 gallons of cooked grits had been sitting in there all night. I use white grits, but these had turned a milky brown color like iced coffee. Obviously, I didn't want to throw them out; we didn't have any more grits in the pantry. I decided to taste them, which is not what a sane person would do with food that's been sitting in a hotbox for a whole day. They were amazing. They tasted 100 times creamier than our normal grits. The corn had fully absorbed the liquid and become completely soft instead of having that "gritty" texture. They also had a nutty taste because the milk sugars caramelized overnight (hence the brown color). I made sure they were safe for human consumption, then brought our "caramelized grits" to the Slow Food dinner. People went apeshit for them. But I couldn't admit that it was an accident until now.

Second story: In September 2011, I was competing in the Chef's Challenge at Kendall Jackson's 15th Annual Heirloom Tomato Festival in Santa Rosa, California. The chefs can pick whatever they want from the winery's gardens, but you have to make three dishes in 25 minutes and each has to include tomatoes plus the secret ingredient, which is revealed *Iron Chef*–style at the last second. Chicken was the secret ingredient, and I served it with young collard greens that I found in the gardens. The greens are a variation on classic Southern braised greens, but I learned on a hunch that adding tomatoes speeds up the cooking because the acid in the tomatoes helps break down the greens, making them tender faster. I won the challenge not because of the acid in the tomatoes but because the greens tasted awesome. I knew they would be even better with the caramelized grits, so I tried the combo when I got back home. Try it yourself and see.

LET'S GET STARTED →

OVERNIGHT GRITS
WITH TOMATO-BRAISED GREENS

FEEDS 8 TO 10 FOLKS

Butter
½ cup

Onion
1 baseball-size,
sliced lengthwise into
thin strips

Salt
2 teaspoons

Whole milk
2 cups

Water
3 cups

Grits
1 cup
coarse-ground,
preferably
Anson Mills

**Tomato-braised
greens**
4 cups (recipe
follows)

1. Heat a Dutch oven over medium-high heat. Add 4 tablespoons of the butter, the onions, and ½ teaspoon of the salt. Cover and cook until the onions start to caramelize, about 8 minutes. Take off the cover and add the milk and water. Crank the heat up to high and bring the mixture almost to a boil. Start whisking, and slowly add the grits, whisking nonstop. After the grits are all in, whisk for another 30 seconds, then pull from the heat.

2. Pour the grits into a slow cooker, cover, and cook on low for 8 hours or overnight. If you don't have a slow cooker and don't mind keeping your oven on for a while, put the covered Dutch oven in a 200°F oven for 8 hours or overnight. The long cooking time and low temperature give you amazingly creamy grits.

3. Before serving, stir in the remaining 4 tablespoons of butter and remaining 1 teaspoon salt. Then mound a large spoonful of grits on each plate and top with a generous portion of greens.

TOMATO-BRAISED GREENS

MAKES 4 CUPS

**Tender young greens
(collards, kale, or turnip)**
about 2 pounds

Bacon
¾ cup chopped, about 4 ounces

Onion
1 cup diced into ½-inch pieces

Garlic
8 cloves, minced, about ¼ cup

Canned peeled whole tomatoes
2 cans, 28 ounces each

**Smoked pork or chicken stock
(page 293)**
1 cup

Brewed coffee
¾ cup

Jalapeño chile pepper
1, sliced crosswise, about ¼ cup

Salt
1 tablespoon

Dried red pepper flakes
2 teaspoons

Fresh thyme leaves
2 teaspoons

1. Fill a 4-quart stockpot about three-quarters full with water and bring to a rapid boil. Fill a large bowl with ice water. Line a baking sheet with a dry kitchen towel.

2. Cut off and discard the tough stems from the greens, then coarsely chop the leaves. Drop the greens into the boiling water and blanch until the greens are a shade brighter than they were and just start to wilt, about 2 minutes. Using tongs, transfer the greens to the ice bath and swirl to cool. Transfer to the kitchen towel to drain.

3. Heat a Dutch oven over medium-high heat. Add the bacon, stir, and cook until the bacon is crispy and the fat has rendered, about 5 minutes. Stir in the onions and garlic and cook until soft, about 3 minutes. Using your hands, squeeze and crush the tomatoes into the pot, breaking them up and adding all of the juice. Stir in the stock, coffee, jalapeño, salt, red pepper flakes, thyme, and drained greens. Bring the mixture to a boil, then cut the heat down and simmer until slightly thickened, about 1 hour.

SOUTHERN REVIVAL POTATO SALAD

I remember old ladies bringing dishes like this one to church revivals and potluck suppers when I was a kid. I created the recipe from memories of creamy potato salad, crammed full of hard-cooked egg yolks with a sharp kick of mustard. Southerners love that puckery quality in potato salad. On a potluck plate, you'll already have sweetness in the coleslaw. So we like the potato salad to have some piquancy to it. This is one of the few recipes in the book that calls for a store-bought product. I specifically recommend Duke's mayonnaise. Duke's is a Southern product, and it's different from other commercial mayonnaises because it's not sweetened. You could use Hellmann's, Blue Plate, or another commercial brand, but your potato salad will come out sweeter than I like it. I suppose you could replace some of the sweet relish with more cornichons to offset the sweetness, but it's easy enough to buy Duke's online. Either way, a store-bought mayo is preferred here because it won't break as easily as homemade mayo. That's important because you add the hot potatoes to the mayonnaise to create the creamy texture that's crucial to the dish. The hot potatoes need to absorb some of the mayo, sort of like stirring butter and milk into hot potatoes for mashed potatoes. Believe me.

I served this dish in July 2010 to a crowd with several notable food professionals. It works. The dinner was $175 a plate and hosted by Wholesome Wave, chef Michel Nischan's organization that brings farmer's markets to underfunded areas of the country. The event was billed as a Southern potluck, and I knew this dish would strike a chord. It was a hit. Even fine-dining chefs appreciated the taste of a humble dish properly executed and driven by loving care. If you're cooking a fancy meal, try it as a side dish with the crispy sweetbreads with celery relish (page 47).

1. Peel the potatoes and slice them about 1 inch thick. Put the potatoes in a Dutch oven and add enough water to cover the spuds. Add 2 tablespoons salt and stir to combine. The water should be salty, like seawater. Bring the potatoes to a boil over high heat, then cut the heat down to maintain a simmer. Cook until the potatoes are fork-tender, about 15 minutes.

2. Put the eggs in a saucepan and add enough water to cover them. Bring to a boil over high heat, then pull the pan from the heat and put a lid on it. After 13 minutes, take off the lid, pour out the hot water, and run cold water over the eggs until they are completely cool. Peel the eggs.

3. Meanwhile, in the bowl of a stand mixer fitted with the paddle attachment, mix the cornichons with the sweet relish, vinegar, Espelette pepper, mayonnaise, and mustard to make the dressing. It will be light orange in color from the mustard and Espelette pepper.

4. When the potatoes are done, drain them in a colander and add to the mixer bowl while hot. Turn the mixer on low just until the potatoes are combined with the dressing. The hot potatoes melt the dressing to make a really creamy mixture. It will be a little thin when it's hot but will thicken up when it cools. Add the peeled, boiled eggs (yes, whole). Turn to low speed, gradually cranking up the speed as the potatoes and eggs break up. Beat the potatoes and eggs until they are a creamy mess, a little chunky but really creamy. Taste and season with salt as needed.

5. Spread the potato salad on a baking sheet and cover with plastic wrap. Place in the refrigerator to cool. Serve cold.

ESPELETTE PEPPER / The French don't like chile peppers too much, but in the Basque region, they like a little heat. Espelette tastes pretty mild as far as chile peppers go, but it has this beautiful floral aroma. It's perfect when cayenne pepper would be too hot and black pepper just doesn't fit the bill. I find that a little bit of heat can be extremely important in a dish. It adds an exciting edge to foods with a soft, delicate flavor—like potatoes. Just a pinch of chile wakes up the whole palate. A lot of retailers carry Espelette pepper these days (see Sources, page 327), but if you can't find it, you could replace it with hot paprika or pure New Mexican chile powder in a pinch.

SHOULD BE ENOUGH FOR 8 PEOPLE

Yukon gold potatoes
about 3 pounds

Salt

Eggs
2 large

Cornichons or dill pickle relish
¼ cup finely chopped

Sweet relish
2 tablespoons

White wine vinegar
2 tablespoons

Espelette pepper
1½ teaspoons

Duke's mayonnaise
(see Sources, page 327)
1 cup

Sauer's yellow mustard
(see Sources, page 327)
¼ cup

BOILED PEANUTS

My wife thinks peanuts should only ever be roasted or made into peanut butter. I, on the other hand, would come just short of wrecking my car to pull to the side of the road for boiled peanuts. I've been trying to figure out how to get a boiled peanut tattoo. If you're new to boiled peanuts, you basically take freshly dug, raw green peanuts and boil them in salty water. When green peanuts are available—which is twice a year in Georgia—you need to stop what you're doing, call in sick to work, and make boiled peanuts. You can soak them overnight in water like you would with beans; or you can just boil them longer. For the cooking liquid, some go with plain salted water; some go with spicy liquid. I once had boiled peanuts in the mountains of Rabun Gap, north of Mountain City, Georgia, from a guy who cooked his peanuts with a piece of hambone in the water. He sold Confederate flags, chairs made from braided saplings, boiled peanuts, and a big jacked-up truck that I thought about buying. The peanuts were so good that now I would never even think of boiling peanuts without a hambone, bacon, or some kind of cured pork. And it's critical to cool the peanuts in the cooking liquid so that they can soak up the seasoning. Give them a stir once or twice as they cool, so the seasoning doesn't settle to the bottom.

ENOUGH FOR 10 HUNGRY SNACKERS

Green peanuts
3 pounds in the shell, soaked overnight in water

Bacon
4 ounces, diced

Salt
⅔ cup

Dried thyme
1 tablespoon

Garlic powder
1 tablespoon

Cayenne pepper
1 tablespoon

Celery seeds
1 tablespoon

GREEN PEANUTS / **Like beans, peanuts are legumes. Green peanuts are the raw legumes. They're not green in color, just freshly harvested.**

1. Rinse the peanuts of all dust and dirt. Combine the peanuts, bacon, salt, thyme, garlic powder, cayenne, and celery seeds in a Dutch oven and cover with water; the peanuts will float, so add about a third more volume of water than peanuts. Put on the lid and bring to a boil over high heat. Cut the heat down so that the liquid bubbles and cook at an aggressive simmer until the peanuts are tender, about 3 hours. Cooking time depends on how green, fresh, and dry-cured the peanuts are. The first batch of the season may cook for 5 hours, while a batch from a few weeks later might be good and done at 3 hours. After 3 hours or so, start tasting the peanuts every 15 minutes.

2. If you're eating these now, let them cool a bit, then fish them out with a slotted spoon and serve them in a bowl, with an extra bowl for the shells. If you're eating them later or have leftovers, cool them to room temperature in the cooking liquid, stirring a few times as they cool. Drain off the cooled liquid and discard it; if you leave the nuts in the cooking liquid for too long, they'll absorb too much salt. Store the peanuts in the refrigerator for up to 1 week or zip them shut in plastic bags and freeze them for up to 6 months. You can pop them in the microwave to warm them up before serving.

MY GRANNY'S POLE BEANS

Gena Berry, our recipe guru on this book, cried when she tasted these beans. Gena said it was like her mamaw was standing right there next to the stove. I love my granny's food because it tastes like there's love in it. It tastes genuine and heartfelt. It's hard to make food that tastes like that. You have to believe in something more than just following the steps of a recipe. You have to believe that food can transcend a moment, like you're in a time machine. That usually happens with the simplest foods, like braised pole beans. Why bother to put such a basic recipe in a chef's cookbook? Because when it's done right, it's a helluva lot more important than just a pot of cooked beans. As for the recipe itself, I will say first that your cooking liquid has to be well seasoned because the beans will never absorb the entirety of the seasoning in that liquid. Second, you are cooking these with fatback, so skim off the fat before serving them so the beans don't taste greasy. Most important, when they're done, take the beans off the heat and let them cool to room temperature in the cooking liquid. If you don't have time to do this step, pick a different recipe. Some things benefit from time. And that time will come back to you in soulful, satisfying flavor. For the beans, don't dig out your super-tender haricot verts for this recipe. You want older, more rugged, fibrous beans like Blue Lake, Romano, Rattlesnake, or Provider beans. I use an heirloom variety called Cherokee Trail of Tears. This variety is on the Slow Foods "Ark of Taste" list because it's in danger of being lost to history from disuse. If you come across some of these beans, buy them, braise them, and enjoy them.

1. Cut the pole beans into 1-inch pieces and put them in a Dutch oven. Add the onion, garlic, fatback, salt, red pepper flakes, bay leaf, and enough chicken stock to generously cover the ingredients. Cover the pot and bring the beans to a boil. Cut the heat down and simmer, covered, until a knife goes straight through a bean with no resistance, about 30 minutes. The beans should be quite tender but not mushy. Turn off the heat and stir in the vinegar. Taste and add salt if needed. Uncover and let the beans cool to room temperature in their liquid. This is where Granny got it right: She'd start the beans early in the morning, set them aside, and let them finish cooking as they cooled down. It's a slow-cooking method that most folks don't think about today. But the extra time off the heat brings the flavors together like no other method can. Be sure to make this recipe at least 2 hours in advance so the beans have time to cool in the cooking liquid. Then just skim the fat from the surface and reheat the beans before serving.

ENOUGH FOR 6 FOLKS

Pole beans
1 pound, strings and tips removed

Onion
1 baseball-size, quartered

Garlic
1 clove, mashed

Smoked fatback
2 ounces, cut into 1-inch cubes

Salt
1 teaspoon

Dried red pepper flakes
½ teaspoon

Bay leaf
1

Chicken stock
about 4 cups

Apple cider vinegar
2 teaspoons

FRIED GREEN TOMATOES WITH SPICY RAITA

There are as many ways to fry a green tomato as there are to scramble an egg. My granny always dredged them in cornmeal and cooked them in bacon grease. I liked the bacon, but the breading got soggy. I like my fried green tomatoes supercrunchy. You have to crisp them up fast enough so that the tomato doesn't get mushy. I use flour, egg, and panko bread crumbs for crunch. It's not traditional. But it works a lot better than anything else I've tried. I totally ripped this method off my friends Kevin and Lisa Clark, who run Home Grown restaurant in Atlanta. However, I serve the tomatoes with a creamy, spicy sauce, which is hardly ever done in the South. In this dish, I experimented once again with crossing Southern and Indian cuisine. The spice trade routes naturally bring these two cuisines together. So I made a raita out of whole goat's milk yogurt spiced up with Indian green chile pickles. The spicy-tart, creamy yogurt works perfectly with the fried green tomatoes. If you can't find goat's milk yogurt, use the milder cow's milk variety. For the Indian chile pickles, try an Indian food market or order them online (see Sources, page 326). Hot mango pickle also works well in a pinch. Or substitute any Indian pickle and add some finely minced jalapeño chile pepper.

ENOUGH FOR 6 AS A SIDE DISH

Grapeseed oil
about 2 cups for frying

Green tomatoes
3 baseball-size

Salt and ground black pepper

All-purpose flour
1 cup

Eggs
3 large

Panko bread crumbs
1 cup finely ground and sifted

Espelette pepper

Spicy raita (recipe follows)
about ¾ cup

1. Line a platter with paper towels and set aside.

2. Heat a deep skillet over medium-high heat and add 2 inches of oil to the pan. Heat the oil to 350°F. Or heat the oil in a deep fryer to 350°F.

3. Cut the tomatoes into ½-inch-thick slices and season with salt and pepper. Bread the tomatoes using the 3-step fry prep with the flour, egg, and panko (see page 7). Add the tomatoes to the oil and fry until GBD, about 3 minutes per side. If you're using a deep fryer, the cooking time will be about 4 minutes total. Transfer the tomatoes to the paper towels and immediately sprinkle with salt, black pepper, and Espelette pepper. Serve with a generous portion of the raita.

SPICY RAITA

MAKES ABOUT 1 CUP

Plain yogurt, preferably goat's milk
¾ cup

Garlic
1 clove

Carrot
1 peeled

Lime
1

Spicy Indian green chile pickles
1 tablespoon finely chopped

Dijon mustard
1 teaspoon

Cumin seeds
2 teaspoons

1. Spoon the yogurt into a medium mixing bowl. Grate the garlic on a Microplane grater directly into the yogurt. Again, using the Microplane, grate and measure out 3 tablespoons of the carrot and mix it into the yogurt, carrot juice and all. Squeeze 1 tablespoon lime juice into the mixture, then stir in the pickles and mustard.

2. Toast the cumin seeds in a small dry skillet over low heat until they turn a shade darker and develop a deep nutty aroma, about 4 minutes, shaking the pan now and then. Slow toasting gives the cumin a real depth of flavor that releases into the sauce over time. Tilt the cumin from the skillet directly into the yogurt. Let stand for at least a few hours before using. The raita is best made a day in advance so the flavors can fully develop. Store it, covered, in the refrigerator for up to 1 week.

GREEN TOMATOES / A green tomato is not a particular variety of tomato, but rather an unripe tomato of any variety. They're generally available twice a year. At the beginning of tomato season, farmers thin the plants by pulling off the less-than-perfect tomatoes while they're still green, leaving more nutrients for the perfect tomatoes. They do the same thing at the end of the season to improve their crop. A green tomato should feel hard like a softball. When you slice it open, it should look green all the way through. If it has any red specks, it will cook really fast and get mushy. A properly cooked fried green tomato should be crunchy on the outside and just starting to get soft on the inside. It should taste a little sour and a little crunchy, like lightly pickled cucumbers. Rutgers is my favorite variety for frying green. It's the perfect tennis ball size. Beefsteaks are too damn big. But if you can't find Rutgers, try a Cherokee Purple, Brandywine, Green Zebra, or other midsize tomato that doesn't get much bigger than a baseball.

TOMATO TARTINE WITH ARUGULA SALAD AND COUNTRY HAM

A tartine is a fancy French open-faced sandwich, but country ham personalizes it for me and makes it more American, more Southern. I wouldn't say it's a challenging dish to make, but the flavors are sophisticated. You get the sweetness and acidity of tomatoes up against the bracing bitterness of the arugula—a no-brainer matchup. I also like to partially cook the tomatoes. That makes them not quite raw but not quite softened and clingy like fully cooked tomatoes either. They take on this fondue-like quality and just melt on your tongue. That texture screams out for cheese. The smell, taste, and texture of toasted cheese are what elevate this sandwich to something special. Everyone loves toasted cheese. Even vegans dream about it! I like to use an alpine cheese like aged Gouda or Ossau-Iraty because alpine cheeses melt so well. Cheddar would be too sharp and wouldn't ooze over the tomatoes as easily.

SHOULD BE ENOUGH FOR 4 PEOPLE

Country bread
4 slices, each about ½ inch thick

Olive oil
5 tablespoons

Garlic
1 clove, peeled and halved on the diagonal

German Striped, Brandywine, or other beefsteak tomato
1 softball-size or larger, ripe and ready to eat

Aged Gouda or Ossau-Iraty cheese
2 cups finely grated, 4 ounces

Lemon
1 plump

Salt and ground black pepper

Arugula
2 cups

Country ham, preferably Benton's (see Sources, page 326)
4 very thin slices

Finishing-quality olive oil

1. Adjust an oven rack to the second highest position and preheat the broiler.

2. Put a baking rack on top of a baking sheet. Brush both sides of each bread slice with 1 tablespoon of the olive oil and place on the baking rack. Toast the bread just until it's crunchy and the edges are deep brown; the toast should be crisp on the outside but still soft on the inside, about 2 minutes per side. While the toast is warm, rub each slice with the cut garlic and set aside.

3. Rinse the tomato, cut out the core and, with a serrated knife, slice crosswise into ¾-inch-thick rounds. Place the slices on a baking sheet lined with a silicone baking mat, parchment paper, or nonstick foil and mound ½ cup of the grated cheese on each tomato. Watching carefully, broil the tomatoes until the juices are bubbling and the cheese is lightly browned and bubbly, about 3 minutes.

4. Mix the remaining 1 tablespoon olive oil, ½ teaspoon lemon zest, 1 tablespoon lemon juice, a Kevin pinch of salt, and 4 grinds of pepper in a large bowl. Gently toss the arugula with the dressing and divide into four bundles. Wrap each bundle with a slice of ham.

5. Place a slice of tomato on each slice of toast. If the tomato is small, use 2 slices; the toast should be completely covered with tomato. Lay an arugula bundle on top of each tomato and drizzle with 1 tablespoon finishing oil. Serve immediately.

CORNBREAD PANCAKES WITH SLICED BRANDYWINE TOMATOES AND BACON MAYONNAISE

As a kid, I ate tomato sandwiches all summer long. My favorite was a plain-Jane, stripped-down, white bread tomato sandwich with Duke's mayonnaise. But instead of replicating that juicy, standing-over-the-sink kind of sandwich, I thought back to the fresh tomatoes beading up with warm juice after being sliced and sprinkled with salt. That's really what I wanted to capture. I also needed the fat of the mayo to grab hold of the tomato's flavors. I needed the recipe to be stone-cold simple, but different. So I made cornbread pancakes. My favorite part of cornbread is the toasted caramelized cornmeal—the part that hits the pan. You get more of that with pancakes because there's more surface area. I spread a pancake with bacon mayonnaise—like you would with bread—then topped it with a salted slice of ripe tomato. You taste the tomatoes in all their soft, sweet, acidic brilliance. Then, for a split second, you get the caramelized crunch of toasted cornmeal.

---

1. Use a serrated knife to cut out the tough cores of the tomatoes. Slice the cored tomatoes crosswise into ½-inch-thick rounds. Put the tomatoes on a baking sheet in a single layer and sprinkle the tops lightly with salt. Let them sit for at least 30 minutes or up to an hour. The tomatoes will release some water, which will dissolve the salt; and after a while, the tomatoes will soak most of that salt water back up. Essentially, you're brining the tomato.

2. In a large mixing bowl, whisk the cornmeal, bacon, baking powder, and 1 teaspoon salt to blend. In another bowl or 4-cup liquid measuring cup, whisk the buttermilk, eggs, and 2 tablespoons of the bacon grease until blended. Stir the mixture into the dry ingredients to form a fairly smooth batter. Set the batter aside to rest for a few minutes.

3. Heat a flat griddle or very large skillet over medium heat. Brush the pan with bacon grease (or just smear on a thin layer with a pancake turner). Spoon on the batter, forming pancakes about the same diameter as your tomatoes; leave plenty of room between the cakes. Cook until bubbles just start to break on top and the edges start to set and dry, about 3 minutes. Gently flip the pancakes and continue cooking until lightly browned and cooked through, about 2 more minutes. Transfer to a warm plate.

4. To serve, spread each pancake with bacon mayonnaise and top with a tomato slice. Add a quick grind of black pepper and garnish with basil.

SHOULD BE ENOUGH FOR 10 SMALL PLATES

Brandywine tomatoes
2 ripe

Salt
1 teaspoon + more for the tomatoes

Cornmeal, fine-ground
2 cups

Crisp-cooked bacon
¼ cup finely chopped, about 4 slices

Baking powder
2 teaspoons

Buttermilk
2 cups

Eggs
2 large

Bacon grease
2 tablespoons + more for the pan

Bacon-basil mayonnaise
about ½ cup (page 299)

Ground black pepper

Basil sprigs for garnish

Heirloom Tomatoes

When I was a kid growing up in Locust Grove, Georgia, I would stay at my granny's house up the street after school. Granny always had a garden full of tomatoes. They were a constant for lunch … in a sandwich, in a salad, or eaten straight off the vine like an apple. Tomatoes grow great in Georgia because it's so hot in the summer. My favorite way to eat them is sliced raw on a plate sprinkled with salt. I would wait all year to eat juicy, warm tomatoes picked fresh from vines in Granny's garden. Just writing about it makes my mouth water for this summer's crop.

What a Tomato Is Made Of

I challenge anyone to reject the taste of an heirloom tomato grown with care on a small-scale organic farm, hand-picked from the vine when fully ripe, and served while still warm from the heat of the sun and the earth in which it grew. It's completely delicious! Most foods have a single flavor that dominates, but a fully ripe tomato tastes sweet, acidic, bitter, savory, and aromatic all at once. You taste the sweetness first, then the sharpness or acidity, which concentrates in the water and gel around the seeds. You also taste a fair amount of savoriness or umami in the flesh and skin. And the seeds have a slight bitter taste but a delicious crunch. And, like most fruits, a tomato's aromas are off the charts. Depending on the variety, a tomato can smell anywhere from herbal, fruity, and floral to meaty, musky, and grassy. Keep in mind, too, that tomatoes are about 95 percent water, which is a higher percentage than watermelon!

Beefsteaks are the big, heavy, not-perfectly-round heirloom tomatoes like Brandywine, Arkansas Traveler, German Striped, and Cherokee Purple. These are the ones you see mostly at farmer's markets. They have super-juicy, meaty yet tender flesh and work best raw or with almost no heat. I usually use beefsteaks for salads and sandwiches. Cornbread pancakes with sliced brandywine tomatoes and bacon mayonnaise (page 77) and tomato tartine with arugula salad and country ham (page 76) are two of my favorites. But sometimes I'll cut a beefsteak in half and sear the cut side on a hot grill to serve with steak or eggs.

Globe or slicing tomatoes

include the common round and medium hybrid varieties like Better Boy, Early Girl, and Rutgers, as well as some less common heirlooms like Green Zebra and Kumato. Slicing tomatoes don't chop up easily because of all their interwoven walls of flesh. But those walls of flesh make slicing tomatoes stand up to heat better than beefsteaks. To see what I mean, try the stuffed Rutgers tomatoes with Savannah red rice and creamed shrimp (page 80).

Paste tomatoes are the familiar plum tomatoes with the fat bullet shape. Roma and San Marzano are the most common varieties, and these are the best cookers. They have thick, dense, dry flesh with very little gel. There's so little liquid that paste tomatoes cook down and thicken up real quick. They're perfect for sauce, canning, and preserving.

Cherry and grape tomatoes are the smallest and come round, oblong, or teardrop shaped with names like Sun Gold, Purple Haze, Juliet, and Tiny Tim. These include some of those supersweet varieties that taste best popped right into your mouth or cut and served raw. Sometimes I'll confit them to balance all that sweetness with a little fat.

More Than 4,000 Varieties

The key to cooking a tomato is knowing which variety you're working with. Certain varieties lend themselves to certain preparations. There are more than 4,000 varieties, but you really only need to know about four main types.

No matter which variety you're working with, you want to use the plumpest, heaviest fruits. A ripe tomato will also have a sweet, floral aroma when you lift it to your nose. It's best to keep tomatoes at room temperature because refrigerating them makes the flesh turn mealy and dampens the flavors. They'll last longest at room temperature stored away from apples, pears, bananas, and other fruits, which naturally produce a ripening ethylene gas.

Experiment with as many varieties as you can, but keep in mind the dominant tomato flavor: sugar. It makes up about 3 percent of the fruit, which is more than twice the amount of acidity, bitterness, or savoriness (umami). That sugar content is why I treat tomatoes as fruits and not vegetables. Tomatoes work incredibly well in desserts. In fact, vanilla is a classic addition to preserved tomatoes in old Southern cookbooks. You preserve ripe, sweet tomatoes in syrup like you would peaches or any other fruit, and add vanilla to the syrup. Then you spoon the soft, vanilla-scented tomato preserves over ice cream in the summertime.

STUFFED RUTGERS TOMATOES WITH
SAVANNAH RED RICE AND CREAMED SHRIMP

Sounds very Southern, right? It is, but Granny never would have made this dish. She's from the mountains, and it doesn't fit her food style. When you take a good look at Southern culture, you realize it's not as simple as "this is Southern food and that is not." The South spans from Louisiana to Virginia, and each region has its own landscape, microclimate, ingredients, techniques, and traditions. This dish is characteristic of low-country Southern food, the plantation cuisine of the wealthy. Shrimp is everywhere in coastal Georgia, and cream makes it taste luxuriously rich. Another low-country classic, Savannah red rice, gets its red color from tomatoes, but I always thought the tomato itself kind of slips by unnoticed. I wanted to highlight the tomatoes even more. So I put the rice inside a big, fat, hollowed-out tomato. Rutgers tomatoes came to mind first because they're the most stable tomato when cooked. You can peel 'em; you can stuff 'em; you can bake 'em; and they still come out looking like a tomato. All in all, they're the perfect vehicle for creamy shrimp and pilaf-style red rice.

ENOUGH FOR 6 SMALL PLATES

Rutgers tomatoes
6 ripe

Bacon
4 ounces, cut into
¼-inch dice,
about ¾ cup

Basmati rice
¾ cup

Onion
¾ cup cut into
¼-inch dice

Celery
1 stalk, cut into
¼-inch dice,
about ¼ cup

**Red gypsy or
other small sweet
bell pepper**
1, cut into ¼-inch
dice, about ¼ cup

Garlic
1 teaspoon minced

**Smoked pork broth
(page 293)**
1 cup warm

Canned tomato puree
1¼ cups

Frank's RedHot sauce
1 tablespoon

Thyme sprigs
2

Salt
2 teaspoons

Ground black pepper
1 teaspoon

Scallions
4, white and light
green parts thinly
sliced, about ½ cup

Lemon
1 plump

Butter
2 tablespoons

**Creamed shrimp
(recipe follows)**
about 2 cups

1. Bring a large pot of water to a boil. Fill a large bowl with ice water.

2. Spray a 2-quart rectangular baking dish with nonstick spray.

3. Using a paring knife, remove the core from the stem end of the tomatoes and score a small X on the bud end. Using tongs, drop the tomatoes into the boiling water for 20 seconds and transfer directly to the ice bath to "shock" the tomatoes and stop the cooking. Swirl the tomatoes in the ice bath for 1 minute, then transfer to a cutting board. Using a paring knife, peel the loosened skin from the bud end of the tomatoes and discard. Carve a larger hole, about the diameter of a poker chip, in the stem end of each tomato. Using a melon baller, scrape out and discard the inner core and seeds to hollow out the tomatoes. Nestle the tomatoes, hollow side up, in the baking dish.

4. Heat a 4-quart Dutch oven over medium-high heat until very hot, about 2 minutes. Add the bacon and stir the hell out of it with a wooden spoon. Cut the heat down to medium and keep cooking, stirring now and then, until the bacon is crisp and light golden brown, about 5 minutes. The bacon will give up its fat, which is called rendering. Stir in the rice and toast it to a nice light golden brown, about 3 minutes, stirring a couple of times. Add the onion, celery, sweet pepper, and garlic, and cook until the vegetables soften, about 5 minutes. Add the smoked pork broth, cover, and cut the heat down so the mixture simmers gently. Simmer for 5 minutes. Stir in the tomato puree, hot sauce, thyme, salt, and pepper. Crank the heat up so that the mixture boils, then cut the heat down so that it simmers. Cover and cook for 15 minutes. Pull the pan from the heat and let it rest, covered, for 15 minutes.

5. Preheat the oven to 500°F.

6. Uncover the rice and remove and discard the thyme sprigs. Fold in the scallions, ½ teaspoon lemon zest, and about 1½ teaspoons lemon juice. Aggressively stir in the butter.

7. Spoon the rice into the tomatoes, filling to the top, and bake for 10 minutes.

8. Set a tomato on each serving plate, top with a generous portion of the creamed shrimp, and serve.

CREAMED SHRIMP

MAKES ABOUT 2 CUPS

Georgia white shrimp 8 ounces 26/30 count	**Dry sherry** ½ cup	**Heavy cream** 1 cup	**Lemon** 1
Grapeseed oil 1 tablespoon	**Garlic** 1 teaspoon minced	**Salt** ½ teaspoon	**Butter** 1 tablespoon

1. Line a plate with paper towels. Peel, devein, and cut the shrimp into ½-inch pieces and transfer to the paper towels–lined plate, patting them dry. Drying the shrimp gives you a better sear on the surface.

2. Heat a 10-inch sauté pan over high heat until very hot, 1 to 2 minutes. Add the oil and swirl to coat the bottom of the pan; the oil should just start to smoke. Wearing oven mitts, add the shrimp. If you have a gas stove, tilt the pan away from you, allowing the flames to creep up over the pan and ignite the shrimp. This flambéing technique will singe the outside of the shrimp and create awesome flavor. Once the shrimp are lit, shake the pan and toss the shrimp nonstop until the flames die down, about 30 seconds. Transfer the shrimp to a shallow bowl.

3. Pull the pan off the heat and add the sherry. Put the pan back over the heat and tilt it away from you as before, igniting the sherry (you can also ignite the sherry with a lighter or long match). When the flames die down, stir all of the browned bits from the bottom of the pan into the sherry. Add the garlic and cream and cut the heat down to medium. Simmer until the cream is thick and reduced in volume by half, about 4 minutes, stirring almost nonstop. Return the shrimp and any accumulated juices to the pan, then season with the salt and 1 tablespoon lemon juice. Bring to a boil over high heat. Pull the pan from the heat and swirl in the cold butter until melted.

PREP AHEAD / For a party, you can make the red rice and the creamed shrimp a day ahead. For the shrimp, stop the cooking right after you add the lemon juice, then cool down the shrimp, cover, and refrigerate. Don't forget to flambé the shrimp: it's a crucial step that creates a subtle roasted flavor. About 15 minutes before serving, gently reheat the shrimp and swirl in the butter. You can also blanch and core the tomatoes on party day and leave them to cool, so that all you have to do is assemble the dish and pop it in the oven 10 minutes before party time. Georgia white shrimp are ideal here (see Sources, page 326); they're sweeter and firmer than typical brown shrimp. But you can use whatever domestic shrimp is local to you, such as Gulf shrimp. Just steer clear of imported shrimp, which tend to be farmed using questionable methods or wild-caught with massive dragnets that damage the environment in a pretty serious way.

ONE-POT HOG SUPPER

This is my granny's dish, and one that I ate pretty often growing up. She first made it in the early fall, when she had fresh tomatoes, fresh cabbage, and fresh potatoes all at the same time. I haven't altered it much from her original recipe. Granny would render fatback for cooking oil, but she didn't use the fatback pieces. I chopped up the cracklings and mixed them with a fresh herb salad to contrast the concentrated, slow-cooked flavor of the dish. To find out why it's called one-pot hog supper, see page 59.

1. Using a mandoline, slice the potatoes and garlic into rounds and slice the onions into lengthwise strips—all about ⅛ inch thick.

2. Remove the tough, dark green outer leaves from the cabbage (save them for another use, like the cabbage dumplings on page 92). Peel the inner leaves from the core and tear them into 3-inch-wide strips.

3. Heat a 4-quart Dutch oven over medium heat. Add the fatback in a single layer and cook until lightly browned, about 9 minutes; turn each piece and cook until lightly browned, an additional 2 minutes. Line a plate with paper towels and, using a slotted spoon, fish out the fatback cracklings to drain on the paper towels. Leave about 1 tablespoon of fat in the bottom of the pan, setting aside the rest.

4. In this order, layer the potatoes, onions, garlic, cabbage, and tomatoes in the Dutch oven, aggressively seasoning each layer with salt and pepper as you go. Pour 1 cup of water and 3 tablespoons of the reserved fat over the top of the tomatoes. Crank the heat up to high and bring the mixture to a boil. Cut the heat down to medium-low, cover, and simmer until the vegetables are tender, about 45 minutes. To test for doneness, take off the lid and slide a knife into the center of the pot. The knife should easily slide through the vegetables. If it doesn't, put on the lid and continue cooking until it does. Once the vegetables are tender, take off the lid and cook uncovered until the liquid reduces in volume and sits well below the top of the vegetables, about 30 minutes more.

5. Pull the pot from the heat and let rest for 10 minutes.

6. Finely chop 2 tablespoons of the fatback cracklings and toss in a small bowl with the celery leaves, chives, parsley, and tarragon. Drizzle with the lemon juice and finishing oil and season with a grind of black pepper. Toss to combine.

7. Serve a generous portion of vegetables, making sure you get a little of everything in each serving, then top with the crackling herb salad.

SERVES 4 HUNGRY FOLKS

White potatoes
4 tennis ball–size, about 12 ounces

Garlic
3 cloves, peeled

Onion
1 softball-size, peeled

Green cabbage
1 head, 2½ pounds

Fatback
6 ounces, rinsed and sliced into ⅛-inch-wide strips

Heirloom beefsteak tomatoes
4 baseball-size, cored and sliced into ¼-inch-thick rounds

Salt

Ground black pepper

Celery leaves
¼ cup coarsely chopped and loosely packed

Fresh chives
¼ cup coarsely chopped and loosely packed

Fresh parsley
¼ cup coarsely chopped and loosely packed

Fresh French tarragon
¼ cup coarsely chopped and loosely packed

Lemon juice
about 1 teaspoon

Finishing-quality olive oil
about 1 teaspoon

SHRIMP-STUFFED PAN-FRIED CATFISH

Most people have this idea that catfish tastes muddy and dirty. That's only true for river-caught catfish, and this recipe is not designed for that fish. It's designed for the farm-raised catfish that's widely available in grocery stores around the country. Farm-raised catfish tastes super-clean, and it's better for the environment than other farm-raised seafood. Most fishery watch groups rank farm-raised catfish among the healthiest, most sustainable seafood choices you can make. Still, farm-raised catfish is not the single most flavorful fish on earth. I wanted to give it more flavor, and I wanted it fried because cornmeal-fried catfish is about as old-school as old-school Southern gets. To keep the fish from tasting bland, I made a filling of highly seasoned shrimp paste. You sandwich two catfish fillets around the shrimp filling, bread it, and fry it, and it becomes one stuffed piece of fish. The filling keeps the fish moist, and a creamy avocado puree adds a luxurious quality to the whole dish. The only downside is that it takes a tiny bit longer to prep and cook than a single fillet of catfish. And sorry: no dice on frozen catfish here. It will leach out too much water and soggy up the filling. Use fresh only. In a pinch, you could sub in fresh, farm-raised tilapia.

ENOUGH FOR 4 FOLKS

Catfish
8 skinless center-cut fillets, about 2 ounces each

Fresh shrimp paste (recipe follows)
about ⅓ cup

Canola oil for frying

Cornmeal, fine-ground
¾ cup

Salt

All-purpose flour
¾ cup

Eggs
2 large

Avocado puree (recipe follows)
about ½ cup

1. Pat the fillets dry with a paper towel. Trim the fillets so that they are the same size and thickness. Set 4 of the fillets skin side up (where the skin used to be) on a paper towel and spread each with about 1 tablespoon shrimp paste; you want a nice thick layer evenly covering the fillet. Top each with a second fillet, (former) skin side down. Refrigerate to allow the shrimp paste to set and kind of "glue" the fillets together, about 10 minutes.

2. Heat the oil in a deep fryer to 325°F. Or heat 1 inch of oil in a deep skillet to 325°F. This frying temperature is lower than normal to allow the heat to reach the filling before the outside burns.

3. Line a baking sheet with a cooling rack. Season the cornmeal with salt.

4. Bread the fish using the 3-step fry prep with the flour, eggs, and seasoned cornmeal (see page 7). Fry the fish until GBD, 5 to 6 minutes. If you are pan-frying, fry for 4 to 5 minutes, flip over, and fry for another 3 to 4 minutes, until all sides are GBD. Transfer the fish to the rack to drain.

5. To serve, use a thin-bladed knife to cut each fish bundle in half crosswise. Spoon a pool of avocado puree onto the center of each serving plate and stand the two halves cut side up on the puree.

FRESH **SHRIMP** PASTE

MAKES ABOUT 2 CUPS

Egg whites
2, at room temperature

Shrimp
12 ounces, peeled, deveined, and diced

Sweet herb blend (page 6)
1 tablespoon

Salt

---

1. Fit a mixer with the whisk attachment and add the egg whites to the mixer bowl. Beat on low speed until frothy, then crank it up to high and beat until soft peaks form when the whisk is lifted.

2. Fit a food processor with the metal blade and add the shrimp to the work bowl. Pulse about 6 times, or just until the mixture is nearly smooth. Add the egg whites, herbs, and a Kevin pinch of salt. Pulse to a smooth paste, about five 5-second pulses. Transfer to a bowl and refrigerate until ready to use. This is best used the day you make it.

AVOCADO PUREE

MAKES ABOUT ½ CUP

Avocado
1 ripe

Lime
1 plump

Water
1 tablespoon

Salt
½ teaspoon

---

1. Cut the avocado in half from the north pole to the south pole and remove the pit. Cut the flesh into small chunks and transfer to a mini chopper or small food processor with about 1 tablespoon lime juice, the water, and the salt. Puree until smooth, about 30 seconds. Press the puree through a fine-mesh strainer to make it even more velvety. Cover and refrigerate. If you are making and storing the puree overnight, squeeze some more lime juice over the surface of the puree before covering so that it won't turn dark.

PREP AHEAD / You'll have some leftover shrimp paste. Use it to make shrimp toast as an appetizer: Remove the crusts from white sandwich bread and cut the bread diagonally into quarters. Spread each triangle with about 2 teaspoons shrimp paste and fry, shrimp side down, in an oiled skillet over medium heat until GBD, about 3 minutes. Flip and fry the toasts for another minute to brown the bottom crust. Transfer to a paper towel to drain.

PAN-SAUTÉED TROUT WITH GREEN GARLIC AND PEACHES

I got my first pair of hiking boots in the third grade. That's when my dad started taking me on a guys-only camping trip in the mountains of north Georgia. When I say *camping*, I mean more like survival training. My dad and his brothers hiked deep into the woods, created temporary shelters, slept on the ground, and foraged for just about everything. It was pretty intense for a third-grader. They would bury cast-iron pans in the ground and mark them so we could find them when we returned. We didn't pack in much food. We hunted and foraged, and we caught a lot of trout. The Chattooga River is full of them. You couldn't swing a dead cat around that river without hitting a trout. We'd hike down to the gorge; fish morning, noon, and night; then hike back up. As a kid, I wasn't much of a fish eater, but I always liked the pan-seared trout. We'd bring in cornmeal or flour, bread the fish, and eat it pan seared—bones and all. The downside to cooking whole trout is that some of it inevitably overcooks.

To solve the problem, I now take a single fillet off the bone, dredge it in cornmeal, and cook it on the skin side only. Trout skin is nice and thin, so it gets super crispy, and the fillet is thin enough to finish cooking from carryover heat. It's one of the easiest methods for cooking fish. The dish won't work with frozen trout, though, because freezing the fish softens the flesh tremendously. This dish is all about freshness and seasonality. Make it in the spring when green garlic, peaches, and trout are all coming up. It's the perfect combination of pungency from the green garlic, sweetness from the peaches, and superclean richness from the trout. This dish proves the old adage about combining ingredients: What grows together, goes together.

FEEDS 4 FOLKS

Trout
4 skin-on fillets, about 3 ounces each

Salt and ground black pepper

Cornmeal
about ¼ cup

Butter
4 tablespoons

Super-sweet Florida white corn
2 ears

Onion
¼ cup finely diced

Green garlic
3 stalks finely sliced, about 2 tablespoons

Chicken stock
⅓ cup

Peach
1 baseball-size, pit removed, diced into ¼-inch pieces with skin on

Lemon juice
1 squeeze

Fresh chives
1 tablespoon finely sliced

Caramelized turnip and potato puree (page 303, optional)
about 1 cup, warmed

1. Pat the trout fillets dry with a paper towel. Season the flesh side with salt and pepper and lightly dust both sides with cornmeal. Place a 12-inch skillet over medium-high heat and add 2 tablespoons of the butter. When the butter starts to foam, transfer the trout, skin side down, to the skillet. Cook until the skin is golden brown, 5 to 6 minutes. Flip the fillets and, just when the last one is flipped, immediately remove them to a plate to rest, skin side up.

2. Meanwhile, remove the husks and silks from the corn and, using a sharp knife, cut the corn off the cob. Melt another 1 tablespoon of the butter in the same pan over medium heat and sauté the onion and green garlic until they just begin to soften and start to brown around the edges, about a minute. Add the corn and sauté for 1 minute. Crank the heat up to medium-high and add

the chicken stock. The stock will sizzle and immediately start to reduce in volume. Add the peaches, a squeeze of lemon juice, a Kevin pinch of salt, 2 grinds of pepper, and the remaining 1 tablespoon of butter. Pull the pan from the heat and, using the washing machine method (see page 12), stir and emulsify the butter into the sauce. Gently fold in the chives.

3. Swirl a puddle of the caramelized turnip puree in the center of each serving plate. Center one piece of trout, skin side up, over the puree and spoon the peaches over the top. Season with a pinch of salt, and drizzle with a little of the sauce.

CAST-IRON SKILLET
CHICKEN
WITH FARRO AND
BRUSSELS SPROUTS

Everyone likes the taste of fried chicken but maybe not the extra fat. I wanted to get the crispy skin of fried chicken without the frying. It took me a few years to figure out that roasting the chicken pieces in a cast-iron pan gives you a similar result. It's a simple technique that can easily become standard in your repertoire. Just make sure the surface of the chicken is really dry so that the skin crisps up when it hits the pan. You pan-roast the chicken pieces almost exclusively on the skin side, then transfer the pan to the oven to cook the meat all the way through. To switch things up, I pair the chicken with Middle Eastern flavors. Farro is a form of wheat berry brought to the Southern United States from Europe; it's prepared much like bulgur wheat is prepared in Lebanese cuisine. I give it a crunchy texture similar to fried rice by toasting the farro grains in the rendered chicken fat. They puff up and take on a glossy sheen, sort of like Honey Smacks cereal. Then I mix in some lemon juice and Brussels sprout leaves for a crisp, bright flavor. A traditional Lebanese tahini sauce rounds out the flavors with some bitterness. When these flavors stand alone, the chicken might taste too salty, the farro too sour, or the tahini too bitter. But when tasted together, they strike a balance. It's a very satisfying take on a traditional Southern favorite.

LET'S GET STARTED →

FEEDS 4 HUNGRY FOLKS

**Semi-pearled farro,
preferably Anson Mills**
1 cup

Water
3 cups

Brussels sprouts
*a generous pound,
about 32 golf ball-size sprouts*

Chickens
2, about 4 pounds each

Salt and ground black pepper

Grapeseed oil
2 tablespoons

Garlic
3 cloves, shaved on a mandoline

Chicken stock
*2 cups, warm, preferably
homemade (page 293)*

Olive oil
2 tablespoons

Lemon juice
¼ cup

Tahini sauce (page 307)
about ¼ cup

1. Preheat the oven to 500°F.

2. Soak the farro in the water for 30 minutes. Drain off the water and rinse the grains with cold water. Put the farro in a 2-quart saucepan and add enough fresh cold water to cover. Bring to a boil, then cut the heat down to low, cover, and simmer until tender yet still chewy, about 20 minutes. Drain off any excess liquid and spread the farro on a baking sheet to cool. You should end up with about 2 cups of cooked farro.

3. Meanwhile, peel off the outer green leaves of the Brussels sprouts until you have 4 cups. Reserve the inner heads for another use.

4. Cut up the chickens into leg-thigh and breast-wing portions with the skin still attached. For each leg-thigh portion, bend the leg away from the body, cut down to the joint, then bend the joint to break it. Cut between the ball and socket, then down around the carcass to remove the entire leg-thigh portion. For each breast-wing portion, cut down along one side of the breastbone, then run the knife along the contour of the rib cage and around the wishbone to begin removing the breast from the body. When you get to the joint connecting the wing to the body, grab both wing and breast together and cut through the wing joint to remove breast and wing in one piece. Score the meat around the next wing joint closest to the breast, cutting down to bone and scraping with the knife so the bone is fairly clean. Bend the joint to break it and remove the wing. The resulting boneless breast with the first wing bone attached and exposed is called an airline breast. It looks nicer than the boneless breast by itself, and the wing bone helps keep the meat moist during cooking.

5. Cut off any excess flaps of skin and pat the chicken very dry with a paper towel. Generously season the chicken on all sides with salt and pepper. Heat two large cast-iron skillets over medium heat. Add enough grapeseed oil to coat the bottom of each pan. Put the chicken legs in one pan, skin side down, and put the breasts in the other pan, also skin side down. Crank the heat up to medium-high and cook until the skin is nicely browned, about 4 minutes. No need to peek; just let the chicken cook undisturbed. When the skin is browned, it will release easily from the pan and the meat will start to pull away from the bone. Turn the leg-thigh portions and cook for 1 more minute skin side up, but let the breasts cook skin side down the entire time.

6. Place both skillets in the oven and roast for 5 minutes. Carefully pull out the pan with the legs, turn the legs skin side down once again, and return to the oven for 3 more minutes. The breasts will still be skin side down, remember; they do not get turned at all. After a total of 8 minutes, carefully pull both skillets from the oven, transfer the chicken to a large plate, and tent with foil to keep warm.

7. Using mitts, carefully pour out and discard the accumulated fat from the pans. Heat one pan over high heat until smokin' hot. Add the cooled farro to the pan, spreading to evenly cover the bottom (save any leftover farro for another use; it makes a great salad). Again with the mitts, grab the handle and shake and toss the farro so it heats through evenly. After about 3 minutes, the farro will begin to cara-melize and puff. Add the Brussels sprout leaves and stir nonstop for 1 minute. Add the garlic and warm chicken stock, then shake and toss the mixture for 2 more minutes, until almost all of the liquid is gone. The farro will absorb the stock and release its starch to thicken the remaining liquid, creating a creamy mixture.

8. Stir in the olive oil, lemon juice, a pinch of salt, and any accumulated chicken juices from the plate. Taste and adjust the seasonings as needed; with all that lemon juice in the farro, the dish screams for salt to balance it out.

9. To serve, drizzle a circle of tahini sauce in the center of the plate, and top with a scoop of farro and a chicken breast and leg.

CABBAGE DUMPLINGS WITH COUNTRY SAUSAGE

I created this dish when Meridith Ford Goldman, the restaurant critic for the *Atlanta Journal-Constitution,* visited in October 2008, just after I became executive chef at Woodfire Grill. It was a slow night, and I was bored. I put together this cabbage dumpling to go with a pork loin dish I was making. I ground up some chicken thighs to make a country sausage, then rolled it up in cabbage leaves. Like I do with our greens, I braised the dumplings in seasoned stock above the wood grill. I'm not sure why I thought to wing it and try this dish on the night a restaurant critic was coming in. But she raved about it and wrote about it. A year later, I made the same dish but with pork sausage. Andreas Muller from Sweden was working with me at the time, and he went crazy for them. He said his grandmother made dumplings almost exactly like these. He was having a nostalgic moment even though the dish wasn't supposed to be Swedish or Southern. It's just slow-cooked, handmade, homey food. It makes a simple supper with a piece of cornbread or a biscuit for sopping up the braising juices. You could also serve the dumplings with oven-roasted tomato sauce (page 311) or on a root vegetable puree (page 302). Either way, try to buy your cabbage at a farmer's market. It will be much more tender than grocery store cabbage that's been sitting in cold storage for days on end. Use only the outer leaves for this recipe, and save the rest for skillet-roasted cabbage (page 29), chili slaw dawgs (page 271), or one-pot hog supper (page 83).

FEEDS 4 FOLKS

Cabbage
8 dark green outer leaves

Country sausage (page 249)
1¼ pounds

Smoked pork broth (page 293)
about 4 cups

1. Fill an 8-quart Dutch oven three-quarters full with water and bring to a rapid boil. Fill a large bowl with ice water.

2. Completely submerge the cabbage leaves in the boiling water, using tongs to press each one down into the water as you add it. Blanch the leaves until they are bendable, about 3 minutes. Use the tongs to transfer the leaves to the ice bath and dunk them in the ice bath to cool. Pluck the leaves from the ice bath and pat dry. Remove and discard most of the tough stems from each leaf. Discard the blanching water and reserve the pot.

3. For each dumpling, scoop up about ¼ cup sausage and shape it into a small brick. Set the sausage brick on the upper third of a cabbage leaf. Fold the top of the leaf down just about to the middle of the sausage and then diagonally fold the two sides of the cabbage in toward the middle. The leaves will cross over where you removed the stem. You'll have a little parcel that looks like an envelope with the bottom flap still open. Fold the entire packet toward you, over the cabbage leaf, to completely enclose the sausage. You'll have a nice, neat dumpling with the veins of the cabbage showing a design on the top.

4. Place the dumplings in a single layer in the Dutch oven. Add just enough smoked pork broth to cover the dumplings. Cut a circle of

parchment paper to fit the diameter of the Dutch oven and press it directly onto the surface of the stock; the parchment circle helps to keep the dumplings in contact with the stock. Bring the stock to a low simmer over medium heat, then cut the heat down so the liquid is just below a simmer, and poach the dumplings until the largest top vein in the cabbage is tender when tested with a knife, 20 to 30 minutes. You can also test with a thermometer, which should read about 180°F when inserted into the center of a dumpling. But tender cabbage leaves really are the way to tell when your dumplings are done. When the cabbage is tender, it won't have a tendency to unwrap, but will stay folded in the dumpling shape.

5. Carefully remove the dumplings and trim off any excess cabbage sticking out of the bottom. Re-season the poaching liquid. To serve, set 2 dumplings in each shallow serving bowl and spoon in about ½ cup of the seasoned poaching liquid.

PREP AHEAD / The fully cooked dumplings will keep for up to 4 days in the refrigerator; just separate the dumplings and poaching liquid to keep the cabbage from getting mushy. You can also vacuum-seal the dumplings and freeze them for up to 3 months. Thaw, if frozen, and then gently reheat the dumplings in a Dutch oven with some pork stock and the parchment circle as described at left.

PAN-ROASTED PORK CHOPS WITH APPLES AND REDEYE GRAVY

Pork chops are not easy to cook. The loin, where the pork chop comes from, is the single most difficult part of the animal to cook properly. It has the least flavor and the least fat and is the most likely to dry out. To get something delicious, your seasoning has to be aggressive and your technique flawless. I built the flavors here from two iconic foods that work consistently well with pork—apples and redeye gravy. The apples play up the sweetness of the pork and the gravy emphasizes the earthy diet of pigs, which root around eating nuts and seeds. If you're not familiar with redeye gravy, it's a thin sauce made in the South by cooks who used what they had available to them. After cooking ham, they would deglaze the pan with brewed coffee. When you put the gravy in a white bowl, the coffee sinks to the bottom and the pork drippings rest on top. Viewed from above, it resembles the iris and pupil of a human eye. Redeye gravy doesn't have much fat, so it's important that the pork chops stay nice and juicy. You want the heat high enough to brown the meat but not so blazingly hot that the chops dry out. Medium-high heat is about right. It's also important to let the pork rest after cooking so the juices can redistribute throughout the meat. That way, every bite tastes juicier.

FEEDS 4 HUNGRY FOLKS

Fuji apples
3 crisp

Apple cider vinegar
1 tablespoon

Honey
¼ cup

Salt

Turnips
4 golf ball–size baby purple-top turnips or 1 baseball-size

Grapeseed oil
2 teaspoons

Butter
2 tablespoons + 1 teaspoon

Country ham, preferably Benton's (see Sources, page 326)
about ⅓ cup cut into ¼-inch dice, 2 ounces

Pork loin chops
4 thick chops, each about 8 ounces and 1½ inches thick

Ground black pepper

Strong brewed coffee
1½ cups

Chicken stock
1½ cups

Lemon juice
½ teaspoon

1. Peel and core the apples. Using a mandoline, slice one of the apples into very thin rounds and put the rounds in a microwave-safe bowl. Cover and seal with plastic wrap, then microwave on 100 percent power until the apple is very soft and the kitchen smells of pure apple, about 5 minutes. Carefully remove the bowl from the microwave and let the plastic wrap shrink around the dish, creating a vacuum. Just let it sit there as the juices soak back into the apple. Cut the other 2 apples into ½-inch wedges and, in a small bowl, toss with the vinegar.

2. Line a baking sheet with a silicone baking mat, parchment paper, or nonstick aluminum foil and set aside.

3. Add the honey to a 10-inch ovenproof sauté pan and cook over high heat, shaking and agitating the pan nonstop. When the honey starts to boil, the bubbles will be very large, and as it continues to caramelize, the bubbles will get smaller and smaller. It will only take about 2 minutes for the honey to caramelize. When the bubbles are small and the honey is caramelized, pour in the apple wedges and vinegar. Toss in a pinch of salt and return to a boil. Cook just until the edges of the apples start to soften, another 3 minutes. The apples will continue to cook and soften during the cooling process, so don't worry if the centers are still pretty firm. Using a heatproof silicone spatula, scrape the apples and honey into a small mound at one end of the lined baking sheet. The apples will release a little liquid and form a small puddle of juice as they cool. The juice will be added to the sauce later.

4. Preheat the oven to 475°F.

5. Peel and quarter the turnips if they're small. If you're using one large turnip, peel it, cut it in half across the equator, and then cut each half into 8 wedges. This way, the pieces will be the right size and the cooking time will be perfect.

6. Add the oil and 2 tablespoons of the butter to the sauté pan and, over medium heat, swirl the pan until the foam subsides, about 30 seconds. Add the ham and sauté until it's golden brown, about 2 minutes, shaking the pan so the butter doesn't burn. Using a slotted spoon, transfer the ham to a small mound on the other end of the baking sheet from the caramelized apple wedges. Reserve the ham drippings in the sauté pan.

7. Pat the pork chops dry and season both sides generously with salt and pepper. Heat the sauté pan with the ham drippings over high heat and add the pork. Cook for 30 seconds. Spread the turnips in a single layer over and around the pork and transfer the pan to the oven. Cook for 5 minutes, then carefully remove the pan from the oven. Flip the chops over and redistribute the turnips in a single layer over and around the pork. Return the pan to the oven and cook until the pork chops reach an internal temperature of 140°F, another 5 to 6 minutes. The turnips should be fork-tender. Transfer the chops and turnips from the pan to a plate and tent with foil to keep them warm. Remember that the pan handle is still hot, so use a towel or potholder to pick up the pan and pour out the fat. Return the pan to high heat, add the coffee and chicken stock, and stir with a wooden spoon, scraping all the browned bits into the sauce.

8. Carefully pour the sauce into a blender and set the pan aside. Using a slotted spoon, scoop the microwaved apples into the blender, reserving the juice. Add the cooked diced ham to the blender and blend until smooth, stopping and scraping the sides of the pitcher to incorporate everything into the sauce. Strain the sauce through a fine-mesh strainer and discard the solids. Return the sauce to the sauté pan and bring to a boil over medium-high heat. Cut down the heat so the sauce is at an aggressive simmer and cook, stirring now and then, until the sauce is thick and reduced to about ⅔ cup, 15 minutes or so. Remove the pan from the heat and whisk in the lemon juice and the reserved juice from the apple wedges. Swirl in the remaining 1 teaspoon of butter.

9. Pop the apple wedges into a microwave-safe container and heat in the microwave just to re-warm them, about 30 seconds.

10. Slice each pork chop in half on the diagonal, lay one piece flat in the center of each plate, and prop the other piece cut side up along the cut side of the flat piece. Spoon the turnips over the pork and drizzle about 2 tablespoons of the sauce on and around the pork. Garnish with the apple wedges.

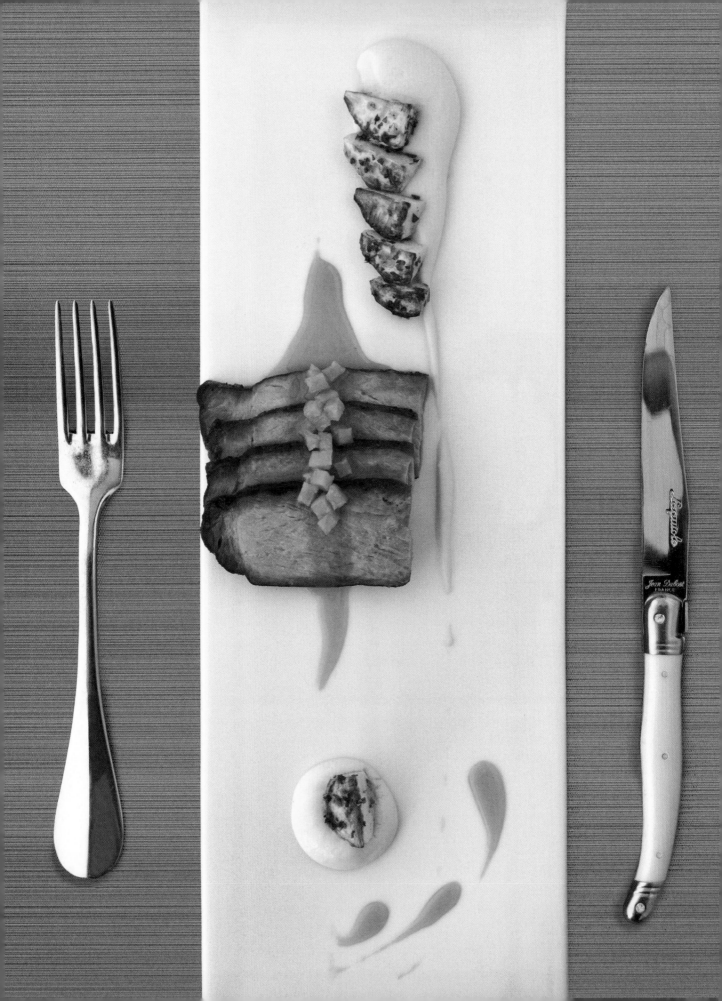

SLOW-ROASTED
PORK SHOULDER
WITH TURNIPS
AND RUTABAGAS

This is what I served to my granny when she came into my restaurant for the first time. I had been cooking professionally for ten years, but Granny never really leaves Locust Grove except for family reunions in the mountains. A few family members said to her, "We're taking you to Atlanta to eat at Kevin's restaurant." I was surprised that she agreed, and I had no idea what to serve her. Something she'd never eaten before? Or one of her favorite recipes? I landed in the middle. I made a dish with ingredients she could easily identify—pork, turnips, and rutabagas—but prepared them in a way that she had never tried before. The funny part is that when my family got halfway to Atlanta on the night of the dinner, she said, "Wait! We have to turn around and go back. I left something at the house." Everyone rolled their eyes, saying, "What? We're not driving a half hour back to the house and then back on the road again to Atlanta." "Yes, we are," she insisted. "I made Kevin a pound cake." That cracked me up. But it shows you the importance of some old Southern traditions. In her mind, my restaurant was like my home. She would never show up to someone's home for dinner without bringing something for the host. She made them turn the car around and get the pound cake. They were about half an hour late for their reservation. The pound cake was delicious, of course. What did she think of the food I made for her? She was so proud of me; she beamed, "Them is some good rutabagas!"

LET'S GET STARTED →

FEEDS 4 TO 6 FOLKS

Pork shoulder steak
*1 thick bone-in steak, about
2 pounds and 2 inches thick*

Salt and ground black pepper

Grapeseed oil

Hakurei turnips
*8 golf ball–size or 2 baseball-size,
about 8 ounces*

Butter
1 tablespoon

Sweet herb mix (page 6)
about 1 tablespoon

**Rutabaga and turnip puree
(page 303)**
1 cup, warm

Pickled rutabaga (page 319)
about 1 cup

1. Heat a smoker to 290°F. Or set up a covered charcoal or wood grill with indirect heat and wood chips (see page 10).

2. Pat the pork steak dry and liberally season both sides with salt and pepper, patting the seasoning into the meat. Scrape the smoker rack clean and coat it with grapeseed oil. Place the steak on the grate over indirect heat. Smoke the steak until the meat is tender and starts separating from the bone but not falling off it, about 3 hours. Check the smoker every hour and make sure you maintain a consistent temperature of 290°F. Transfer the steak to a baking sheet, tent with foil, and let the meat rest for 30 minutes.

3. Preheat the oven to 375°F.

4. Peel and quarter the small turnips. If you're using the larger turnips, peel them, cut them in half across the equator, and then cut each half into 8 wedges. This way, the pieces will be the right size and the cooking time will be perfect.

5. Heat an ovenproof skillet over medium-high heat and add the butter. Swirl the pan until the butter melts and starts to foam. Add the turnips to the butter and cook until the edges start to brown, about 2 minutes. Turn the turnips, transfer the pan to the oven, and roast the turnips until they are fork-tender, about 5 minutes. Remove the pan from the oven, add a pinch of salt and the sweet herb mix, and toss to combine.

6. Using a sharp boning knife, carve the pork to remove the bone. Thinly slice the meat across the grain. Smear about ¼ cup of the rutabaga and turnip puree in an arc in the center of each serving plate and shingle a few slices of pork on top of the puree. Arrange the turnips around the pork and garnish the meat with a spoonful of the pickled rutabaga.

WARM BANANA PUDDING

My great-grandmother on my mother's side always hosted Thanksgiving when I was a kid. It was a family reunion with 70 to 100 people at her house in Fayetteville, Georgia. There was always banana pudding. But there was only one big baking dish of it, and it was hidden somewhere in the house. When it was announced that it was time to look for the banana pudding, whoever found it got the first bowlful. There was never enough for everybody. When I was about eight years old, watching TV in my uncle's basement apartment downstairs, I opened the cupboard to get a water glass and saw the banana pudding. I climbed on the counter and pulled it down. This was hours before the main meal. I knew it was well before the time to hunt for the pudding, but I did the only thing an eight-year-old could do. I ate the whole damn thing! This was the first time I ever tasted the banana pudding because I was way down the family totem pole. My mom and I were joking about this incident a few years ago, and I asked her, "Who has the recipe?" She said it died with my great-grandmother. But the dish was pretty clear in my head after eating the whole thing that one time. The pound cake. The vanilla pudding from scratch. The meringue. I added a couple of things: I toast the pound cake so it doesn't absorb as much pudding. And I brush brewed coffee over the cake because I love coffee and bananas together. Otherwise, this is built from my flavor memory of my great-grandmother's banana pudding. My mom tells me it's spot-on.

FEEDS ABOUT 12 FOLKS

Half-and-half
2 cups

Whole milk
2 cups

Vanilla bean
1, split

Vanilla extract
1½ teaspoons

Eggs
8 large

Sugar
2½ cups

All-purpose flour
1 cup

Salt
1 teaspoon

Butter
6 tablespoons, cut into chunks

Pound cake
1 store-bought loaf, about 12 ounces

Strong brewed coffee
about ½ cup

Bananas
8 to 9 very ripe ones, peeled and cut into ½-inch coins

Cream of tartar
½ teaspoon

1. Preheat the oven to 375°F.

2. In a large saucepan, combine the half-and-half, milk, vanilla bean and ½ teaspoon of the vanilla extract and heat over medium-high heat until bubbles start forming around the edges of the pan, about 4 minutes. Pull the pan from the heat. Fish out the vanilla bean and use a paring knife to scrape the vanilla beans and pulp from the pod into the milk mixture. Discard the pod.

3. Separate the egg yolks from the whites using the three-bowl method: one small bowl to separate the eggs over, one large bowl for the yolks, and a third bowl to collect all of the whites. Crack one egg at a time, straining the white into the small separating bowl and placing the yolk in the yolk bowl. If the yolk did not break, transfer the white to the white collection bowl. This method ensures that no broken yolk gets into the main batch of whites. If you break a yolk, you'll only lose 1 white instead of the whole batch. For meringue, it's imperative to have whites with absolutely no yolk at all or the whites won't whip up properly.

4. Add 2 cups of the sugar to the yolks and whisk until very thick and light yellow, about 1 minute. Pour the flour into a strainer over the yolk bowl and shake the flour into the yolks. Whisk the flour and salt into the egg yolks until smooth. Slowly whisk ¾ cup of the milk mixture into the yolk mixture to gradually warm the eggs so they won't scramble; this is called tempering. Whisk all the yolk mixture into the milk mixture and return the pan to medium heat. Cook the mixture until it thickens, about 8 minutes, stirring nonstop. There will be some lumps, which is fine. Remove the pan from the heat and whisk in the butter, one piece at a time, until it's all incorporated. Blend the pudding with an immersion blender for 1 minute. Press the pudding through a fine-mesh strainer to remove any remaining lumps.

5. Slice the pound cake ¼ inch thick and arrange the slices in a single layer on a baking sheet. Toast in the oven until they are lightly browned, about 6 minutes. Flip the slices and toast again until lightly browned, about 4 minutes more. Remove the toasted cake from the oven and brush both sides with the coffee.

6. Spoon about 1½ cups of the pudding into the bottom of a 2-quart deep casserole dish. Layer the pound cake and bananas on top of the pudding and repeat the process, ending with a layer of pudding.

7. In a small bowl, whisk the remaining ½ cup sugar and cream of tartar to combine. Whip the egg whites in a mixer fitted with a whisk attachment until they are thick and frothy, about 2 minutes. With the mixer running, slowly add the sugar mixture to the egg whites. Add the remaining 1 teaspoon vanilla extract and beat until the mixture holds soft peaks when the whisk is lifted.

8. Mound the meringue on top of the pudding and spread to completely cover and seal at the edges. Using the back of a spoon, swirl the meringue into peaks. Bake until the peaks are browned, about 5 minutes. The top should be brown while the center of the meringue stays soft and creamy. Let the dish cool for at least 15 minutes. Serve warm.

CARAMELIZED PEACH ICE CREAM

I was lucky to grow up a mile from Gardner's peach stand in Locust Grove, Georgia. Gardner's sells at least twenty varieties of peaches like the Elberta, one of the original types cultivated in Georgia and a delicious heirloom that has mostly disappeared in favor of peaches that grow faster and hardier. Don't rely on grocery stores for your peaches. They will sell whatever variety is good for packing, which means the peaches will be hard and bland instead of soft and sweet. Find a good orchard and buy peaches from them. Go to your farmer's market. The whole point of this recipe is to make ice cream that tastes like peaches. The majority of peach ice creams don't taste like peaches because they use artificial peach flavoring.

It's difficult to make real peach ice cream because the water in peaches turns to ice crystals when it freezes. And when you cook peaches, they start to lose their peach flavor. I start with a base of peach butter made from unpeeled ripe peaches cooked down with brown sugar and cinnamon and then caramelized in a hot pan. The water evaporates and the crystallization problem is replaced with the fantastic flavor of peaches and caramel. I add a little apricot kernel extract to boost the peach flavor lost from cooking. You could use almond extract instead. Almonds, apricots, and peaches all share the same kernel of truth: Their unique flavor comes from the stone or kernel at their core.

MAKES 1 QUART

Whole milk
1 cup

Heavy whipping cream
1 cup

Egg yolks
4

Sugar
½ cup

Fine sea salt
a small pinch

Peach butter (page 317)
1 cup, chilled

Almond extract
⅛ teaspoon

1. Pour the milk and cream into a heavy saucepan. Put the pan over medium heat and heat to just below the boiling point (called scalding); a small ring of bubbles will form around the edge of the pan. While the milk and cream are scalding, put the egg yolks, sugar, and salt in a large bowl and whisk vigorously until thick and butter-colored; the mixture should start to pull away from the sides of the bowl as it thickens.

2. Pull the milk mixture from the heat and stir ⅓ cup of the mixture into the thickened yolks. This will temper the yolks and help prevent the mixture from curdling/scrambling. Slowly whisk the tempered yolks into the scalded milk and cream and "rinse" the yolk bowl with some of the milk mixture to make sure you capture all the yolks. Return the pan to low heat and stir gently but nonstop with a rubber spatula. I like a rubber spatula so I can feel the bottom of the pan and get into the corners to make sure nothing scorches or sticks. Cook until the mixture starts to thicken and registers 180°F on a thermometer; it should have a super-creamy texture and the aroma of lightly cooked eggs. Strain the custard through a fine-mesh strainer and refrigerate until cold, at least 2 hours or up to 3 days (see Prep Tip).

3. Stir the cold peach butter and almond extract into the cold custard. Freeze the mixture in your ice-cream maker according to the manufacturer's directions. For a standard electric "pre-freeze canister" machine meant for home use, it should take about 18 minutes for the ice cream to freeze to a thick, rich, smooth, and velvety soft texture. Pay close attention to the ice cream after about 15 minutes; it's very common to over-churn and "butter-up" the ice cream. You should take it out of the machine just when it is the texture of shiny soft serve. If you let it go for too long, the ice cream will start looking coarse and mealy, like wet sand, and literally will start churning into butter. Scoop out the custard and pack it into a freezer-safe container, cover, and freeze until firm, about 2 hours.

PREP TIP / The custard is best made and chilled ahead of time—up to 3 days in advance. If you're making the custard to use immediately, pour the cooked custard into a large metal bowl set in an ice water bath and gently stir until the mixture is cool to the touch, about 40°F. The metal bowl will help to quickly cool down the custard. As for the ice cream itself, it tastes best when it's churned, frozen, and eaten within a day.

PEACH PARTY LIQUOR

The name is inspired by the show *Squidbillies on* Cartoon Network's Adult Swim. I recently became a *Squidbillies* cast member, playing myself. The show is hilarious. It's not for everyone, but I love how it explores the idea of these ultra-redneck characters that are, absurdly, squids. One of the characters, Early Cuyler, makes something he calls "party liquor." One weekend when the cooks at Woodfire Grill were getting together on Sunday for some fun, I said, jokingly, that I would bring some "party liquor." And it would include moonshine. "You can't bring moonshine," they said. "We'll all go blind!" I wanted to show them it wasn't so bad, so I mixed the moonshine with really strong tea and juiced peaches. It tasted like Snapple peach tea and you could barely detect the moonshine. It was so good that we drank all of it. We got to goofing around and thought it would be fun to have a dart tournament. Someone had brought a blow dart gun. Before long, one of us had a brilliant idea and asked, "What if we shot someone with one of these?" That soon digressed into a series of retaliatory dart wounds. That's when I knew it was time for me to go. Just as my wife, Valerie, and I were walking out the door, I felt this pain in the back of my leg. I craned around, and there was a blow dart sticking out of my calf.

1. Bring the water to a boil in a medium nonreactive saucepan. Add the tea bags, and steep the tea in the hot water for about 30 minutes; you want to end up with very strong tea. Add the agave nectar to the tea and stir until blended. Cool the tea to room temperature.

2. Using a juicer, food processor, or heavy-duty blender, puree the peaches until they are completely smooth. Pour into the pan of tea along with the moonshine and lemon juice, stirring to blend. Strain the mixture through a fine-mesh strainer and discard the solids. Cover, chill, and serve ice-cold.

MOONSHINE / *White lightning* or *moonshine* refers to any illegally distilled, unaged white whiskey made in an unregulated still at home. But you can find perfectly legal white whiskey called *moonshine* in just about every liquor store across the country. Any corn-based liquor will do just fine in this recipe. If you can't find white whiskey, 80-proof Cathead Vodka from Mississippi is finished with corn and makes a great substitute.

GETS 4 SENSIBLE PEOPLE PRETTY LIT UP, OR 1 SOMEBODY WHO'S GONNA BE HURTIN' FOR CERTAIN

Water
2 cups

Black tea bags
4

Agave nectar
½ cup

Peaches
8 ripe baseball-size ones, pitted and peeled

Moonshine
2 cups

Lemon juice
¼ cup

WATERMELON COOLER

I was never much of a beer or wine drinker. I prefer cocktails. And while I admire the skill set required to make the amazing cocktails that are cropping up around the world, I unfortunately do not possess that skill set. I use whatever ingredients I have lying around to make drinks. I employ simple techniques. The inspiration for this cooler is *agua fresca, the* fresh fruit juice drink found on Mexican menus. It has spectacular flavor. I've always loved the taste of watermelon, especially with some added acidity to spark it up. Grapefruit juice and lemon juice are just the thing here. For the liquor, I prefer white whiskey. People always ask me, "Are you a brown liquor man or a white liquor man?" I'm usually a brown liquor man, but here I like the whiskey white so that it doesn't darken the drink. If you can't find unaged white whiskey, use white rum or silver tequila.

1. Put the watermelon in a large bowl, then squeeze in 1 cup grapefruit juice and ¼ cup lemon juice. Using a sturdy whisk, mash the mixture to a pulp. Mashing by hand is important because it will bring out all of the deliciousness of the watermelon and leave behind the tasteless pulp and seeds. Don't use a blender. It would blend in the seeds and pulp, which would make the mixture bitter and watery. Strain the hand-mashed mixture through a fine-mesh strainer into a pitcher and discard the solids. You'll end up with about 2 cups of liquid.

2. Using your fingers, gently slap or bruise the mint leaves and then stir them into the mixture. Stir in 1 tablespoon of the agave nectar and taste. Depending on the sweetness of your watermelon and grapefruit, you may need to add additional agave nectar to taste. You just want the sweetness of the agave to balance out the bitterness of the grapefruit and the tartness of the lemon juice.

3. To serve, stir the whiskey into the juice and pour into ice-filled glasses. Garnish with a skewer of cubed watermelon, a sliver each of lemon peel and grapefruit peel, and a mint leaf.

ENOUGH FOR 4 DRINKS

Watermelon
*3 cups diced small
+ a little for garnish*

Grapefruit
2 softball-size

Lemon
1 fat one

Fresh mint leaves
3 + more for garnish

Agave nectar
1 tablespoon + more as needed

High West Silver Western Oat

Whiskey
½ cup

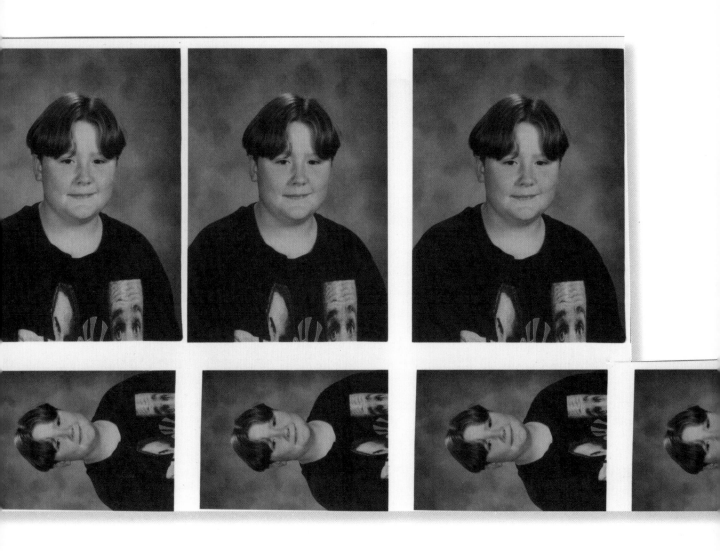

My fifth-grade teacher, Mrs. Robinson, wanted her students to learn more than what was in the class textbooks. She encouraged individuality. One of our assignments was to do a demonstration in front of the class for 5 to 10 minutes. We could demonstrate whatever we wanted. The idea was to encourage our ability to speak publicly.

I decided to cook crepes Suzette. I have no idea why. I had not decided to become a chef—or anything else, for that matter. I was only in the fifth grade! I had never eaten crepes Suzette. I had never cooked crepes Suzette. I'd merely seen the dish prepared on a television cooking show called *Great Chefs* on PBS. I thought it would be fun.

When I told my mom, she said, "That's perfect. I have a crepe maker." She had one of those inverted electric crepe pans that you dip into a wide bowl of batter. To do research for my assignment, I went to the public library and found a classic Continental cookbook. The book didn't have a single food photograph in it. But it had a recipe for crepes Suzette.

I checked out the book and brought it home. My mom helped me get the ingredients together. And I made crepes Suzette in our kitchen. I thought they were terrible. The sauce was too sweet and too harsh from too much alcohol. So I changed it. This was just before Christmas, around the time that my aunt makes wassail. She makes it with orange juice and cinnamon, and in my young mind, OJ and cinnamon went well together, so I used that. I added some almond extract because I thought that would taste good. I swapped out some of the white sugar for brown sugar because I liked brown sugar better. And I used less Grand Marnier and added amaretto. I had no moral dilemma about messing with the classic recipe. It didn't occur to me that it was sacrilegious. I just wanted to enjoy the dish more.

Once I got the crepes to where I thought they tasted good, I practiced the recipe again and again. I must have made 100 crepes before I set foot in that classroom. And I made a total wreck of my parents' kitchen.

On demo day, I made up a bunch of crepes in the morning to make sure everyone would have a taste. I got up in front of the class, plugged in the crepe maker, and showed everyone how to make the batter. I showed them how to dip the pan in the batter and cook the crepes. How to fold them. And how to flambé the sauce. That was the fun part. It was so cool to light something on fire in school! But my demo must have taken at least 20 minutes, twice as long as the allotted 5 to 10 minutes.

No matter. Everyone loved it. Mrs. Robinson. The ten-year-olds. Even the school principal, whom Mrs. Robinson had called in to the class. I just stayed up there and kept making crepes.

I feel certain that Mrs. Robinson, a classy, well-educated, well-to-do woman with a wealthy husband, had tasted crepes Suzette before. But every time she saw me, even years later when I was in high school, she remarked on how good my version was.

Once I decided to become a professional chef and went to culinary school, I learned that you weren't supposed to destroy and bastardize the classics. Oops! You were supposed to try and make the classics as perfectly as possible. But my cooking demo also taught me that sometimes it's okay to revisit a classic. Sometimes a recipe becomes a classic not because it's the best way to cook something, but because it is the accepted way. Maybe some flavors will taste better to you when you make them more pronounced. Maybe other flavors should be more subdued. It's your right as a cook and an eater to ask those questions and change a recipe until it tastes good to you. After all, the whole point is to enjoy what you're eating.

This chapter takes both approaches to classic dishes from around the world. In some recipes, like eggs Benedict (page 120), I revert to the original idea of the dish and make it a point to perfectly execute each component. In other recipes, like beef pot roast (page 113), I change the classic version so it tastes better to me.

I get angry when I hear anyone proclaim that they don't like a classic dish like eggs Benedict, beef pot roast, or crepes Suzette because "it's just not a good dish." These dishes exist for a reason. They've been around for so long because there is something of merit in them. Part of my job as a chef is to find out why a dish was made in the first place and amplify its best qualities.

COCA-COLA BRAISED POND ROAST

My mom made pot roast the same way every time. She put the beef, vegetables, seasonings, and water in a slow cooker, turned it on, and let it go. I never liked it. Now I know why: All of the flavors blended into one and tasted flat. Here, I braise the meat with some vegetables to create a flavorful brown sauce, but I cook different vegetables separately to put on the plate; that way they don't taste bland. For the beef itself, I like a boneless chuck blade roast. It's also called a 7-blade steak and is made up of several overlapping muscles, so it has tons of connective tissue that softens, melts, and turns to rich-tasting gelatin in the sauce. It's a relatively flat cut, which gives you a better sear on the meat. That's important because a dark brown surface on the beef is what creates a rich, dark, beefy sauce. To create an even silkier sauce, I add a little veal demi-glace, a type of superconcentrated veal stock (see Sources, page 327). For the cola, I use Mexican Coke, the kind in tall glass bottles. It's made with real sugar instead of corn syrup, which would just taste nasty in pot roast.

---

1. Tie a piece of kitchen twine around the circumference of the roast; tie it tight like a belt. Tie a few pieces of twine over and around the top of the roast to compact it for even cooking. Pat the roast dry with a paper towel and generously season both sides with salt and pepper. Heat a 4-quart Dutch oven over medium-high heat. Add enough grapeseed oil to generously cover the bottom of the pot. When the oil is hot, add the roast; you should hear it sizzle immediately. Sear the meat on one side without disturbing it for about 4 minutes; you want to develop a deep brown color right out of the gate.

2. Transfer the meat to a cutting board and return the pot to the heat for 30 seconds; this gives the pot a chance to recover heat so both sides of the roast will be evenly and deeply browned and caramelized. If the pot looks dry, add a little more oil to cover the bottom and, when the oil is hot, return the meat to the pot, browned side up. Slightly tilt the pot and, using a large spoon, baste the top side of the roast with the hot oil and juices. This will help to brown all the little pockets and crevices in the roast. Continue this process of removing the meat, letting the pot get hot, then returning the meat to the pot and basting it until all sides are deeply browned, 5 to 8 minutes. Transfer the roast to a plate, tent with foil, and set aside. Pour the cola into the pot, crank the heat

CONTINUED →

SHOULD BE ENOUGH FOR 6 PEOPLE

Chuck blade roast
4 pounds boneless

Salt and ground black pepper

Grapeseed oil
about ¼ cup

Mexican Coca-Cola
2 bottles, each 250 ml

Veal demi-glace (see Sources, page 327)
1 cup

Chicken stock
8 cups

Espelette pepper
1 teaspoon

Carrots
3 small, peeled and sliced 1 inch thick

Celery
3 stalks, sliced 1 inch thick

Yellow onion
1 softball-size, peeled and cut into 1-inch cubes

Butter
2 tablespoons

Glazed vegetables (recipe follows)
about 2 cups

Fresh chives
2 tablespoons very finely sliced

up to high, and bring to a rapid boil. Add the veal demi-glace, chicken stock, 1 tablespoon of salt, 2 teaspoons of black pepper, and the Espelette pepper, and return to a boil. Cut the heat down so that the liquid simmers aggressively and cook until the liquid reduces in volume by half, about 30 minutes.

3. Rearrange your oven racks so the Dutch oven will slide in and out easily. Preheat the oven to 350°F. Cut a 20-inch square of cheesecloth and lay the carrots, celery, and onion in a single layer in the center. Gather the corners together over the vegetables and tie the packet closed with a piece of twine. This packet makes it easy to pull the vegetables from the pot roast when the cooking is done.

4. Transfer the roast back to the pot and top with the single-layer vegetable packet. Pour the reduced braising liquid over the top; it should just cover the roast and the vegetables (add more stock if needed). Slide the pot into the oven and cook, uncovered, for 2 hours. Check the roast every 30 minutes or so, pressing the vegetables down into the braising liquid. After 2 hours, put the lid on the Dutch oven and continue cooking another hour, for a total cooking time of 3 hours.

5. Pull the pot from the oven and remove and discard the cheesecloth bundle. Cut, remove, and discard the twine. Put the roast back into the Dutch oven, put on the lid, and keep warm until ready to serve.

6. Transfer the roast to a warm, shallow platter and tent with foil. Measure out 4 cups of the braising liquid and pour the remaining braising liquid into a separate bowl. Return the 4 cups braising liquid to the pot and bring to a rapid boil over medium-high heat. Boil until the liquid reduces in volume by half, about 5 minutes. Remove the pot from the heat and whisk in the butter. Spoon the sauce over and around the roast, top with the glazed vegetables, and sprinkle with the chives. Store the remaining braising liquid with any leftovers.

GLAZED **VEGETABLES**

*Make these while the roast
is cooking.*

MAKES 4 CUPS

Purple-top turnip
1 baseball-size

Hakurei or Tokyo white turnips
4 golf ball–size

Rutabaga
1 baseball-size

Golden beets
4 golf ball–size or 1 baseball-size

Carrots
2

**Sunchokes
(Jerusalem artichokes)**
8

New potatoes
6 golf ball–size

Celery
2 stalks

Chicken stock
1 cup

Butter
2 tablespoons

Salt and ground black pepper

1. Fill a 2-quart saucepan three-quarters full with water and bring to a rapid boil. Fill a large bowl with ice water. Line a baking sheet with a clean, dry kitchen towel.

2. Peel the turnips, rutabaga, beets, and carrots. Cut each into ¾-inch dice and pile in separate mounds on the towel. Wash and cut the (unpeeled) sunchokes, (unpeeled) new potatoes, and celery into ¾-inch dice.

3. Drop the turnips and potatoes into the boiling water and blanch for 4 minutes. Using a spider strainer or slotted spoon, transfer the vegetables to the ice bath and swirl to cool. Transfer to a section of the towel to drain. Using the same cooking, cooling, and draining method, blanch the carrots and sunchokes for 2 minutes each. Lastly, blanch the beets and rutabagas for 6 minutes each. You blanch the beets and rutabagas last because they release some color into the blanching water that would stain the other vegetables. Celery does not need to be blanched because it is the least dense of the vegetables and will cook quickly.

4. Evenly spread the turnips, potatoes, carrots, sunchokes, beets, and rutabagas in a deep 12-inch sauté pan. Add the chicken stock and bring to a boil over high heat. Scatter the celery over the top of the vegetables. Cut the heat down to medium and let everything simmer aggressively until the vegetables are fork-tender and almost all the liquid is gone, about 8 minutes. Pull the pan from the heat and swirl in the butter, ½ teaspoon salt, and about 6 grinds of black pepper.

PREP AHEAD / **Pot roast tastes awesome reheated. You can braise the roast at least 4 days ahead and refrigerate it in the braising liquid in the Dutch oven. About 45 minutes before serving, reheat the roast and braising liquid in a 350°F oven until warmed through, then remove the roast from the Dutch oven, boil down 4 cups of the liquid until reduced to 2 cups, and whisk in the butter. (You'll have some leftover glazed vegetables from this dish. You can refrigerate them for up to 2 days and reheat them gently before serving.)**

SALAD LYONNAISE

In the United States, this salad is a mound of lettuce mixed with bacon bits, croutons, and mustard dressing, with a poached egg on top. I always thought it was a bastardization that would never exist in France. Like when you order Mongolian beef in a Chinese restaurant and think: This is not what they serve in Mongolia! In 2010, I went to Lyon, France, to eat at Paul Bocuse and a few other French haute cuisine restaurants. I visited some old bistros, too, like Café Comptoir Abel, which has been there forever. Salad Lyonnaise was on the menu at Abel. I had to get it. It was fried chunks of bacon with little chunks of bread fried in bacon fat and a soft-cooked egg all broken up and mixed with bacon dressing and a few greens. The "salad" came in a crock, not on a plate, and it was ten times heavier than any Lyonnaise I'd had in the States. I thought, "I'll need a nap after eating this salad!" But it was delicious, so I made this version as a tribute.

---

1. Place the whole eggs in a bowl of warm water to take off the chill. Bring 4 cups water to a boil in a small saucepan. Gently slide the eggs into the boiling water and cook for 6 minutes at a full boil. Fill a bowl with about 8 cups ice water. Using a slotted spoon, transfer the eggs directly to the ice bath. Gently tap the eggs with the back of a spoon until they crack. This will let some cold water into the eggs to slow down the cooking and allow for easier peeling.

2. Preheat the oven to 350°F. Evenly scatter the blocks of bacon in a cold skillet and place over high heat. Cook until the bacon starts to brown and the fat starts to render, about 2 minutes. Cut the heat down to medium-high and cook for another 5 minutes. Turn the bacon pieces and cook until all sides are golden brown, about 3 minutes more per side. Pull the pan from the heat, pour off the bacon fat, and reserve the fat.

3. Add the chicken stock and veal demi-glace to the pan with the bacon and bring to a simmer over medium heat. Cover the pan with a tight-fitting lid or with foil and place in the oven for 20 minutes.

4. Pull the skillet from the oven to the stove and carefully uncover. Don't forget that the handle is HOT! Put the pan over high heat and bring the liquid to a boil. Swirl in the vinegar and mustard and continue boiling for about 2 minutes to reduce the volume of liquid. Cut the heat down to very low just to keep the mixture warm.

5. Peel the eggs and cut cleanly in half lengthwise. Wipe your knife between cuts because the yolks will be slightly runny.

6. To serve, place 3 bacon blocks on each plate and top with frisée. Top the frisée with 3 egg halves, yolk side up, and sprinkle a tiny pinch of salt on each egg yolk. Divide the croutons among the plates and drizzle about 2 tablespoons of the reduced bacon sauce over each salad. Serve immediately.

SHOULD BE ENOUGH FOR 4 PEOPLE

Eggs
6 large

Slab bacon
about 14 ounces, well chilled, cut into twelve 2 by ½-inch blocks

Chicken stock
1 cup

Veal demi-glace
(see Sources, page 327)
⅓ cup

Champagne vinegar
1 tablespoon

Dijon mustard
1 teaspoon

Frisée
1 cup

Fried croutons
(page 314)
1 cup

Salt

CHICKEN POT PIE

All-butter pie crust
2 deep-dish 9-inch crusts

Chicken stock
2½ cups

Chicken breasts
1 pound boneless and skinless

Butter
5 tablespoons

Carrots
2, peeled and cut into ¼-inch dice, about 1¼ cups

Onion
1 baseball-size, peeled and cut into ¼-inch dice, about 1 cup

Celery
2 stalks, cut into ¼-inch dice, about ½ cup

Salt
1 teaspoon

All-purpose flour
⅓ cup

Dried culinary lavender
1 teaspoon crumbled

Fresh thyme
1 tablespoon leaves

Lemon
1 plump

Egg yolks
2

Heavy cream
2 tablespoons + a little more for brushing the crust

Petite peas
1½ cups frozen

Coarse sea salt and freshly ground black pepper

When I was a kid, my mom worked a lot, so we always had a Swanson or Banquet chicken pot pie in the freezer. I ate it, but I never liked the crust. It tasted mealy, didn't bake evenly, and was either burned or raw in spots. A few years later I started buying Boston Market chicken pot pie because it had a better crust. This was when I started cooking professionally. The irony of being a chef is that you rarely have time to cook good food for yourself. As a new cook I was dirt-poor, and frozen chicken pot pie was a cheap, hearty, easy dinner after a long day of work. I developed a taste for it. This recipe is a homemade version of commercial frozen chicken pot pie. I know it sounds crazy, but I like certain things about the prefab variety, like perfectly cubed chicken and a rich, luscious filling. I use a premade all-butter crust, so the whole thing actually takes less time to cook than a frozen pot pie.

---

1. Preheat the oven to 400°F.

2. If the piecrusts are frozen, let them thaw for a few minutes while you gather all of your ingredients. Use a fork to evenly stab holes in the bottom of one of the pie crusts. This is called docking and helps to prevent the dough from puffing. Cover with foil and put pie weights or dried beans on the foil to prevent puffing. Bake until the edges start to brown, about 15 minutes. Remove the crust from the oven and carefully remove the weights and foil. Cut the heat down to 375°F, return the crust to the oven, and bake until golden brown, another 10 to 12 minutes. Remove and let the crust cool to room temperature. This process of baking the unfilled piecrust is called blind baking. It prevents the crust from getting soggy when you fill it with something liquidy. Keep the remaining piecrust chilled.

3. Heat the chicken stock over medium-high heat to a gentle simmer. Cut the chicken into bite-size pieces, add to the stock, and poach for 3 minutes. Using a slotted spoon, transfer the chicken to a shallow bowl, spoon a little of the stock over the top, and refrigerate until cold. Cut the heat under the stock down to low.

4. Heat a 4-quart Dutch oven over medium-low heat. Add 3 tablespoons of the butter and when the butter starts to bubble, add the carrots, onion, celery, and salt. Cook, stirring now and then, until the vegetables release their juices and soften, about 5 minutes. Stir in the remaining 2 tablespoons of butter until melted. Stir in the flour so that all the vegetables are coated with a thick flour paste. Cook for 2 minutes. Start stirring, then slowly pour the stock into the vegetables and cook until thickened, about 2 minutes, stirring nonstop. Stir in the lavender, thyme, ¼ teaspoon lemon zest, and about 1 teaspoon lemon juice.

5. In a small bowl, whisk the egg yolks with the cream. Whisk about ¼ cup of the hot filling into the yolks; this will temper the yolks so they won't scramble when you combine them with the filling. Whisk the tempered yolks back into the filling in the Dutch oven and cook for 1 minute to fully incorporate the egg, whisking nonstop. The egg will give the sauce a velvety texture and a rich flavor.

6. Remove the cream sauce from the heat and gently fold in the chicken and the peas, which will cool the filling down to room temperature and help ensure a flaky crust. Taste the filling and add a little salt and/or lemon juice if you think it needs it. Mound the filling into the baked crust.

7. Put the unbaked pie crust on a lightly floured board and gently flatten to an even thickness. Set the unbaked crust on top of the chicken filling, pressing the edges with a fork to seal the top crust to the bottom crust. Using a sharp knife, cut a few slits in the top crust to allow steam to escape during baking. Brush the top with cream and sprinkle with coarse salt and a grind of pepper.

8. Bake until the filling is bubbling and the crust is golden brown, 50 to 60 minutes. Remove the pie from the oven and let rest for at least 25 minutes before serving.

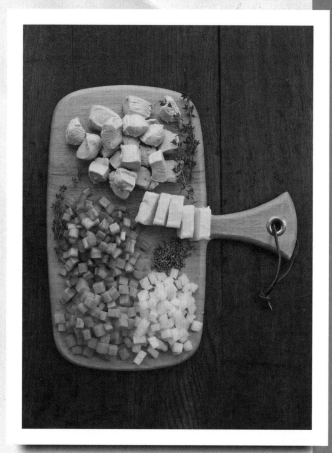

PREP AHEAD / **You can bake the bottom crust and then cover and refrigerate it up to 2 days ahead of time. Then all you have to do is cook the filling, assemble the pie, and bake. Look for a premade all-butter crust or at least one that's nice and flaky. Whole Foods and Trader Joe's make decent premade pie crusts. For the lavender, check the gourmet spice aisle. McCormick sells it.**

EGGS BENEDICT

Most people only know eggs Benedict in its poorly done, half-assed form. Here I go back to the basic components: English muffin, Canadian bacon, poached egg, hollandaise. The goal is to make each component from scratch and make it properly. When you taste homemade English muffins, you'll understand why they are far and away better than anything that comes out of a package. When you try real Canadian bacon (see Sources, page 326), you'll know that it's nothing like what Hormel sells. Canadian bacon is a wet-cured pork loin coated in cornmeal. As for the hollandaise, it's just amazing. If you don't like classic hollandaise prepared from scratch, you might have a screw loose. All of these components add up to one of the most perfectly designed dishes that has ever existed. That's why it has lasted so long. The dish takes a little advance planning (you can make the English muffins ahead), but the payoff is well worth it. Highly recommended for brunch.

MAKES ENOUGH FOR 4 PLATES

Apple cider vinegar
½ cup

Eggs
8 large

Clarified butter
3 tablespoons

Canadian bacon
8 slices

**English muffins
(recipe follows)**
4

**Hollandaise sauce
(page 304)**
about 1 cup, warmed

1. Pour the vinegar into a medium mixing bowl. Carefully break the eggs one at a time into the vinegar, making sure the yolks stay whole. Fill a Dutch oven about three-quarters full with water and bring to a rolling boil over high heat. Stir the boiling water vigorously with a wooden spoon to create a whirlpool. Gently slide the eggs and vinegar into the whirlpool. Cut the heat down to medium and bring the water back to a gentle simmer. The eggs will magically separate into single eggs. Cook for 4 minutes for a warm, runny yolk; 6 minutes for a firm, moist yolk; and 7 minutes for a firm, dry yolk that is completely cooked through. Line a shallow bowl with a double layer of paper towels. Using a slotted spoon, carefully transfer the eggs to the paper towels to drain.

2. Line a plate with a double layer of paper towels. Heat a 10-inch skillet over medium-high heat and add 2 teaspoons of the clarified butter. Pat the Canadian bacon dry and pan-fry the bacon just until the edges start to brown, about 2 minutes on each side. Transfer the bacon to the paper towels to drain. Heat a little of the remaining clarified butter in the same skillet, add the fork-split muffins, split side down, and pan-fry until golden brown, 2 to 3 minutes. You will need to do this in batches.

3. For each plate, set 2 muffin halves, browned side up, in the center. Top each with a slice of Canadian bacon, an egg, and a generous spoonful of warm hollandaise.

ENGLISH MUFFINS

MAKES 6

Bread flour
*4 cups + enough to dust
your work surface*

Active dry yeast
*0.25-ounce packet,
or 2¼ teaspoons*

Baking soda
½ teaspoon

Sugar
a reasonable pinch

Water
1¼ cups, at 110°F

Egg whites
2

Salt
1½ teaspoons

Canola oil
about 1 tablespoon

Cornmeal
about 2 tablespoons

1. In a large bowl, whisk together 1 cup of the flour, the yeast, baking soda, and sugar. Add the warm water and whisk until smooth. Let rest until the yeast has proofed or bubbles up and forms a layer of foam on the surface, about 10 minutes.

2. In a mixer fitted with the whip attachment, whip the egg whites until soft peaks form when the whip is lifted. Remove the mixer bowl and, using a rubber spatula, scrape the flour mixture into the whipped egg whites. Fit the mixer with the dough hook and return the bowl to the mixer. On low speed, gently mix the egg whites and flour mixture just until combined and no more clouds of white remain, about a minute. With the mixer set to medium-low, add the remaining 3 cups of flour and the salt and knead until smooth, about 4 minutes. The dough will go through several stages: it starts out as a scrappy mess, then gathers into a wobbly ball, then separates into 3 or 4 balls. After about 3 minutes, you will hear a whop, whop, whopping sound as the dough comes together and turns around the sides of the bowl. When you hear that sound, mix for 1 minute more, and then remove the bowl from the mixer and remove the dough ball from the bowl.

3. Pour the canola oil into the mixer bowl and, using a piece of plastic wrap, rub the oil around the bowl. Place the dough ball back in the bowl and roll around to coat the ball with oil. This will prevent the dough from sticking to the bowl as it rises. Cover the dough ball with the oily plastic wrap and set in a warm place (about 90°F) until the dough doubles in bulk, about 1 hour.

4. Lightly dust a work surface with flour. Using your hands, gently transfer the dough to the work surface. Lightly dust the top of the dough with flour. Work gently; if you mash the dough, you'll deflate the bubbles that bake up into all those delicious nooks and crannies. Using a rolling pin, start at the center of the dough ball and, gently and minimally, roll the pin away from you. Rotate the dough a quarter turn and, gently and minimally, roll the pin away from you again. Repeat the rotating and rolling two more times until you have a ½-inch-thick dough round. You don't need roll back and forth; in fact, you shouldn't; just use soft little rolls from center to edge to get the dough to a ½-inch-thick circle. Let the dough rest for 5 minutes.

5. Lightly sprinkle a rimmed baking sheet with cornmeal. Using a 3¼-inch round cutter, press straight down without twisting and stamp the dough out into 6 rounds. You'll have to punch the circles very close together, as

CONTINUED →

this dough will not stand up to re-rolling. Set the rounds on the cornmeal and gently turn each one over so both sides are lightly dusted with cornmeal. Cover loosely with a kitchen towel or plastic wrap and let the dough rest for 45 minutes.

6. Heat a large, dry skillet over medium heat for 1 minute. Carefully set the dough rounds in the pan so there is plenty of room between them. Four muffins in a 10-inch skillet is perfect. Cook until the muffins are golden brown and cooked through, gently turning every 4 minutes, for a total cooking time of 18 to 20 minutes. Each turn should reveal a little added color; you turn them often because otherwise they would brown too quickly on the outside before the centers cook through. When they are cooked through, most of the moisture will have evaporated and the muffins will feel pretty light.

7. Transfer the muffins to a wire rack to cool for 10 minutes. This cooling time allows the muffins to finish cooking all the way through. Insert a fork in even intervals all the way around the circumference of each muffin, poking the fork through to the center of the muffin. Using your fingers, gently split each muffin into halves. Using a fork and your fingers will preserve all those delicious nooks and crannies you've worked so hard to create.

PREP AHEAD / You can make the English muffins up to 4 days ahead. Let them cool until just warm, then split them with a fork and your fingers into halves. Reposition each muffin back together as a whole, then cool completely. Cover tightly with plastic wrap and refrigerate for up to 4 days. Make sure you bring these back to room temperature before using.

SCOTCH EGGS

My grandmother made Scotch eggs every Christmas morning. I looked forward to them every year, but I have to admit, I popped out the yolk and tossed it in the trash. It was too hard-cooked. That's the knock against Scotch eggs. They're too dry. You start with hard-cooked eggs, wrap them in sausage, bread them, and drop them in the deep fryer, where the hard-cooked eggs get even harder and drier. Plus, the fat runs out of the sausage, making that part dry too. I didn't set out to reinvent the wheel with this dish. I just wanted to plug the hole in the tire. I start with soft-boiled eggs; they have fully cooked whites but only partially cooked yolks. I also add bacon to the sausage so it stays nice and moist even after it's breaded and fried. You won't need any sauce here. The runny yolk gives this well-made Scotch egg built-in saucing technology. Although I do like to season the yolk with some pickled horseradish, salt, and black pepper.

1. Place 4 of the whole eggs in a bowl of warm water to take off the chill. Bring 4 cups water to a boil in a small saucepan. Using a slotted spoon, gently slide the eggs into the boiling water and cook for 6 minutes at a full boil.

2. Meanwhile, fill a 2-quart bowl three-quarters full with ice water. Using the same slotted spoon, transfer the eggs to the ice bath. Gently tap the eggs with the back of a spoon until they crack. This will let some cold water into the eggs, stopping the cooking process and making the eggs easier to peel. Swirl the cracked eggs in the ice bath until they are cooled, about 2 minutes. Carefully (remember, these eggs are soft-boiled) peel the eggs and pat dry. Reserve the ice bath.

Eggs
5 large

Bacon
3 fatty slices

Country sausage (page 249)
8 ounces

Canola oil for frying

All-purpose flour
about ¼ cup

Panko bread crumbs
about ½ cup finely ground and sifted

Pickled horseradish (page 319)
about 1 tablespoon

Salt and ground black pepper

LEFT TO RIGHT: Robert Higgins (grandfather), Coylene Higgins (grandmother), Kayla (sister), mom, some weird kid, dad, Richard Edwards (uncle).

3. Using kitchen scissors, snip the bacon lengthwise into very thin strips. Chop the strips crosswise so you end up with a very fine dice. You want the bacon pieces to be just as fine as the sausage. The bacon gets added to the sausage mostly for the fat, but it will also add a little flavor. Put the sausage in a bowl and place the bowl in the ice bath to keep the sausage cold while you are working. If you have kitchen gloves, this is the perfect time to use them; if you don't have them, thoroughly wash and dry your hands. Using your hands, mix the bacon and sausage to combine. You want to mix it kind of aggressively but not so much that the mixture gets hot from the heat of your hands. Divide the sausage mixture into 4 equal portions and roll quickly into balls. One at a time, pat each ball into a flat disk in your hand, 5 to 6 inches in diameter. Wrap each disk carefully around an egg (be gentle with the soft eggs). Make sure that you completely encase the eggs in the sausage mixture. As each egg is wrapped, transfer it to a plate. Cover with plastic wrap and refrigerate until the sausage firms up, at least an hour. You can certainly refrigerate the eggs overnight to make for an easy breakfast or brunch the next morning.

4. Heat the oil in a deep fryer to 350°F or heat a pot with 2 inches of oil to 350°F. Line a plate with a double layer of paper towels.

5. Bread the cooked eggs using the 3-step fry prep with the flour, remaining raw egg, and panko (see page 7). Fry the eggs until GBD, about 4 minutes. Keep in mind that you only need to cook the thin coating of sausage, but you should leave the egg yolk runny. If you are pan-frying, fry the egg for 4 minutes, then turn and fry for another 4 minutes. Using a spider strainer or slotted spoon, transfer the eggs to the paper towels to drain.

6. For each plate, pierce an egg with the tip of a knife and gently cut in half lengthwise. Arrange both halves yolk side up on the plate, and spoon a little of the horseradish on the yolk. Sprinkle with salt and a few grinds of black pepper. Serve hot.

PREP AHEAD / You can soft-boil the eggs, wrap them in sausage, bread them, and refrigerate them up to 24 hours ahead of time. Then all you have to do is fry the eggs and serve—perfect for Christmas morning or a quick lunch.

WELSH RAREBIT

In Wales, cheese is the poor man's meat. Welsh rarebit is simple tavern food—a thick cheese sauce mixed with draft beer and melted over rustic bread. It's cheap and it's good. And when done right, it's super flavorful and super rich. My mom and uncle liked it, so my grandmother used to make it for them. The Welsh make it with local, well-aged cheddar. Buy the best cheese that you can because it's the star of the dish. For the bread, the heartier the better. Whole-grain brown loaves work really well. You could even use one with nuts in it, like pecan-raisin bread. The sturdy bread forms a dense backdrop for the velvety melted cheese sauce. Not everything should have the same texture, which is part of what makes this dish fun to eat. It might look like an open-faced sandwich, but this is definitely knife-and-fork food.

1. Preheat the oven to 425°F.

2. Toast the bread on the oven rack until crispy on both sides, about 3 minutes. Leave the oven on.

3. In a heavy saucepan over medium heat, whisk the clarified butter and flour until the flour dissolves, about 3 minutes. Keep whisking, then add the cream and cook until thickened, about 2 minutes, whisking nonstop. Whisk in the beer, mustard, Worcestershire, cayenne, and salt and cook for 10 minutes, stirring several times. You've got a lot of flavors that need time to fully develop, so give it the time it needs to get tasty.

4. Pull the pan from the heat and let the sauce cool for about 5 minutes; cooling the sauce will help keep the cheese from separating when you add it to the sauce. Add the cheese and stir until you see the texture change completely from a kind of grainy mess to a smooth, silky sauce; that's when the cheese is completely melted. Press the sauce through a fine-mesh strainer, and discard any remaining solids.

5. Line a baking sheet with a silicone baking mat, parchment paper, or nonstick aluminum foil. Or, just use some oven-to-table sizzle plates (see Sources, page 327). Set the toasts on the pan and generously spoon the cheese sauce over each piece. Bake until brown and bubbly, about 4 minutes.

ENOUGH FOR 2 HUNGRY PEOPLE OR 8 NIBBLERS

Rustic, dark-crusted whole wheat bread
4 thick slices

Clarified butter
4 tablespoons

All-purpose flour
¼ cup

Heavy cream
2 cups

Porter, stout, or other dark, slightly bitter beer
½ cup

Dry mustard
1 teaspoon

Worcestershire sauce
1 teaspoon

Cayenne pepper
¼ teaspoon

Salt
1 teaspoon

Grafton or extra-sharp yellow cheddar cheese
1 cup freshly grated, 4 ounces

CUCUMBER AND ALMOND GAZPACHO

I came back to be the chef at Woodfire Grill in the summer of 2008, at the height of cucumber season. We needed soup on the menu but it was 1,000 degrees out—way too hot to serve hot soup. I didn't want to make fruit soup or traditional tomato-based gazpacho. But I remembered an almond-based white gazpacho in a Spanish cookbook someone had given me. I did a little more digging in a few other cookbooks and online and then decided to wing it. Cucumbers and Marcona almonds would be the base. The Marcona almond is a Spanish variety that's rounder and sweeter than most almonds; it's sold pre-roasted and salted. I added lemon-infused olive oil to the soup for brightness and silkiness. It came out this gorgeous sea green color, and I garnished the soup with diced ripe peaches for contrast. Guests went crazy for it, especially vegans. It's incredibly refreshing on a hot summer day. I served it in tall shot glasses as shooters, but you could also serve it in small bowls.

MAKES 4 BOWLS OR 12 SHOOTERS

Cucumber
2, cut into chunks, about 4 cups

Water
2 cups

Marcona almonds
¾ cup

Garlic
1 marble-size clove, peeled

Citrus vinegar
1 tablespoon

Salt
1½ teaspoons

Olive oil
⅔ cup

Lemon olive oil
(see Sources, page 327)
2 tablespoons + more for drizzling

Peach
1 ripe Hacky Sack–size peach, cut into ¼-inch dice

Espelette pepper
a pinch

1. Blend the cucumbers (peel, seeds, and all), water, almonds, garlic, vinegar, and salt in a heavy-duty blender until smooth, about 2 minutes. A high-speed blender such as a Vitamix or Blendtec will produce a much creamier consistency. With the blender running, slowly drizzle in the oils. Strain the mixture through a fine-mesh strainer, forcing the mixture through with a ladle. Discard the solids. Refrigerate until cold, at least 1 hour.

2. Just before serving, reblend the soup, then taste and adjust the seasoning: It takes a while for the flavors to develop and for the salt to fully dissolve. You may or may not need to add more salt, as the almonds usually come pretty heavily salted. You'll just have to taste and decide. Serve chilled and garnished with a little spoonful of diced peaches, a pinch of Espelette pepper, and a drizzle of the lemon olive oil.

SUGAR SNAP PEAS <u>AMANDINE</u>

Every version I've had of this 1950s classic is basically steamed green beans with slivered almonds on top. For the life of me, I can't grasp how that makes any sense. It's like the old yearbook photo, and the almonds are grudgingly standing next to the green beans. The flavors should marry better on the plate. Here, I use sugar snap peas and Spanish Marcona almonds. The sugar snaps are so sweet that they make you notice the meaty quality of the almonds right away. I crush the almonds so you get some almond flavor in every bite. I also cook the almonds along with the green beans, so the almond oil comes out and coats the beans. And I fold in some sautéed mushrooms to deepen all the flavors. It's still a simple dish. But I'm hoping it's a little more satisfying than what you've had in the past.

---

1. Fill a 2-quart saucepan three-quarters full with water and bring to a boil over high heat. Fill a large bowl with ice water.

2. Drop the peas all at once into the boiling water and cook for 1 minute. Using a spider strainer or slotted spoon, transfer the peas to the ice bath, swirling until the peas are completely cool, about 1 minute. Then transfer the peas from the ice bath to a kitchen towel. Cut the peas in half on the diagonal and set aside.

3. Wipe any dirt from the mushrooms and remove the tough, woody root ends. Slice into thin strips. Heat a 10-inch sauté pan over medium heat and add 2 tablespoons of the butter. Swirl the pan until the butter melts and foams up. Add the mushrooms and onion and cook until the mushrooms are browned and crispy, about 10 minutes, stirring now and then. Add the almonds and another 1 tablespoon butter and cook for 3 to 4 minutes, stirring a few times. Add the peas, the remaining 1 table-spoon butter, a Kevin pinch of salt, about 1 teaspoon lemon juice, and 1 tablespoon ice water. Cook and stir, using the washing machine method (see page 12) for 1 minute. Serve immediately.

PREP AHEAD / You can blanch the peas up to 8 hours ahead; just keep them chilled in the fridge. You can also cook the mushroom mixture ahead of time up to the point of adding the peas. Hold off on the peas, cool the pan to almost room temperature, cover, and refrigerate for up to 4 hours. When you're ready to serve, reheat the cooked mixture over medium heat and start with the step where you add the peas.

ENOUGH FOR 4
AS A SIDE DISH

Sugar snap peas
8 ounces, strings removed

Hen of the woods or oyster mushrooms
4 ounces

Butter
4 tablespoons

Vidalia onion
2 tablespoons finely chopped

Marcona almonds
¼ cup crushed or coarsely chopped

Salt

Lemon
1 plump

Water
1 tablespoon, ice cold

GLAZED ROOT VEGETABLES

Roasted root vegetables are something of a cliché. These roots are not roasted. They are blanched and sautéed in a pan until they develop good, brown color. The real technique is in the glaze. The goal is to completely blend and emulsify butter and chicken stock so that every piece of every vegetable takes on a beautiful sheen. When the butter and liquid are entirely combined as a glaze, they thoroughly convey the seasoning to the vegetables, which makes them taste fantastic. Just make sure you use warm stock so it doesn't slow down the cooking, and pull your pan off the heat before stirring in the butter to keep the butter from separating. I like to serve these with oven-roasted chicken (page 137).

1. Fill a 2-quart saucepan about three-quarters full with water and bring to a rapid boil. Fill a large bowl with ice water. Line a baking sheet with a dry kitchen towel.

2. Peel the carrot, turnips, parsnip, and rutabaga, then cut each into ½-inch dice; measure out ¼ cup of each and reserve the rest for another use. Cut the (unpeeled) sunchokes into ½-inch dice.

3. Drop the rutabaga into the boiling water and blanch until it gets a little brighter in color, about 5 minutes. Using a spider strainer or slotted spoon, transfer the rutabaga to the ice bath and swirl to cool. Transfer to the towel to drain. Using the same cooking, cooling, and draining method, blanch the turnips for 3 minutes and then the parsnips and carrots together for 1 minute. The sunchokes are not blanched so that they will retain their crunchy texture.

4. Heat a 12-inch sauté pan over high heat. Add 1 tablespoon of the grapeseed oil and swirl to coat the bottom of the pan. Add the sunchokes in a single layer and cook, tossing now and then, until lightly caramelized and starting to soften, about 3 minutes. Add the remaining 1 teaspoon oil and the rutabaga and cook until golden brown, another 4 minutes, tossing a few times. You'll have a really good, deep brown color on the sunchokes at this point, which is what you want. Add the turnips, parsnips, and carrots and cook until they start to caramelize, about 3 minutes, tossing a few times. Add the warm chicken stock, ½ teaspoon lemon juice, and salt. The liquid will bubble wildly and quickly reduce in volume. When almost all the liquid is gone, after about 2 minutes, pull the pan from the heat and use the washing machine method to swirl the lemon dill butter into the vegetables until they are evenly glazed. Serve hot.

ENOUGH FOR 4 AS A SIDE DISH

Carrot
1

Hakurei turnips
2 small

Parsnip
1

Rutabaga
1

Sunchokes (Jerusalem artichokes)
8 ounces

Grapeseed oil
1 tablespoon + 1 teaspoon

Chicken stock
¾ cup, warm

Lemon
1

Salt
½ teaspoon

Lemon-dill butter (page 295)
1 tablespoon

SMOKED TROUT PUFFS WITH BACON JAM

These are fantastic hors d'oeuvres for a party. All of the components can be made ahead so that you only have to assemble the puffs before your guests arrive. Choux pastry is what makes them so good. It's the dough used for cream puffs, gougères, and other stuffed appetizers. Even though it's French, choux pastry is not hard to make. It's just a buttery pastry dough that you mix on the stovetop. Then you squeeze it into little mounds and bake it. It's such reliable, classic dough that there's no sense in reinventing it. This one is from *On Cooking*, my culinary school textbook. The smoked trout filling comes from E.J. Hodgkinson, my chef de cuisine at Woodfire Grill. I added a smear of bacon jam to anchor the trout with a punch of salty, meaty flavor.

MAKES 24

Eggs
3 large

Butter
4 tablespoons, cut into small cubes

Milk
2 tablespoons

Water
¼ cup

Salt
½ teaspoon

All-purpose flour
¾ cup, sifted after measuring

Bacon jam (page 309)
about ½ cup, at room temperature

**Smoked trout mousse
(recipe follows)**
about 2 cups

1. Preheat the oven to 425°F with the rack set in the middle position.

2. Line a baking sheet with a silicone baking mat, parchment paper, or nonstick aluminum foil.

3. In a liquid measuring cup, using a small whisk or fork, beat 2 of the eggs. Separate the egg white and yolk of the third egg and add just enough of the egg white to measure ½ cup total. Beat until completely combined and smooth. Reserve the remaining egg white and yolk together in another bowl.

4. Combine the butter, milk, water, and salt in a shallow saucepan. Set over high heat and bring to a boil, stirring once or twice. Dump the flour into the pan all at once and, using a flat wooden spoon, beat the hell out of the mixture while removing the pan from the heat. This goes completely against everything you've ever heard about stirring flour into hot liquid; it will clump and lump and look like you've done it wrong. Keep going; you're doing it right! Keep beating the bejesus out of the mixture off the heat until it comes together and forms a paste-like ball of dough. Return the pan to low heat and cook, while stirring and flattening the dough ball across the bottom of the pan, for 1 minute. The mixture will be a little shiny and some of the butter will leak out in tiny drops in the pan.

5. Transfer the dough to a stand mixer fitted with the paddle attachment and, with the mixer set to low, very slowly drizzle in the ½ cup beaten eggs. Turn off the mixer and, using a rubber spatula, scrape down the batter; then turn the mixer on low for another 30 seconds. The batter will look like rubber cement—kind of sticky, kind of stretchy.

6. Fold down a 3-inch cuff on a pastry bag or gallon-size plastic zip-top bag; fit a ½-inch plain pastry tip into the corner of the bag (snip off a ¼-inch corner if using a plastic bag; or if you're fresh out of plain tips, skip it and just snip off a corner). Scrape the dough into the bottom of the bag and unfold the cuff. Press excess air out of the bag, then twist and fold the top closed.

7. Pipe the dough onto the baking sheet in poker chip–sized mounds, leaving space between each. You should be able to get all 24 puffs onto your baking sheet.

8. Beat the leftover egg with 1 tablespoon of water to make an egg wash; lightly brush the tops of each round with the egg wash. Transfer the pan to the oven and bake for 15 minutes. After 15 minutes, cut the heat down to 350°F and continue baking until golden brown, another 7 minutes or so. The puffs will be crispy and firm on the bottom, very light, and hollow. Remove the pan from the oven and turn off the oven. Using a paring knife, make a small slit in the top of each puff to allow steam to escape. Return the pan to the oven and allow the puffs to cool down in the oven for about 30 minutes. The puffs will be hollow, crisp, and deeply browned.

9. Using a small serrated knife, slice a 1-inch-diameter disk off the top of each puff. Spread a teaspoon of bacon jam all around the inside of each puff. Fold a 3-inch cuff on a pastry bag or a gallon-size plastic zip-top bag and, using a rubber spatula, spoon the trout mousse into the bag. Squeeze the excess air out of the bag and twist the top closed. Fit a ½-inch plain pastry tip into the pastry bag or cut ¼ inch off the corner of the plastic bag and pipe the mousse into the puffs, filling them to a little over the top edge. Serve at room temperature.

SMOKED TROUT MOUSSE

MAKES ABOUT 3 CUPS

Cream cheese 8 ounces, 1 cup	**Garlic powder** ¾ teaspoon
Water ⅓ cup	**Onion powder** ¾ teaspoon
Lemon 1 plump	**Smoked trout fillet** 12 ounces, skin removed
Salt ¼ teaspoon	**Fresh chives** 2 tablespoons thinly sliced

1. In a food processor fitted with the metal blade, blend the cream cheese, water, ¼ teaspoon lemon zest, 1 tablespoon plus 1 teaspoon lemon juice, the salt, garlic powder, and onion powder until smooth, about 30 seconds. Remove the top and, using a rubber spatula, scrape down the sides of the work bowl. Flake the trout into the mixture and blend until smooth, about 15 seconds. Add the chives and pulse just until incorporated.

PREP AHEAD / **All three components for these hors d'oeuvres can be made ahead. But wait until just before serving to assemble the hors d'oeuvres, because they can get soggy pretty fast. The unfilled puffs can be made up to 2 days ahead and stored in an airtight container at room temperature. If they get soft, place them on a baking sheet and crisp them up in a 325°F oven for about 5 minutes before filling and serving. The bacon jam keeps covered in the fridge for up to 2 weeks. And the trout mousse will last in the refrigerator for the better part of a week. Just take it out of the fridge about 30 minutes before assembling the hors d'oeuvres to take the chill off.**

BUTTER-BASTED SCALLOPS WITH CAULIFLOWER

I get criticized by other chefs for making things too simple, but sometimes simple sings. This dish gives you two different tastes of the same vegetable along with the best-tasting scallops ever. The first is a velvety puree of cauliflower. I cook the florets in heavy cream because it diminishes cauliflower's sulfurous quality. For a contrasting taste, I pan-roast the florets so they get crunchy at the tips. The sweetness of the scallops balances out the mineral taste of the cauliflower. The trick is to butter-baste the scallops. You add butter to the pan, let it turn a hazelnut color, and then spoon it over the scallops for a perfectly even, golden brown crust. Just be careful not to overcook the scallops or they will turn rubbery. Each one should still look a little translucent in the center when you take it off the heat.

1. Trim the cauliflower into same-size small florets for even cooking.

2. Spoon the cauliflower purée into a small saucepan over medium-low heat and gently heat through, 3 to 4 minutes.

3. Pat the scallops dry and generously salt both sides. Heat an 8-inch sauté pan over high heat, add 1 tablespoon of the grapeseed oil, and swirl to coat the pan. Add the scallops, cut the heat down to medium, and cook undisturbed for 2 minutes. Do not shake the pan or poke at the scallops or you won't get a good sear on the scallops. One tablespoon at a time, add 3 tablespoons of the butter, swirling the pan to melt each tablespoon as it's added. Add the thyme and garlic and crank the heat up to high. The butter will start to foam and you will hear a crackling sound, which is the thyme leaves popping. Keeping the pan on the heat, tilt the pan and, using a large tablespoon, spoon the hot butter over the top of the scallops to baste them. Spoon the butter over the scallops for 2 minutes nonstop. Pull the pan from the heat, transfer the scallops to a plate, and tent with foil.

4. Heat a 10-inch sauté pan over high heat. Add the remaining tablespoon oil and swirl to coat the pan. Add the cauliflower florets and cook for 30 seconds. Toss and add the remaining 1 tablespoon butter. Stir occasionally until the florets start to brown, about 3 minutes. Toss in the rosemary, Espelette pepper, and 1 teaspoon salt and cook for 30 seconds more.

5. Spoon ¼ cup cauliflower puree in the center of each serving plate. Arrange one-quarter of the florets around the puree and top with a scallop, seared side up. Spoon a little of the browned butter from the scallops over the top and scatter on some finishing salt.

ENOUGH FOR 4 AS A STARTER

Cauliflower
½ head

Cauliflower puree (page 302)
1 cup

Scallops
4, large day-boat about 2 ounces each (U10)

Salt

Grapeseed oil
2 tablespoons

Butter
4 tablespoons, cut into tablespoon-size pieces

Thyme
2 sprigs

Garlic
2 cloves, peeled and crushed

Rosemary
1 sprig, stripped and leaves finely minced

Espelette pepper
1 teaspoon

Finishing salt such as Maldon

PAN-ROASTED LAMB CHOPS

Overcooked lamb is noticeably bad. It tastes like your grandma's sweater, and you really don't want to make that mistake. The problem is that lamb chops are not very forgiving. The chop is small, the meat is lean, and just a few minutes can make the difference between a tender, rosy chop and a cardboard hockey puck. Make things easier on yourself by buying an entire rack of lamb and cutting the chops yourself. All you have to do is cut between the bones to make chops. Buying a whole rack allows you to cut chops that are two bones wide, so each chop is thicker and less likely to overcook. You also want to trim the surface fat. Lamb fat doesn't render well and tends to get bitter when roasted. I trim it off, slowly render the fat (the low heat prevents the bitterness from developing), then cook diced new potatoes in the rendered fat. This method coaxes more lamb flavor out of the entire dish while avoiding the potential drawbacks of roasted lamb. Sugar snap peas on the side echo the unique taste of lamb and its diet of foraged grass.

MAKES ENOUGH FOR 4 PLATES

New potatoes
12 ounces, cut into ½-inch dice

Lamb racks
2, each about 1¼ pounds

Grapeseed oil
½ cup

Salt and ground black pepper

Lemon
1 plump

Sugar snap peas
4 ounces, sliced in half on the diagonal, about 1 cup

Scallion
1, thinly sliced on the diagonal

Lemon olive oil (see Sources, page 327)

1. Fill a medium pot three-quarters full with water and bring to a rolling boil. Fill a 1-quart bowl three-quarters full with ice water. Line a plate with a double layer of paper towels.

2. Drop the potatoes in the boiling water and blanch for 3 minutes. Using a spider strainer or slotted spoon, transfer the potatoes to the ice bath, swirling until they are cool, about 30 seconds. Again with the spider or slotted spoon, transfer the potatoes to the paper towels and pat dry.

3. Preheat the oven to 350°F.

4. Remove the cap of fat from the top of the lamb rack and set it aside. Trim and clean the bones, scraping them clean all the way down to the eye of meat; reserve all of the trimmings. This is called frenching. You can have your butcher do it for you, but make sure you ask him or her to give you all the trimmings. Slice each rack into four 2-bone chops; you will end up with 8 double chops. Using butcher's twine, tie each double chop between the bones and around the eye of meat so it stays in a compact cylinder shape. Cut the fat trimmings into 1-inch pieces.

5. Combine the grapeseed oil with the lamb trimmings in a 2-quart saucepan. Cook over medium-low heat until the trimmings are brown and crispy, about 15 minutes. Strain the oil and return it to the pan; discard the trimmings. Rendering the fat gives the oil a great lamb flavor for cooking the rest of the dish.

6. Season the chops on both sides with salt and pepper. Heat a 10-inch ovenproof skillet over high heat until smokin' hot. When the meat is added, the pan will smoke quite a bit, so turn on your range hood or open a window. Add 2 teaspoons of the lamb-flavored oil to the pan and swirl to coat the bottom. Add the chops in a single layer, cut side down, and cook until they form a deep, dark, caramelized crust, about 3 minutes. Use tongs to flip the chops over, then transfer the skillet to the oven and cook until a meat thermometer registers 120°F, another 4 to 5 minutes. Pull the pan from the oven and transfer the lamb to a cutting board or platter; remove the twine. Tent the lamb with foil and let rest while the vegetables are cooking.

7. Using a vegetable peeler, cut a 2-inch piece of peel from the lemon. Cut the peel into long, thin strips (julienne) and set aside.

8. Line a baking sheet with a double layer of paper towels.

9. Heat the remaining lamb-flavored oil in the saucepan to 375°F. Add the potatoes and cook until fork-tender and lightly browned, about 5 minutes. Add the peas and cook for another minute, tossing and stirring a couple of times. Add the lemon peel and pull the pan from the heat. Use a slotted spoon to transfer the vegetables to the paper towels and sprinkle them with salt, pepper, and a squeeze of lemon juice.

10. For each plate, arrange a nice mound of vegetables a little off-center and sprinkle with the scallions. Place two double chops in the center of the plate, pointing up the bones and hooking them together if you like, then drizzle everything with lemon olive oil.

OVEN-ROASTED CHICKEN

A roasted chicken can be incredibly satisfying when it's done the right way. It can be equally disappointing when it's done poorly. My goal is to make sure the bird, come hell or high water, stays juicy and flavorful. So I separate the skin from the meat and slather it with flavored butter. I like lemon, dill, and honey as basic seasonings for the butter, but you could take the flavors almost anywhere. For Latin flavors, try jalapeño-lime butter (page 295). If you like Indian food, add curry powder to the butter. Either way, the cooking method stays the same. I truss the bird into a tight ball to cover up the parts that tend to dry out. No one eats the ends of the wings, so I sacrifice them and cross them over the breasts to shield the delicate breast meat from the heat. You lose a little crispness on the skin over the breast, but remember, my goal is juicy meat. The single most important thing you do is let the bird rest, breast side down as if it is standing on its head, after it comes out of the oven. Cooking chicken forces moisture out of the meat, and gravity draws the juices to the bottom of the bird. I let the chicken rest inverted so that the juices get reabsorbed into the breast meat. When you carve it, chicken should be bursting with juices.

---

1. Adjust the oven racks so your chicken can roast upright. Preheat the oven to 450°F.

2. Cut the head of garlic and the lemon in half across the equator, and cut the shallot in half lengthwise.

3. Remove the packet of goodies from the chicken cavity and pat the cavity dry with a paper towel. Stuff two paper towels into the chicken while you are prepping the bird to absorb any additional juices.

4. Thoroughly wash and dry your hands. If you're a glove user, by all means, this is the ideal time to slip on some nice tight food-handling gloves and work away! Gently slip your fingers between the skin and meat on the breast and thighs, working your fingers across the meat to separate the skin from the meat. Take care not to tear the skin. Generously slather ¾ cup of the honey-dill butter under the skin of the breast and thighs.

FEEDS 2 HUNGRY FOLKS

Garlic
1 head

Lemon
1 fat one

Shallot
1 peeled

Poulet Rouge chicken
1, about 3 pounds

Honey-dill butter (page 295)
1 cup, at room temperature

Salt and ground black pepper

CONTINUED →

5. Remove the paper towels from the cavity of the bird and discard. Sprinkle the cavity liberally with salt and pepper. Push one lemon half, skin side first, into the cavity of the chicken, wedging it up into the neck end. Stuff both shallot halves into the bird, then stuff in half the head of garlic, cut side in. Stuffing the cavity full helps the chicken to cook evenly by slowing down the transfer of heat from inside the bird to the breast meat. Reserve the remaining lemon half and half head of garlic for another use.

6. To truss the bird, start with a piece of butcher's twine about 5 feet long. Lay the chicken, breast side up, on your work surface. Fold the twine in half and put the center point of the twine under the butt end of the chicken. Taking a piece of twine in each hand, wrap the twine up and around the chicken and securely bundle the legs and tail nub together. Cross and pull the ends of the twine up and around the top end of the chicken and tuck through the joints of the wings. Cross and loop each end of twine around the wing tips so that you can pull and bundle the wings together. Cross the wings over the breast of the bird and pull the ends of the twine back around to the rear of the bird and tie securely, making a nearly round ball out of your chicken. Your chicken will look fat and happy with its little arms crossed over its chest.

7. Slather the remaining ¼ cup honey-dill butter over the entire outside of the bird. Sprinkle all sides liberally with salt.

8. Thoroughly wash your hands. Again.

9. Cut a 3-foot piece of heavy-duty aluminum foil and fold it into a long 1½-inch-wide strip. Mold it into a 4-inch-diameter ring and place it in the center of a 10-inch ovenproof skillet. Set the chicken in the pan, breast side down, so the ring supports the chicken. The chicken will look like it's doing a headfirst cannonball into the pan. You'll have to fiddle with this a bit to wedge the bird in place; you want the bird tilted at a slight angle, breast side down, while it roasts. Fold a small piece of aluminum foil in half and tent it over the tail end of the bird.

10. Transfer the chicken to the oven and roast for 40 minutes. Remove the chicken from the oven and turn it on the foil so the breast side is up. Remove the tent from the tail end and discard. Insert a meat thermometer into the thigh of the chicken, return the pan to the oven, and cook to an internal temperature of 160°F, 15 to 20 minutes more. The chicken should be nicely browned.

11. Remove the chicken from the oven and adjust the foil so the chicken rests breast side down. Let rest for 20 minutes before carving.

POULET ROUGE / For the bird itself, I prefer Poulet Rouge de Fermier, a heritage French chicken breed. If you can't get Poulet Rouge from a local farmer or butcher shop, you can mail-order Niman Ranch Poulet Rouge from Lobster Gram or Ashley Farms Poulet Rouge from Joyce Foods (see Sources, page 326). Use any leftover roasted chicken in the shawarma (page 188) or pair it with glazed root vegetables (page 129), crispy green beans with salsa brava (page 227) or Brussels sprout gratin (page 34).

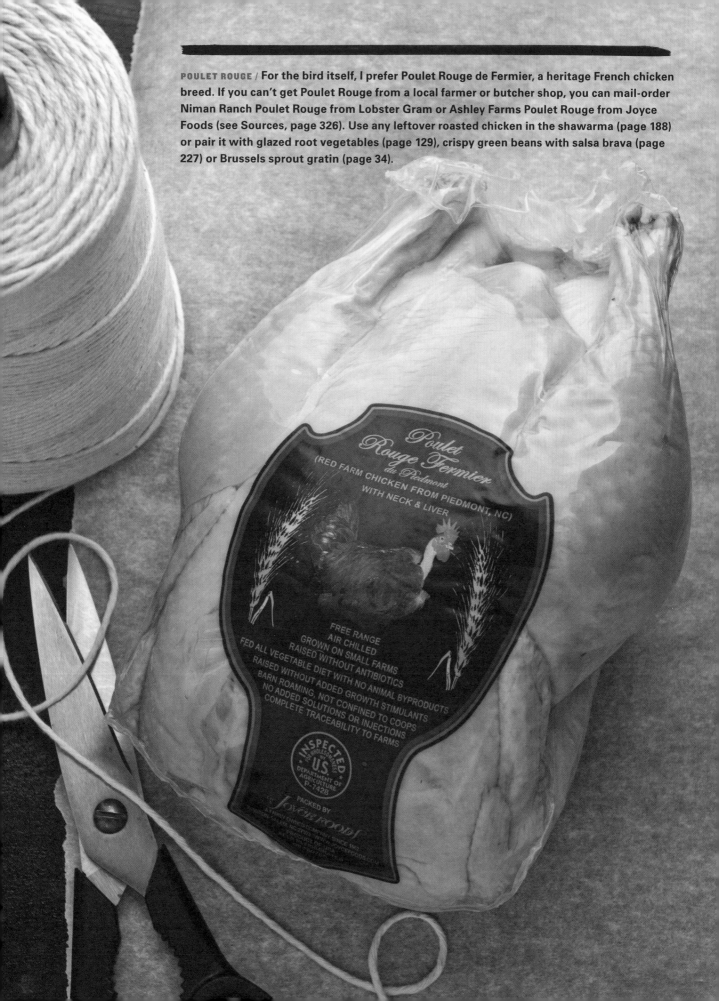

TURKEY AND RICE

From India to Spain to Mexico to the American Midwest, every culture seems to have its chicken and rice. In South America, it's *arroz con pollo,* and I love the creamy, risotto-like quality it takes on. But I don't have a grandmother who made chicken and rice for me as I was growing up. My strongest tie to this near-universal dish comes through one of the owners at Woodfire Grill, Nicolas Quiñones. Nick is Cuban, and he's made *arroz con pollo* at least a dozen times for staff meal at the restaurant. It's different every time, and each time he asks my opinion. It always tastes good, but I tell him, "If you remember, I'm not Cuban. I don't know what it tasted like when your mother made it." Over the years, I've picked out the things I like best about the dish: dark meat, creamy rice, and lemon for brightness. This recipe intensifies all of those qualities. I like to use dark-meat turkey instead of chicken because it's more flavorful. I poach turkey thighs in chicken stock. The stock takes on a deeper flavor, which then makes the rice taste better. I use Carolina Gold rice, a starchy risotto-like rice, so the dish gets good and creamy. The only downside to the classic dish is that you mix everything together, which mutes all the flavors. I changed that here. A squeeze of lemon juice and some fresh tarragon keep everything tasting bright. All of a sudden, the dish goes from humdrum to exciting.

FEEDS ABOUT 8 FOLKS, WITH LEFTOVERS

Turkey thighs
4, about 1 pound each

Chicken stock (page 293)
8 cups

Carolina Gold rice
2 cups

Salt and ground black pepper

Lemons
2 fat ones

Fresh tarragon
2 tablespoons finely chopped

Butter
3 tablespoons

1. Put the turkey and chicken stock in a Dutch oven and bring to a boil over high heat. Cut the heat down so that the stock simmers gently and cook until the meat is tender enough to start falling off the bone, about 1 hour. Transfer the turkey to a baking sheet and pour the stock into a saucepan; keep the stock warm over low heat. Let the turkey cool, then remove the skin and reserve. Shred the meat from the bones, removing and discarding all of the fat and tendons. Put the shredded turkey in a bowl and cover with a few ladles of the stock to prevent it from drying out.

2. Preheat the oven to 450°F.

3. Skim off and save ⅓ cup of the fat from the stock; skim off and discard the rest of the fat. Add the ⅓ cup fat and the rice to the Dutch oven and toast over medium heat until the rice turns light gold in color, about 10 minutes, stirring now and then. The process is similar to cooking risotto, if you've ever done that. Slowly stir in 1 cup of the stock and stir until the rice sucks up the stock. Stir in another cup of stock and cook until almost all of the liquid is absorbed, 3 to 4 minutes, stirring now and then. Repeat the process until the rice is cooked through but a little chewy; you'll probably need to stir in a total of about 4 cups of stock. Once the rice is tender yet chewy, add the shredded turkey and the remaining stock to the rice. Season with 1 teaspoon salt and 4 grinds of pepper. Cover, cut the heat down to low, and simmer for 10 minutes so the flavors can fully develop.

CAROLINA GOLD RICE / Prior to the Civil War, rice accounted for a huge portion of the economy in the South. Carolina Gold is an heirloom variety that was grown back then and has since been replanted and revived. It was originally brought to the South from Italy, so it's similar to Italian varieties like Arborio and Carnaroli. Even though it has a long grain, it's starchy and cooks up creamy like risotto. You can find Carolina Gold rice from Anson Mills and other retailers (see Sources, page 326). Or you can use any starchy short-grain rice like Arborio, Carnaroli, or Vialone Nano.

4. Put the turkey skin in a cast-iron skillet and roast in the oven until browned and crispy, about 20 minutes. Pour off the rendered fat and discard. The skins will stick mercilessly to the pan; just let them cool in the pan and then scrape the crispy skin from the pan with a wooden paddle. Coarsely chop the skin and reserve.

5. Stir 2 tablespoons lemon juice and the tarragon into the turkey and rice. Whip the butter into the rice, again, just like risotto. Stir in the crisped skins. Taste and season with salt, pepper, and more lemon juice if needed. You'll likely need all three in varying degrees. Serve hot.

PREP TIP / If you have leftovers and want to reheat them, do not under any circumstances use a microwave oven. The microwave will steam the rice; the dish will get thick and clumpy and lose its creaminess. Trust me on this one. If you want to reheat leftovers, follow these instructions: Spoon the turkey and rice into a small saucepan and add a little chicken stock (for 1 serving, you'll need about ¼ cup stock). Set the pan over medium-high heat and stir the hell out of it until the turkey and rice are heated through, about 3 minutes.

COQ AU VIN

When I was 11, I saw a French chef (I don't remember who) make this dish on a PBS cooking show. Chicken pieces braised in wine with onions, carrots, celery, and potatoes. "That looks incredible!" I thought. But I never got to taste it until culinary school, in a "classics" class. We split up into groups, tasted everyone's dishes, and the instructor critiqued us. One of the other groups got coq au vin, and I was jealous. When I tasted it, I thought, "This sucks!" Jealousy gone. Everything tasted out of whack. The chicken was bland and the whole thing was too boozy. A few years later, I ordered coq au vin at a restaurant in Jacksonville, Florida. It was tons better. The wine wasn't dominating and the chicken had absorbed the rich flavors; but it still fell victim to the pot-roast phenomenon, where everything tastes too muted, too melded, too unexciting. I tried a few other versions of coq au vin, then tackled the dish with one goal in mind: to preserve that slow-cooked richness but make sure you could pick out every flavor. I cook the wine down thoroughly to soften its boozy edge, but to keep the flavors distinct, I add the vegetables later in the process. Coq au vin is like a pot roast, but that doesn't mean everything should be tossed in the pot at the beginning and cooked together for the entire time.

SHOULD BE ENOUGH FOR 4 PEOPLE

Bacon
3 thick strips, cut into ¼-inch dice

Chicken
1 whole bird, about 3½ pounds

Salt

All-purpose flour
about ¾ cup

Clarified butter
3 tablespoons

Carrots
6 baby ones, tops removed and skins scrubbed off

Red spring bulb onions
4, greens removed

Celery
1 stalk, cut into ½-inch by 1½-inch pieces

Red skin potatoes
4 giant marble-size, halved

Madeira
1 bottle (750 ml or 2 cups + 2 tablespoons)

Chicken stock
4 cups, at room temperature

Ground black pepper

Fresh chives
2 tablespoons thinly sliced

Fresh flat-leaf parsley
2 tablespoons minced

Ramps
6, cut into 2-inch pieces

---

1. Line a plate with a double layer of paper towels.

2. Heat a 4-quart Dutch oven over medium heat for 2 minutes, then add the bacon. Cook until some fat has rendered out and the bacon is golden brown and crispy, about 8 minutes, stirring now and then. Using a slotted spoon, transfer the bacon to the paper towels.

3. While the bacon is cooking, cut up the chicken into leg/thigh and breast/wing portions with the skin attached. For each leg/thigh portion, bend the leg away from the body, cut down to the joint, and then bend the joint to break it. Cut between the ball and socket, then down around the carcass to remove the entire leg/thigh portion. To separate the drumsticks from the thighs, cut down firmly through the joint. For each breast/wing portion, cut down along one side of the breastbone, then run the knife along the contour of the rib cage and around the wishbone to begin removing the breast from the body. When you get to the joint connecting the wing to the body, grab both wing and breast together and cut through the wing joint to remove breast and wing in one piece. To separate the wings from the breasts, cut through the joint at the base of the wings to remove them. Cut the breasts in half crosswise all the way through the bone, making four 2-inch square breast pieces.

Gather the breasts, drumsticks, and thighs for this recipe, and reserve the wings for another use (such as the baked hot wings on page 267).

4. Pat the chicken pieces dry with a paper towel and season on all sides with salt. Spread the flour in a shallow bowl or pie plate and dredge each piece of chicken in the flour, shaking off any excess so you have just a light dusting of flour.

5. Stir the clarified butter into the pot to combine with the bacon drippings. Crank the heat up to medium-high and add the chicken in a single layer, skin side down. Cook until the skin is golden brown, about 10 minutes. Don't fiddle with the chicken; just let it cook, caramelize, and develop a nice, crispy crust. Flip each piece and again let the skin get brown and crisp, another 5 to 6 minutes. The chicken won't be fully cooked at this point, just nice and brown and crispy. Transfer the chicken to a baking sheet.

6. Add the carrots, bulb onions, and celery to the pot and cook until they start to caramelize and brown around the edges, about 4 minutes. Using a slotted spoon, transfer the vegetables to the baking sheet with the chicken. Add the potatoes to the pot, turn them cut side down with tongs, and cook until they are browned, another 4 to 5 minutes. Transfer the potatoes to the baking sheet with the chicken and vegetables and tent with foil to keep warm.

7. Pour off any remaining fat from the pot. Add the entire bottle of Madeira to the pot, scraping all the browned bits into the wine. Bring to a boil over high heat. Cut the heat down to medium-high and boil until the liquid has reduced in volume by half, about 10 minutes. Add the chicken stock and return to a boil. Stir in 2 teaspoons salt and 1 teaspoon pepper, and transfer the chicken and vegetables back to the pot. Bring to a boil, then cut the heat down so that the liquid simmers gently. Partially cover, allowing some steam to escape, and cook for 1 hour.

8. Pull the pot from the heat, uncover, and transfer the chicken and vegetables to a warm shallow serving platter. Sprinkle the crispy bacon over the chicken. Stir the chives and parsley into the sauce left in the pot. Ladle the sauce over the chicken and vegetables and garnish with the ramps.

Good Birds, Good Eggs

Georgia is the largest producer of commodity poultry in the country. We raise more bland mass-market chicken than anyone. For that reason, it's hard for me to buy high-quality chicken locally. I usually have to buy from another state. I'm pretty adamant about finding high-quality poultry that's been raised and processed responsibly and humanely.

Chickens are not the smartest animals in the world. If you put food in front of them, they eat it. When it's light out, they feed. When it's dark, they don't feed. It's very easy to put systems in place that take advantage of a chicken's eating habits. The larger poultry producers keep the birds inside and keep the lights on 24/7 so they eat all the time. The chickens grow faster and go to market sooner. It's more profitable. But it doesn't make better-tasting chicken—especially when you raise garden-variety breeds like White Rock that reach market weight in only 6 weeks. Cheap, commodity chicken tastes bland and boring because great-tasting meat is not the number-one priority. Low price is the priority.

A good breed of chicken raised carefully on pasture develops a complex taste and a firm texture. That's the kind of chicken I prefer to cook, eat, and serve. My favorite breed is Poulet Rouge Fermier, a heritage French breed. It has a longer breast and longer legs than your typical supermarket bird. The legs are more proportional to the breast because the birds actually get to walk around more than commodity birds do. And the flavor difference is monumental. Poulet Rouge just tastes more chicken-y. Look for it at Whole Foods or have it shipped to you from Ashley Farms or Joyce Foods, two North Carolina farms that I trust (see Sources, page 326).

You'll see a lot of marketing terms when you go to buy a chicken. Here is a very brief look at some of them. In most cases, the terms apply to both chickens and eggs.

FREE-RANGE. This term is not highly regulated. It basically means that the birds are allowed to go outside and scratch and peck. It doesn't mean they will actually be outside scratching and pecking; it just means they are given the opportunity. Like I said before, chickens are simple animals. If you give them a big shelter with food in it, they'll probably stay there. So *free-range* sounds a lot more romantic than it really is. *Cage-free* is the equivalent term for eggs. *Cage-free* means that the eggs come from birds that are not kept in cages where they're unable to move around.

ORGANIC. This means that the chickens are fed organic feed. It doesn't mean the birds are free-range or that you're getting a high-quality breed. It just means that the feed is free of synthetic pesticides, sewage sludge, and chemical fertilizers and that the birds are not genetically modi-

fied or given antibiotics. The same goes for eggs. Organic eggs come from laying hens fed organic chicken feed.

PASTURE-RAISED. This is the term I look for. You won't find it in supermarkets. But you will see it in local food co-ops and farmer's markets. Pasture-raised chickens strut around in big open fields. There is some kind of shelter to protect the chickens from hawks and other birds of prey. Otherwise, the chickens are allowed to do their thing: scratch and peck at the grass. Their feed is usually supplemented to produce more nutritious meat and more nutritious eggs. Again, the taste difference with pasture-raised meat is phenomenal. The animals move around more, so their muscles develop more flavor. The meat also echoes the taste of the pasture on which it was raised. Pasture-raised eggs usually have deeply colored yolks with a much richer taste and more beneficial nutrients than commodity eggs. Be prepared for a dramatic cost difference, too. I think the expense is well worth it. But if you're forced to make a choice between supermarket eggs and farmer's market eggs, save the farmer's market eggs for dishes where you'll really taste them, like custards, frittatas, eggs Benedict (page 120), Scotch eggs (page 122), and salad Lyonnaise (page 116).

HOMEMEADE SALISBURY STEAK

Here's another homemade rendition of a frozen dinner classic. I took my cues from the frozen version because the original is basically a hamburger. Back in the mid-1800s, Dr. James Henry Salisbury prescribed a patty of chopped seasoned beef to improve the health and vitality of Civil War soldiers. Then he expanded the recommendation to the entire American population. This was 100 years before Dr. Atkins promoted his high-protein regimen! In the 1950s, new versions of the dish became wildly popular as fancy alternatives to German hamburgers (anything German was avoided in those days). I looked at about 30 recipes from the 1950s, which varied drastically but all included a savory sauce. Here, that savory flavor comes from a splash of Worcestershire sauce, dried porcini mushrooms, and a burger patty made with both beef and pork. This Salisbury steak is not traditional because there isn't really any "tradition." This is a broiled burger with a savory sauce that tastes light years ahead of anything from the frozen foods aisle.

MAKES ENOUGH FOR 6 PLATES

Dried porcini mushrooms
½ ounce, about ¼ cup

Onion
¼ cup finely chopped

Roasted red pepper
¼ cup finely chopped

Tomato paste
3 tablespoons

Fresh flat-leaf parsley
¼ cup finely chopped

Worcestershire sauce
2 tablespoons

Garlic
1 tablespoon minced

Salt
1¼ teaspoons

Ground black pepper

Ground beef chuck
1¼ pounds

Ground pork
12 ounces

Butter
3 tablespoons

Shallot
2 golf ball–size, sliced into thin strips, about ½ cup

All-purpose flour
3 tablespoons

Dijon mustard
½ teaspoon

Cornichons
2, sliced into thin rounds, about 1 tablespoon

Smoked pork broth (page 293)
2 cups, warm

1. Fill a 1- or 2-cup glass measuring cup with ½ cup water and bring to a boil in the microwave. Drop in the dried porcinis, stir, and let them rehydrate for about 30 minutes. Carefully pluck the large mushroom pieces out of the cup without disturbing the sediment on the bottom. Strain the soaking liquid through a very fine-mesh strainer and reserve the liquid. (Dried porcinis usually have a little grit or sand in the package; you've got to be very careful to remove all of the sediment.) Finely chop the rehydrated porcinis.

2. Adjust the top rack of your oven so the rack sits 4 inches below the broiler. Preheat the oven to broil. If your oven has levels of broil, choose low broil.

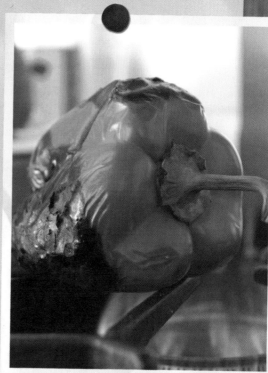

3. Line a broiler pan with foil, spray the top rack of the pan with nonstick spray, and set aside.

4. Thoroughly wash and dry your hands. In a large bowl, mix the porcinis, onion, red pepper, 2 tablespoons of the tomato paste, 2 tablespoons of the parsley, 1 tablespoon of the Worcestershire, the garlic, 1 teaspoon of the salt, and about 10 grinds of black pepper. Add the beef and pork and, using your hands, mix gently just until combined. Too much mixing will give you a tough, dry patty. Shape the mixture into 6 oval patties, each about 1¼ inches thick. Using your thumb, press a shallow divot in the center of each patty.

5. Place the patties on the broiler pan, divot side up, and broil for 5 minutes. Pull the pan from the oven and flip the patties over. Insert a meat thermometer at an angle to the center of the middle patty. Broil until the internal temperature of the middle patty reaches 130°F, another 8 to 9 minutes. The meat should be cooked to medium so it's no longer pink in the center. Pull the broiler pan from the oven and cut the heat down to 350°F.

6. Choose a deep sauté pan that's wide enough to hold all the patties at once. Melt the butter in the pan over medium heat. Add the shallots and sauté until soft, about 3 minutes. Using a wooden spoon, stir in the flour, which will make a roux. Cook and stir until the flour is deep brown and smells nutty, 5 or 6 minutes. Whisk in the remaining 1 tablespoon tomato paste, remaining 1 tablespoon Worcestershire sauce, the Dijon mustard, cornichons, strained porcini soaking liquid, and the broth, and bring to a boil. Season the sauce with a Kevin pinch of salt and 6 grinds of black pepper. Transfer the meat patties to the pan and baste all over with the sauce. Place the pan in the oven for 5 minutes. Remove, flip the patties over, and return to the oven for another 5 minutes. Serve the Salisbury steaks smothered in sauce and garnished with the remaining 2 tablespoons parsley.

SAUTÉED WILD SALMON WITH PEAS AND MUSHROOMS

In 2006, when I was cooking at Fife restaurant in Portland, Oregon, the area was just getting national recognition for its amazing local food. Wild salmon, mushrooms, hazelnuts, and ultra-fresh vegetables are iconic Northwest ingredients. This dish combines them all. I take a classic approach with the fish: It's sautéed and finished with browned butter and lemon juice. That technique is as old-school as it gets. I cook oyster mushrooms in brown butter, too, just enough to bring out their floral aroma.

MAKES ENOUGH FOR 4 PLATES

English peas
1 cup

Wild sockeye salmon
4 Copper River or Columbia River center-cut skinless fillets, each about 5 ounces

Salt

Grapeseed oil
2 teaspoons

Butter
4 tablespoons

Lemon
1 plump

Oyster mushrooms
1 ½ cups trimmed

Sugar snap peas
2 cups with strings removed and pods halved on the diagonal

Hazelnuts
¼ cup toasted and coarsely chopped

Fresh chervil or flat-leaf parsley leaves for garnish

1. Bring a medium pot of water to a boil. Fill a medium bowl with ice water. Drop the English peas into the boiling water and blanch for 1 minute. Using a spider strainer or slotted spoon, transfer to the ice water to stop the cooking.

2. Trim the salmon fillets to an even thickness so they will cook evenly. Pat the fillets dry and season on both sides with salt. Set a large sauté pan over medium-high heat, add the grapeseed oil, and heat until the oil is smoking. Pull the pan from the heat and add 1 tablespoon of the butter. Swirl the pan until the butter melts and starts to foam. With the pan still off the heat, add the salmon fillets, presentation side down (the flesh side, not the skin side), and cook for 2 minutes. Return the pan to medium-high heat, flip the salmon, and cook until it's just a little translucent in the center, another 2 minutes. Line a plate with a double layer of paper towels. Transfer the salmon to the paper towels to drain and rest.

3. Add 1 more tablespoon of the butter to the pan and swirl to melt. With the pan over medium-high heat, shake the pan off and on the heat until the butter foams up and then subsides and starts to turn a golden color and take on a nutty aroma, about 1 minute. Pull the pan from the heat, squeeze about 1 tablespoon lemon juice into the pan, and shake to combine. Set aside the browned lemon butter.

4. Heat a separate sauté pan over medium-high heat. Add the remaining 2 tablespoons butter and swirl the pan until the butter melts and foams up and then subsides. Just when the butter starts to turn a golden color and smell nutty, add the mushrooms and cook for 30 seconds; then add the snap peas, tossing and cooking for 30 seconds more. Add the English peas and toss and cook for 1 minute. Sprinkle with salt.

5. Spoon a nice mound of vegetables in the center of each serving plate and top with a salmon fillet, presentation side up. Scatter the hazelnuts over the top of each plate. Finish the dish with a drizzle of the browned lemon butter, some freshly grated lemon zest, and a few chervil leaves.

AFRICAN SQUASH <u>TART WITH WHIPPED EGGNOG TOPPING</u>

I've never been a fan of pumpkin pie. I like pumpkins. I like cinnamon. But the crust is never good, the filling isn't creamy enough, and the spices are too timid. Here's an alternative dessert I developed with my pastry chef, Chrysta Poulos. It has all the desirable qualities I never found in pumpkin pie. I like a tart crust that's a little crumblier and thicker, like shortbread cookies. And I prefer a super-rich filling. The reality is that pumpkins are too watery for pie filling. I only want pumpkins on my porch, not in my pie. African squash makes a much better filling because it contains less water and more sugar. It also gets silkier when pureed. African squash is a winter variety that came to Georgia via Zaire (now known as the Democratic Republic of the Congo), but it's also grown in other places. If you can't find it, any garden-variety butternut squash makes a good substitute. Either way, the method here is foolproof. You bake the tart crust, let it cool, pour in the filling, and let it set up. For fun, I garnish the tart with whipped eggnog, which thickens up just like whipped cream but tastes even better.

---

1. In a food processor fitted with the metal blade, cream the butter and sugar. While the processor is running, pour in the eggs, just until blended. Remove the lid of the processor bowl and evenly distribute the flour over the top of the mixture. Sprinkle the salt on top of the flour. Pulse to combine and blend just until the mixture comes together, about 20 seconds. The dough will be fairly soft, more like a cookie dough than a tart or pastry dough. Using a rubber spatula, scrape the dough onto a large sheet of plastic wrap. Wrap the dough with the plastic wrap, flatten it to a disk, and refrigerate until the dough is firm, about 2 hours.

2. Spray an 11-inch removable-bottom tart pan with nonstick spray.

3. Dust a clean, flat work surface generously with flour. Unwrap the dough, lay it on the work surface, and dust the top with flour. Rub some flour on your hands and rub the rolling pin with flour. Gently roll the dough into a 15-inch circle that's ¼ inch thick all the way across. To make sure the dough doesn't stick to the work surface, roll it in a single motion from the center to the edge. Turn the dough a quarter turn each time you roll, adding a little more flour to the work surface or the dough if it starts sticking. Four turns and it should be evenly rolled all the way around. Set the rolling pin near one edge of the circle and gently roll toward the center, picking up the dough with the pin. Center and unroll the dough over the tart pan, gently pressing the dough into the pan and up the sides, but being careful to press but not stretch the dough,

MAKES ONE 11-INCH TART

Butter
*1 cup + 1 tablespoon,
at room temperature*

Sugar
½ cup

Eggs
2 large, lightly beaten

All-purpose flour
*3 cups + a little more
for rolling the dough*

Salt
¼ teaspoon

**African squash cremeux
(recipe follows)**
about 3 cups

**Whipped eggnog
(recipe follows)**
about 2 cups

CONTINUED →

AFRICAN SQUASH TART WITH WHIPPED EGGNOG TOPPING

WHIPPED EGGNOG

MAKES ABOUT 2 CUPS

Heavy cream
1 cup

Egg yolk
1

Powdered sugar
2 tablespoons

Spiced rum
1 tablespoon

Freshly grated nutmeg
⅛ teaspoon

Vanilla extract
just a drop

Ground cinnamon
a teeny pinch

---

1. Chill a large mixing bowl and whisk. Or, if you prefer to use an electric mixer, chill the mixer bowl and whip attachment. Add the cream to the bowl and whisk or whip until it starts to thicken up. Add the egg yolk and powdered sugar to the cream and continue beating until the mixture forms soft peaks when the whisk or whip is lifted. Add the rum, nutmeg, vanilla, and cinnamon and beat just to combine.

which could cause it to shrink when baked. Using a sharp knife, cut around the edge of the tart pan and trim off excess crust. Using a fork, evenly prick the entire bottom of the crust. This docking step will ensure the crust does not puff up while cooking. Refrigerate the tart shell until the dough is firm, about 30 minutes.

4. Preheat the oven to 375°F.

5. Bake the crust until golden brown, 20 to 22 minutes. You want the crust to be a nice deep brown, the color of strong iced tea. It should be completely cooked and crispy. Place the tart pan on a cooling rack and cool to room temperature.

6. Fill the tart shell to the rim of the crust with the cremeux filling. Cover and refrigerate until set, at least 2 hours. Serve with a dollop of whipped eggnog.

AFRICAN SQUASH CREMEUX

MAKES ABOUT 3 CUPS, ENOUGH FOR 1 PIE

African squash
2 pounds

Powdered unflavored gelatin
4 teaspoons

Water
¼ cup

Heavy cream
1 cup

Whole milk
½ cup

Salt
½ teaspoon

Ground cinnamon
⅛ teaspoon

Ground cloves
a pinch

Freshly grated nutmeg
a pinch

Egg yolks
9

Sugar
⅔ cup

1. Peel the squash and cut it into chunks; you should have about 4 cups. Transfer the squash to a 4-quart pot and add about 6 cups water, or enough to cover the squash completely. Bring the squash to a boil over high heat, then cut the heat down to maintain a gentle boil and cook until the squash is very tender, about 20 minutes. Drain the squash and puree it in a high-powered blender or food processor until smooth. Run the puree through a sieve and discard the solids. You should have about 1¼ cups puree.

2. Scatter the gelatin over the water in a small bowl and let it soften for a few minutes.

3. Combine the squash puree, cream, milk, salt, cinnamon, cloves, and nutmeg in a 4-quart pot and set over medium-high heat. Bring the mixture up to just under a boil. Bubbles will start forming around the edge of the pan.

4. While the squash mixture is heating, beat the egg yolks and sugar in a large bowl until smooth. Mix some of the hot squash mixture into the yolks to temper them so they won't scramble, and then whisk the tempered yolks into the squash. Return the pot to medium heat and, stirring nonstop, cook the mixture until it thickens, or as my granny would say, "until it coats a spoon." When you dip a spoon into the mixture and take it out and drag your finger across the back of the spoon, the mixture should be thick enough so that the line stays clean. Or, for ultimate precision, you can use a thermometer. The mixture will be ready at 160°F, in about 10 minutes. Remove the pot from the heat and stir a little of the warm squash mixture into the gelatin. Then stir the tempered gelatin into the squash mixture. Stir the mixture until the gelatin is completely dissolved, about a minute. Strain the mixture through a sieve and blend with a stick blender or upright blender. All this straining and blending will result in a velvety, creamy pie. Once it's smooth, cool the filling to room temperature, stirring every now and then.

PEACH MELBA FOSTER JUBILEE

In 2010, I cooked dinner for 300 guests on a chartered sailboat cruise. Every day at 4 p.m., the crew put out a full dessert bar with cookies, cakes, and a special dessert served with vanilla ice cream. One day, the dessert was cherries jubilee. The next it was bananas Foster. Then it was peach melba. They all became so similar, I couldn't distinguish them. I thought it would be fun to take the best qualities of each and combine them into one dish. For instance, the sauce for cherries jubilee is way too sweet for me, but I love fresh cherries. Peach melba usually includes raspberries, but peaches don't ripen in the same season as raspberries in Georgia. And bananas Foster has a brown sugar and cinnamon butter sauce that I could eat every day of my life. So this dessert combines flambéed cherries and peaches in a brown sugar butter sauce. Almond extract intensifies the flavor of both the peaches and the cherries.

MAKES ENOUGH FOR 6 BOWLS

Cornstarch
½ teaspoon

Butter
2 tablespoons

Light brown sugar
½ cup packed

Bing cherries
1 cup pitted

Peach
1 ripe, skin left on and cut into rectangular french-fry shapes about ¼ inch square by 2 inches long

Cognac
3 tablespoons

Orange bitters
2 dashes

Almond extract
⅛ teaspoon

Ground cinnamon
⅛ teaspoon

Salt
⅛ teaspoon

Vanilla ice cream
6 scoops

1. In a small bowl, mix the cornstarch with 1 teaspoon cold water and stir to dissolve; set aside.

2. Heat a 10-inch sauté pan over high heat. Add the butter and swirl the pan until the foam subsides. Add the brown sugar and kind of pat it down into the butter with a wooden spoon. Continue cooking, swirling the pan now and then, until the mixture is a shade darker and doesn't separate, about 2 minutes. Add the cherries and peach and swirl to combine.

3. Now comes the fun part: Move the pan completely away from the heat and pour in the Cognac. You are going to ignite the Cognac in a blaze of glory, so stand back. Flame (flambé) the alcohol by returning the pan to the heat and slowly tilting the pan away from you toward the open flame; if you're working with electric heat, light a long match and touch it to the Cognac. The alcohol will flare up, but don't be scared; it will die down and burn out in about 20 seconds. Cut the heat down to medium, and add 1 tablespoon of water, the bitters, almond extract, cinnamon, and salt to the pan, swirling to combine. The melted brown sugar will seize up and harden; that's okay—the juices will heat up and the caramel will gradually melt into the sauce. Swirl the pan often and cook the mixture just until everything is dissolved into the sauce, 1 to 2 minutes. Stirring nonstop but slowly, stir the cornstarch mixture into the sauce and return to a boil. The sauce will thicken a little and get shiny. The bubbles will flatten out and look totally different than before.

4. Spoon the jubilee into bowls and top each serving with a scoop of vanilla ice cream. You might be temtped by other ice cream flavors. Don't be. Any other flavor will distract from the perfect balance of cherry, peach, orange, and almond.

ABOUT ORANGE BITTERS / Bitters are notoriously unstandardized. Sure, the classic flavor of bitters familiar to most people is Angostura—a middle ground of bitterness extracted from various roots, barks, seeds, herbs, and flowers. But other bitters have other flavors. Peychaud's skews more in the anise/licorice direction. Pommeranzen goes in the orange direction. For this recipe, you really want the bitter orange flavor. You can find that flavor in other ingredients, like orange extract or orange liqueur such as Grand Marnier or Cointreau. If you don't have orange bitters, you can replace it here with ⅛ teaspoon orange extract. If you don't have Cognac, replace it with 3 tablespoons Grand Marnier or Cointreau.

CREPES SUZETTE

A heavy pan is the secret to making good crepes. A thin pan will burn the crepes because it transfers heat too fast. But a heavy pan can handle the drastic temperature changes of cold batter in a hot pan over and over and over. To help spread the batter and make the crepes thin, start swirling the pan before you add the batter. Pour the batter into the middle of the swirling pan and it will instantly spread out to the edges and form a thin crepe. If you're not sure how much batter to pour in, experiment with water. Pour in a ladleful of water and swirl. If the water just coats the bottom of the pan, you have the perfect amount. The basic crepe batter here comes from Alton Brown. I cut back on the sugar and added salt, but otherwise I left Alton's recipe intact. It makes really good crepes. If you happen to have any leftovers, cool them down and store them covered in the refrigerator with wax paper between each crepe to prevent them from sticking together. They should keep for 3 to 4 days.

ENOUGH FOR 6 PEOPLE

Eggs
2 large

Milk
¾ cup

Water
½ cup

Grand Marnier
2 tablespoons

Vanilla extract
1 teaspoon

All-purpose flour
1 cup

Sugar
2 teaspoons

Salt
⅛ teaspoon

Butter
3 tablespoons, melted + a little for brushing the pan

Citrus butter sauce (recipe follows)
about 1 cup

Whipped cream or vanilla ice cream for serving

1. Combine the eggs, milk, water, Grand Marnier, and vanilla extract in a blender and blend quickly to combine. Add the flour, sugar, and salt and blend until smooth. With the blender running, slowly drizzle in the melted butter. Strain the batter through a fine-mesh strainer into a 4-cup measuring cup and refrigerate for 1 hour.

2. Remove the batter from the refrigerator and whisk for 30 seconds to reincorporate the hardened butter; you can also use a handheld immersion blender.

3. Melt about 2 more tablespoons of butter for brushing the crepe pan.

4. Heat a cast-iron skillet or nonstick crepe pan over medium heat. If using a cast-iron pan, brush the pan with melted butter and pour off any excess. Using a 2-ounce ladle or small measuring cup, pour and swirl the batter onto the hot pan in one motion. You want to add the batter and then immediately tilt the pan and swirl the batter around the bottom to get a thin, even coating of batter. Return the pan to the heat and cook until the top of the crêpe is dry and the edges are just starting to curl and brown, about 1 minute. Carefully loosen the edges all around with a rubber spatula, then peel the crepe from the pan with your fingertips and quickly flip it over; cook the other side for 30 seconds. Don't worry if your first crepe doesn't come out perfectly; chefs call it the sacrificial snack (enjoy!). As you cook the crepes, lay them out flat on a piece of parchment or wax paper, with a piece of parchment or wax paper separating each crepe. You may have to cut the heat down a little as you work; adjust the heat so that each crepe turns golden brown on the bottom side just as the top side becomes dry and no longer shiny.

5. Make the citrus butter sauce, then set the sauce-filled skillet back on the stove over the lowest possible heat. Fold each crepe into quarters with the browned side on the outside. One by one, place the crepes into the sauce and baste to coat. About 4 crepes will fit into the pan at one time.

6. Use a flat spoon to transfer 2 crepes onto each serving plate. When all of the plates are served, spoon a little extra sauce over each serving. Serve with whipped cream or ice cream.

ABOUT GRAND MARNIER / Prob- ably the most well-known or- ange liqueur, Grand Marnier is made from a blend of Cognacs sweetened and infused with the distilled essence of Haitian sour orange and sweet orange peels. It's the classic liqueur for crepes Suzette. But if you can't find it, other orange liqueurs can pinch-hit, such as Cointreau (which is clear instead of amber and slightly sweeter), orange curaçao (even sweeter), or, if you're des- perate, triple sec (much less complex).

CITRUS BUTTER SAUCE

MAKES ABOUT 1 CUP

Navel oranges
2

Lemons
2

Sugar
½ cup

Water
1 tablespoon

Amaretto
2 tablespoons

Grand Marnier
2 tablespoons

Salt
a pinch

Almond extract
⅛ teaspoon

Butter
½ cup cold, cut into small cubes

1. Using a Microplane zester, zest 1 tablespoon of orange zest and 1 teaspoon of lemon zest and set aside. Squeeze the oranges to get ½ cup juice. Squeeze the lemons to get 3 tablespoons juice.

2. Spread the sugar in a 10-inch skillet and add the water. Cook over medium-high heat, swirling or shaking the pan often but not stirring with any utensils. Sticking a utensil into the melted sugar will cause it to start crystallizing, which you want to avoid. Cook over medium-high heat with a brief shake or swirl now and then until the mixture starts to caramelize and turn light gold, 4 to 5 minutes.

3. Now the fun part: Pull the pan completely away from the heat and pour in the amaretto and Grand Marnier. This is going to flame up a lot, so stand back. Flame (flambé) the alcohol by returning the pan to the heat and slowly tilting the pan away from you toward the open flame; if you're working with electric heat, light a long match and touch it to the alcohol. The alcohol will flare up, but don't be scared off; it will die down and burn out in about 20 seconds. When it does, cut the heat down to medium, and add the salt, orange juice, and lemon juice to the pan, swirling to combine. The melted brown sugar will seize up and harden; that's okay—the juices will heat up and the caramel will gradually melt into the sauce. Swirl the pan often and cook the sauce to a shiny, glossy syrup, 5 to 6 minutes. Pull the pan from the heat and swirl in the almond extract, orange zest, and lemon zest. Piece by piece, swirl in the butter cubes until completely melted.

I was an overweight kid. But I didn't really care. Like most teenagers, any mention of "healthy food" was an immediate turn-off because it usually meant "less flavorful than cardboard." I never thought "health" and "food" belonged in the same sentence.

In 2003, I graduated from culinary school in Atlanta and cooked in the city's restaurants for the next three years. By the summer of 2006, it was time for a change. I moved to Portland, Oregon, because it was as far away from Georgia as I could possibly get. Plus, the city and the people in Portland had a strong commitment to local, organic food, which is something I care about deeply. After being there for a few weeks, though, it was a little scary because everyone seemed so in tune with the idea of eating a healthy, balanced diet. "My god," I thought, "I'm going to have to start eating tofu at every meal."

Then I realized that they weren't all skinny health food nuts denying themselves the pleasure of eating real food. They were just focused on what was fresh and what was local. They weren't cutting back on flavor; they were diving into flavor. When your backyard has ingredients like juicy sweet berries, rich hazelnuts, and the most succulent salmon ever, you eat them. And you don't need to do much of anything to make them taste good. You actually try to do less. With great ingredients, you end up taking a lighter, softer approach in your cooking.

Of course, I started eating and cooking that way in no time. I fell in love with it. It made me feel better physically. And it made me a better cook. In Portland, I began to fully appreciate the difference between high-quality ingredients and low-quality ingredients. Not that we don't have high-quality ingredients in Georgia. We have truckloads of them. But I wasn't always eating the best stuff. Take summer squash, for example. I never loved it at home. I'd usually eaten squash in some sort of casserole filled with eggs and cheese. It could have been papier-mâché casserole for all I knew. But in Oregon, when the squash was freshly picked and simply prepared, I was blown away by the taste of the squash itself.

I remember when I first started cooking at Fife restaurant in Portland, it was summertime and we got in a delivery of local summer squash. We developed our menus by opening the walk-in and creating dishes from what had come in that day. But zucchini was the last thing I ever wanted to cook with. I took all the good stuff and sheepishly left the squash for Marco Shaw, the chef-owner. He didn't see it as a disadvantage at all. Marco is a brilliant chef. He sautéed the squash with some mushrooms and garlic and served it with rockfish.

Boom. It tasted incredible. "What else did you put in here?" I asked him. "Nothing," he said. I couldn't believe it. It didn't taste bitter. It wasn't limp. It was crunchy, sweet, savory, and delicious. How could I have lived for 22 years without tasting the real flavor of summer squash? As a chef, I'd been preaching the dogma of great ingredients, but there I was having a revelation in Portland about a friggin' squash.

The same thing happened with strawberries. I always thought strawberries kind of sucked. Then once I was talking with Jessica Howard, the pastry chef at Fife, and she was giddy with excitement because it was almost strawberry season. "I can't wait until Sherri brings the strawberries," she said. Sherri was our local strawberry farmer. "Just wait," she told me, "they're so good!" I had to confess to her, "I don't really like strawberries. They taste sort of bland, watery, and grassy to me. And kind of bitter." "You don't know what you're talking about," she said. "You obviously have never had a strawberry from here. When they come in, if you taste one and you don't like it, you are insane."

Two weeks later, the first delivery came. Jessica pulled out a strawberry, tasted it, and said, "Oh my god, these are good. They're going to get even better." The strawberries looked nothing like the oversized ones I'd had back in Georgia. Each one had a really long stem with a small fruit on the end like a cherry. I put one in my mouth, and it totally caught me by surprise. It was the most intense strawberry flavor I had ever tasted. The strawberries were a Mt. Hood variety, red all the way through and so sweet they made candy obsolete. Those perfect little berries completely changed my mind.

Living in Portland helped me realize that fruit could be sweet without adding sugar. Corn could be creamy without adding cream. You didn't need to drown food in heavy sauces to make it delicious. You just needed to start with good ingredients. That one insight finally hit home, and it changed my whole diet.

I came to understand that healthy eating is not simply about substituting low-fat ingredients for high-fat ones. It's not about counting calories or giving up entire categories of food. It's about eating really high-quality fresh food that's bursting with nutrients and flavor. The flavor is so good, you will want to keep eating it. I have eaten mountains of fat-laden strawberry ice cream, butter-rich strawberry pies, and sugary strawberry cobblers, and I'd pass them all up to have just one bite of that fresh, unadorned, low-calorie strawberry that I tasted straight from the vine in Oregon.

You want my dieting advice? Turn your back on processed food. That will be the healthiest dietary move you'll ever make. I've been back in Georgia for several years now, and I brought my Portland experience with me. I make it a point to find the best-tasting local foods in and around Atlanta, like heirloom tomatoes, juicy ripe peaches, mineral-rich greens, and sweet Georgia white shrimp. I shop at farmer's markets and support producers who are putting in the time and effort it takes to grow the highest-quality food possible. Why? Because fresh, high-quality food is healthy and delicious.

BUTTERMILK-MARINATED FENNEL WITH SATSUMAS AND JALAPEÑOS

Most of the dishes in this book have some serious thought behind them. This one was a total experiment. I love the classic flavor combination of oranges and fennel. But I didn't want more orange flavor in this marinade. I didn't want the harsh taste of vinegar either. I wanted the Creamsicle effect you get with oranges and milk. Buttermilk popped into my head. It's acidic and creamy at the same time. I wasn't sure it would work, but it accomplished exactly what it needed to. It softened the raw fennel fibers, and its milk fat mellowed out the other flavors in the dish.

---

1. Rinse the fennel, then remove and reserve the fronds. Slice the bulb in half lengthwise—north pole to south pole—and using a sharp knife, carve around the core, removing and discarding it. Shave the fennel on a mandoline.

2. Mix the buttermilk and salt in a medium bowl until the salt dissolves. Toss the fennel in the buttermilk, cover, and refrigerate. The buttermilk marinade will be very salty, which helps to draw water out of the fennel, and it's the only component in the salad that is seasoned.

3. Cut the oranges into supremes (see photo on page 156): Cut the ends from the fruit, then stand the orange on one flat end. Following the natural curve of the fruit, remove the outer peel and inner white pith with a sharp knife, taking off as little of the flesh as possible. Working over a bowl, carefully run your knife in a V around each side of each segment to remove the segments from the membranes that separate them. Combine the juice and segments in the bowl and reserve.

4. Separate the whites from the green stems of the scallions and trim and discard the roots. Slice the whites into thin rings and thinly slice the greens on the diagonal. Put the whites in a small bowl and the greens in another small bowl. Shave the garlic and jalapeño on the mandoline. Gently toss the scallion whites, garlic, and jalapeño with the satsumas and juice to combine.

5. Pick the fennel fronds from the stems and toss with the scallion greens and a few drops of olive oil. Pluck the shaved fennel from the buttermilk and drain on a paper towel, patting off the buttermilk.

6. For each plate, place a 4-inch ring mold in the center of the plate. Pack the mold with one-quarter of the fennel, pressing with the back of a spoon to compact. Layer one-quarter of the orange mixture on top of the fennel, gently shaping it into the ring mold. Carefully lift the mold straight up to remove it from the plate. Sprinkle with the fennel frond mixture and croutons.

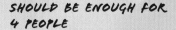

SHOULD BE ENOUGH FOR 4 PEOPLE

Fennel
1 baseball-size bulb with fronds

Buttermilk
½ cup

Salt
2 teaspoons

Satsuma oranges
2

Scallions
2

Garlic
1 clove, peeled

Jalapeño chile pepper
1 fat one

Finishing-quality olive oil

Fried croutons (page 314)
about ¼ cup

MARINATED TURNIP SALAD

In 2008, I was cooking for some guests on a raw foods diet. Well, not exactly "cooking" but preparing food. You are allowed to bring raw food up to about body temperature (98.6°F) but not much warmer than that. One of the tricks is to cut everything up. That breaks apart the tough fibers in food, a job usually left up to heat. The baseline goal is to make raw food easier to chew. And, of course, you want to make it delicious. Slicing and marinating raw ingredients does both. This salad consists of baby turnips cut into paper-thin slices and marinated in honey, salt, fresh rosemary, and orange oil squeezed right from fresh orange peels onto the turnips. To speed up the marinating, I stretch plastic wrap over a rimmed baking sheet, layer on the turnips and marinade, and then stretch another sheet of plastic wrap over the top. This creates a light vacuum effect and keeps the marinade in constant contact with the turnips so they absorb the flavors faster. Pull this dish out for a dinner party because the salad makes a pretty plate. You overlap the sliced turnips, scatter on some orange segments, toasted hazelnuts, and snipped chives, then add a dollop or two of goat cheese mixed with sour cream and horseradish.

ENOUGH FOR 4 AS A SIDE DISH

Hazelnuts
¼ cup

Valencia oranges
2

Blood oranges
2

Hakurei turnips
6 silver dollar–size, about
½ ounce each

Rosemary
1 sprig, leaves very finely chopped,
about ½ teaspoon

Honey
1 tablespoon

Salt

Goat cheese
¼ cup

Sour cream
2 teaspoons

Prepared horseradish
½ teaspoon

Fresh chives
¼ cup thinly sliced

Madras curry powder
⅛ teaspoon

1. Preheat the oven to 300°F.

2. Spread the hazelnuts on a baking sheet and toast in the oven until light golden and fragrant, about 10 minutes. Cool and coarsely chop.

3. Cut the Valencia and blood oranges into supremes (see photo on page 156): Cut the ends from the fruit, then stand the orange on one end. Following the natural curve of the fruit, remove the outer peel and inner white pith with a sharp knife, taking off as little of the flesh as possible. Working over a bowl, carefully run your knife in a V around each side of each segment to remove the segments from the membranes that separate them. Gather the segments and reserve the juice in the bowl and the peels on the side.

4. Wash the turnips and, using the coarse, "scrubby" side of a clean sponge, gently rub off the thin outer skin. With small, tender turnips, a regular vegetable peeler would remove too much of the flesh. Using a mandoline, slice the turnips into paper-thin, almost transparent rounds.

5. Tightly stretch plastic wrap over the top of a rimmed baking sheet so you have a taut, suspended flat layer

of wrap. Evenly spread a single layer of turnips over the wrap and sprinkle with the rosemary. Squeeze the orange peels over the turnips to spritz the oil from the outer peel onto the turnips. Drizzle a little of the honey over the top and sprinkle with a pinch of salt. Stretch a second layer of plastic wrap over the top and seal; this will create a sort of vacuum effect and will help infuse the flavors into the turnips. After about 10 minutes, the turnips will have soaked in the flavors, released some of their juices, and become more pliable.

6. In a small bowl, combine the goat cheese, sour cream, horseradish, and a pinch of salt until smooth.

7. For each plate, shingle one-quarter of the turnip slices in a circle. Sprinkle the turnips with one-quarter of the orange segments, and drop 5 or 6 small dollops of the cheese mixture on top of the oranges. Garnish each plate with 1 tablespoon hazelnuts, 1 tablespoon chives, a pinch of salt, and 1 teeny pinch of curry powder.

ROOT VEGETABLE SOUP

When it was cold outside, my granny made vegetable soup from whatever root vegetables were available. She usually sautéed the vegetables and then simmered them for a few minutes in chicken broth with a piece of ham or other cured pork. It was like a light, brothy chicken soup but with root vegetables in place of chicken. This soup re-creates that dish from memory. Instead of ham, I toss in a few chunks of pancetta (unsmoked bacon) for a savory contrast to the sweetness of the roots. I use rutabagas, carrots, sunchokes, turnips, and parsnips here. If you don't have one of those, leave it out and replace it with more of a root vegetable you do have. The important thing is to dice all the vegetables the same size so they cook quickly and evenly before the liquid is added. The vegetables retain better shape and flavor this way.

1. Heat a large enameled cast-iron pot or other soup pot over medium heat. Add the pancetta, stir, and cook until the pancetta is golden brown, 8 to 10 minutes. Add the onions, rutabaga, celery, and carrots and cook until the vegetables start to soften and the onions become translucent, about 6 minutes, stirring now and then. Add the sunchokes, turnips, and parsnips and cook for an additional 8 minutes, stirring a few times. Stir in the garlic and cook just until fragrant, about 1 minute. Stir in the chicken stock, Espelette pepper, and salt. Bring the mixture to a boil, then cut the heat down to low, cover, and simmer for 5 minutes. The vegetables should be just tender.

2. Remove the pot from the heat, and stir in the turnip greens and about 1 tablespoon lemon juice. Taste and season as needed with additional salt and lemon juice. Ladle into bowls and garnish with the parsley, chives, and celery leaves.

PREP TIP / Don't be tempted to mince the garlic here. It should be sliced. If you mince it, the small pieces will cook faster and develop a bitter taste. The slices also contribute to the texture of the soup. If you want to make the soup ahead, prepare it up to the point of simmering the vegetables in the seasoned stock. Cool it down, and refrigerate it for up to 2 days. Then reheat the soup and add the greens and lemon juice just before serving and garnishing.

SHOULD BE ENOUGH FOR 8 PEOPLE

Pancetta or unsmoked bacon
8 ounces, cut into ¼-inch dice

Onions
2½ cups cut into ¼-inch dice

Rutabaga
1¼ cups peeled and cut into ¼-inch dice

Celery
1 cup cut into ¼-inch dice

Carrots
⅔ cup peeled and cut into ¼-inch dice

Sunchokes (Jerusalem artichokes)
1¼ cups cut into ¼-inch dice

Turnips
1¼ cups peeled and cut into ¼-inch dice

Parsnips
1 cup peeled and cut into ¼-inch dice

Garlic
4 large cloves, thinly sliced on a mandoline

Chicken stock
6 cups

Espelette pepper
1 teaspoon

Salt
2 teaspoons

Baby turnip greens
1 bunch sliced into chiffonade (thin strips), about 4 cups

Lemon
1

Fresh flat-leaf parsley
about ¼ cup minced

Fresh chives
about ¼ cup very thinly sliced

Celery leaves
about ¼ cup minced

ASPARAGUS, <u>MOREL, AND COUNTRY HAM FRITTATA</u>

Frittata is a culinary chameleon. It can be breakfast. It can be brunch. It can be dinner. It can be an hors d'oeuvre. Here, it's an appetizer cut into wedges. The basic technique is even easier than scrambled eggs. You just pour the beaten eggs into a pan and let them cook without stirring. To cook the top, you slide the pan under the broiler for a minute or two. It's dead easy and a completely open book as far as flavors go. I keep the flavors classic. Asparagus loves eggs because eggs are creamy and asparagus is fibrous, so they balance each other out. Mushrooms also taste good with asparagus because earthiness and grassiness naturally complement each other. As for the ham, well, that porky, savory saltiness goes with just about everything.

ENOUGH FOR 4 AS AN APPETIZER

Country ham
4 paper-thin slices, about 1 ounce total

Morel mushrooms
8

Asparagus
3 stalks

Grapeseed oil
1 teaspoon

Salt
¾ teaspoon

Butter
2 tablespoons

Lemon
1

Eggs
4 large

Fresh chives
1 teaspoon thinly sliced or snipped

1. Set the upper rack of your oven so it sits 4 inches below the broiler.

2. Slice the country ham into ¼-inch strips.

3. Trim the ends off the mushrooms and slice in half lengthwise. Using a paper towel, gently brush any dirt or sand from the nooks and crannies. Drop the mushrooms in a small bowl of water and swish to rinse. Let any sand or dirt sink to the bottom of the bowl. Using a slotted spoon, transfer the mushrooms to paper towels to drain. Pat them dry.

4. Snap the tough ends off the asparagus and discard. Using a vegetable peeler, peel off and discard the dark green layer from the stalks. Slice the stalks and tips on the diagonal into ½-inch pieces.

5. Heat a 6-inch broiler-proof skillet (preferably nonstick) over medium heat. Add ½ teaspoon of the oil and swirl to coat the bottom of the pan. Separate the ham strips and drop them in the pan to crisp them up; it will only take about 30 seconds. Transfer the crisped ham to a plate.

6. Crank the heat up to high, add the remaining ½ teaspoon oil, the asparagus, and ¼ teaspoon of the salt to the pan, and toss nonstop just until the edges of the asparagus start to brown, about a minute. Transfer the asparagus to the plate with the ham.

7. Add 1 tablespoon of the butter to the pan and swirl the pan until the butter stops foaming. Add the mushrooms and cook, tossing nonstop, until all of the liquid releases from the mushrooms and the pan goes nearly dry, about 2 minutes. Add a squeeze of lemon juice and the remaining ½ teaspoon of salt to the mushrooms and toss; the clean, citrusy burst of acid makes the perfect counterpoint to the earthiness of the mushrooms. Pull the pan from the heat, leaving the mushrooms in the pan.

8. Preheat the broiler.

9. Crack the eggs into a medium bowl and whisk until blended but not frothy, about a minute. If you overbeat the eggs, the frittata will be airy instead of rich and creamy.

10. Return the mushroom skillet to medium heat and add the remaining 1 tablespoon butter. Swirl the pan until the butter stops foaming and the bottom and sides of the pan are completely coated with butter. Add the ham and asparagus to the pan and toss to combine. Pour the eggs into the pan and cook undisturbed for 4 minutes. Don't get anxious. Don't worry. Don't stir. Just let the eggs cook. Undisturbed.

11. When the eggs start to set on the sides but the top is still wet, transfer the skillet to the top rack of the oven and broil until the eggs are just set, about 2 minutes. Carefully remove the hot pan from the oven and invert a 9- or 10-inch plate directly onto the skillet. Place your hand on top of the plate and quickly flip the frittata onto the plate, lifting off the pan. Let the frittata cool for 2 minutes, then cut into 4 wedges. Serve garnished with the chives.

RICOTTA-STUFFED POBLANO WITH SUMMER VEGETABLE SUCCOTASH

Poblanos are like the Russian roulette of peppers. You can get one as mild as a bell pepper and another as hot as a jalapeño. Either way, a ricotta stuffing improves them. The milk fat in the cheese mellows the tannic, astringent quality of mild poblanos and cools down the spiciness of the hot ones. I roast the poblanos, then core them and trim them so they lay flat, like a thin sheet cake. That allows you to stuff and roll the peppers jelly-roll style into a neat-looking roulade. Underneath the roulade rests a quick sauté of ripe summer vegetables including corn and summer squash. Beneath that sits one of my favorite sauces ever, roasted tomato sauce. I learned it from Jordan Davis, my old sous chef at Woodfire Grill. He would roast summer tomatoes in the wood-burning oven and then pass them through the food mill to create a rustic tomato sauce with awesome fire-roasted flavor but none of the bitter black flecks. As a whole, the dish puts the spotlight squarely on ripe summer vegetables. It makes a great vegetarian entrée if you use vegetable stock instead of chicken stock.

---

1. Char the peppers over an open flame until black on all sides. Set in a bowl and cover tightly with plastic wrap. Let the peppers steam for 15 minutes. Using a clean but ratty towel (one you don't mind ruining), rub off and discard the skins from the peppers. This method is better than using a knife because you don't lose any of the pepper flesh—you just lose the charred skin. Using a sharp knife, cut around and remove the stem and top from each pepper. Cut a slit down the side to open the peppers, then remove and discard the seeds and ribs. Trim each poblano into perfect rectangles. The size will depend on how big the pepper was to start; you just want the long sides to be even and the short ends to be even so you can make a neat and even roulade (roll). Pat the peppers dry with a paper towel. Save the poblano scraps; they can be used in the spicy chanterelles (page 228) or any recipe that calls for chopped roasted poblanos.

2. In a small bowl, combine the ricotta, ¼ teaspoon lemon zest, 1 teaspoon lemon juice, and ½ teaspoon salt. Reserve the rest of the lemon to use in the succotash.

FEEDS 4 PEOPLE AS A MAIN DISH

Poblano chile peppers
8, all about the same size

Whole-milk ricotta cheese
1 cup

Lemon
1

Salt

Butter
2 tablespoons

Onion
½ cup cut into ¼-inch dice

Carrot
¼ cup cut into ¼-inch dice

Celery
¼ cup cut into ¼-inch dice

Summer squash
*½ cup cut into ¼-inch dice
(yellow or green zucchini both work)*

Garlic
2 cloves, minced

Corn
2 ears

Crowder peas
½ cup cooked

Chicken stock or vegetable stock
½ cup + more if needed

Fresh chives
3 tablespoons thinly sliced

**Oven-roasted tomato sauce
(page 311)**
about 1 cup

**Lemon olive oil
(see Sources, page 327)**

CONTINUED →

3. Line up the poblanos on your work surface with the (former) skin side down and a short end toward you. Using a small offset spatula, evenly spread 1 tablespoon of the ricotta mixture on each rectangle, leaving about a ⅛-inch border on all sides. Roll away from you from short end to short end to form a neat cylinder. Wipe any excess filling from the edges.

4. Heat a 10-inch sauté pan over medium-high heat. Add 1 tablespoon of the butter to the pan and swirl the pan until the butter is melted and the foam subsides. Add the onion, carrot, celery, and a pinch of salt and toss to combine. Cook just until the carrots soften, about 2 minutes. Add the squash and garlic and toss to combine. Cook for another 2 minutes. Crank the heat up to high and add the corn, crowder peas, and chicken stock and bring to a boil. Spread the vegetables evenly in the pan and cook for 5 minutes without stirring. It's really hard to let something just cook and not disturb it, but you've got to have patience and just let it go. Eventually, the stock will reduce down to almost nothing. If that happens before the 5 minutes are up, add a little more stock and continue cooking for the full 5 minutes. Pull the pan from the heat and use the washing machine method (see page 12) to stir in and emulsify the remaining 1 tablespoon butter. Stir in the chives, ¼ teaspoon lemon zest, 1 teaspoon lemon juice, and a Kevin pinch of salt.

5. Heat the tomato sauce in a small saucepan just until warm.

6. For each plate, spread about ¼ cup tomato sauce in the center. Top with one-quarter of the succotash and set 2 pepper roulades over the succotash. Drizzle the top of each roulade with lemon olive oil and garnish with a tiny pinch of salt.

WHAT'S A CROWDER PEA? / Most peapods have plenty of room inside for the peas. But when there are too many peas in the pod, they crowd together and the ends of each pea get squared off. I like the square shape of crowder peas here because the square peas blend in with the diced vegetables. But if you can't find crowder peas, any black-eyed pea, zipper pea, pigeon pea, or other cowpea or field pea will work. To cook them, remove the peas from the pod, rinse them, and pour them into a saucepan with enough water to cover the peas by 1 inch. Bring to a boil over high heat, then cut the heat down to low and simmer uncovered until the peas are tender. The total cooking time will depend on how fresh your peas are.

OLIVE OIL–POACHED SHRIMP WITH CUCUMBER AND RADISH SALAD

This dish works best as an hors d'oeuvre, but it could be a light lunch too. It's incredibly beautiful to look at and it can be made ahead in stages, so it's perfect for entertaining. The shrimp are essentially confited, which in French cooking means that they are poached and temporarily preserved in fat. Here the fat is olive oil, so the dish stays nice and light. The advantage of poaching in fat as opposed to water is that it keeps food juicy and tender. You might be surprised to know that meat contains at least 60 percent water, and seafood has even more because it lives in water. When you poach chicken or fish in water, osmosis causes the water inside the food to leave the food and enter the poaching water. But when you poach the food in something more viscous, like oil, fewer juices escape from the meat or fish. That's one reason why confiting creates extremely juicy, flavorful, and tender food. The best part is that you can refrigerate the food in the poaching oil for a few days before using it. For a party, you could poach these shrimp on Friday and serve them on Saturday. Just let the shrimp come to room temperature before you assemble the dish. And once you feel comfortable with the oil-poaching technique, go ahead and confit some vegetables, meat, or anything else that you think would benefit from retaining its juiciness after cooking.

---

1. Peel and devein the shrimp, if necessary; otherwise leave them uncut, as in the picture.

2. Heat the oil in a 1½-quart saucepan over medium-high heat to 180°F. Cut the heat down to medium but maintain the 180°F temperature of the oil. Pat the shrimp dry, add to the oil, and stir to coat evenly with oil. The temperature of the oil will drop to about 100°F; gently bring the temperature of the oil back to 150°F and cook the shrimp just until they begin to curl and lose their translucence, about 5 minutes. Watch them closely so they don't overcook; you want the shrimp tender but just cooked through. Line a plate with paper towels and use tongs to transfer the shrimp to the plate to drain. Refrigerate until cold.

3. Set the radish slices on a cutting board and, using your smallest round cutter, preferably ¾ inch, punch the slices into uniform rounds. In a small bowl, mix the radish rounds, cucumbers, celery, and capers with 1 tablespoon of the herb oil, tossing to combine.

4. Mound 3 shrimp in the center of each serving plate and sprinkle with salt and Espelette pepper. Spoon a little of the cucumber mixture on top of the shrimp, drizzle with some of the remaining herb oil, and garnish with basil leaves.

ENOUGH FOR 4 AS AN APPETIZER

Shrimp
12 large (U30)

Olive oil
about 1½ cups

Watermelon radish
1, sliced into thin rounds on a mandoline

Cucumber
1 peeled, seeded, and cut into ¼-inch dice, about ½ cup

Celery
1 stalk, strings removed and cut into ¼-inch dice, about ½ cup

Capers
1 teaspoon

Herb oil (see Sources page 327)
2 tablespoons

Salt

Espelette pepper
just a pinch

Fresh baby basil leaves for garnish

PAN-SEARED SHRIMP WITH SUMMER VEGETABLES

Here's a completely different take on shrimp than the oil-poached shrimp on page 173. Once the ingredients are prepped, the dish cooks in less than 10 minutes. The advantage of quick cooking here is the browning and flavor that take place when protein meets high heat. Don't be afraid to crank the heat up to full blast. The high heat browns the shrimp, caramelizes the vegetables, and evaporates the juices, concentrating all the flavors. Georgia white shrimp are my hands-down favorite here. Georgia doesn't have a truckload of seafood that trumps everyone else's in the United States. But our shrimp does. They're sweeter and firmer than common brown Gulf shrimp (which you could use in a pinch). They're so sweet that I add a big squeeze of lemon juice to balance their sweetness with some acidity. For the vegetables, use any summer vegetables you like, but make sure you have some ripe tomatoes in there. They release just enough juice at the last minute to create a light sauce.

ENOUGH FOR 4 FOLKS

Grapeseed oil
about 1 tablespoon

Shrimp, preferably Georgia white
24 large (U30), peeled and deveined, about 1 pound

Salt
about 2 teaspoons

Green beans
8 ounces, ends trimmed and halved on the diagonal

Yellow squash
1, ends trimmed and cut into ¼-inch dice, about 1 cup

Padrón chile peppers
2, seeds and ribs removed and thinly sliced, about ⅓ cup

Garlic
1 clove, thinly sliced

Smoked paprika
¼ teaspoon

Tomato
1, core and seeds removed and cut into ½-inch dice, about 1 cup

Lemon juice
1 tablespoon + 1 teaspoon

Fresh Thai basil
3 tablespoons cut into chiffonade (thin strips) + additional sprigs for garnish

Finishing-quality olive oil

1. Heat a 10-inch sauté pan over high heat until smokin' hot. Add just enough oil to cover the bottom of the pan and swirl to coat. Pat the shrimp dry and season both sides with the salt. Stand back, then add the shrimp in a single layer in the pan and sear until they are caramelized and slightly curled up, about 1 minute. The pan should ignite for a split second when you add the shrimp; this is a critical step to getting a lightly caramelized flavor on the shrimp. Once they start to curl, flip the shrimp and cook until just bright pink all over, another 30 seconds; transfer to a plate.

2. Add a little more oil to the pan—again, just enough oil to cover the bottom. Add the green beans, and cook and toss for 2 minutes. Add the squash and cook, using the washing machine method (see page 12), for 1 minute. Add the peppers and garlic and continue shaking the pan and stirring for another 30 seconds. Stir in the smoked paprika, tomatoes, and a pinch of salt and pull the pan from the heat. Squeeze the lemon juice into the pan and toss to combine. Add the basil and toss again; the heat from the vegetables will release the pungent aromas and flavors of the basil.

3. Arrange 6 shrimp on each serving plate and spoon the vegetables over the top. Make sure some of the shrimp are poking out from under the vegetables. Garnish with a generous amount of finishing oil and a fresh sprig of basil.

THAI BASIL IS SPICIER / I like Thai basil in this dish for a couple of reasons. (1) It has a more pronounced licorice flavor than regular sweet basil. (2) It stands up better to heat. Generally, Thai basil has a more pungent aroma than sweet basil, and it's a flavor I really love with these shrimp.

PEPPERS FROM PADRÓN, SPAIN /
Some Padrón chile peppers are
blazing hot and some are very
mild. You never know what you're
going to get. Either way, they
all have a superthin skin, so you
don't really need to remove the
skin like you sometimes do from
a bell pepper. If you can't find
Padrón peppers in your market,
banana peppers are an okay substitute. If you use them, just make
sure to throw in a pinch of dried
cayenne pepper for heat.

LIVORNESE TRADITIONAL FISH STEW

It's challenging to make a dish where everything is cooked and served together yet the flavors are still separate and exciting. When it works, I'm a sucker for it. The key here is not using too much liquid. One way the dish builds flavor is by lightly browning a whole handful of garlic cloves in olive oil to make garlic oil. Then the garlic flavor is in the oil that you use for cooking. To build the rest of the dish, you layer firm white fish and vegetables in the garlic oil in a sturdy pot, then roast the whole thing in the oven.

The fish should be as fresh as possible. The exact variety is less important than its freshness. This is an Italian fishermen's stew; the fishermen would use whatever fish was left over after the fish market closed. Just choose a firm white fish like snapper, grouper, rockfish, or bass so that it doesn't fall apart during roasting. It also helps to use a Dutch oven that's just big enough to hold the fish and vegetables. (I use an enameled cast-iron Le Creuset baking dish.) If there's too much space in there, the heat won't transfer quickly from the pot to the food. Italians aren't big on spicy food, but this dish is an exception. It features spicy red Calabrian chile peppers. But the sweetness of tomatoes, the richness of garlic oil, and the spark of lemon, capers, and olives balance everything out. It's a pretty substantial stew, thanks in part to toasted Italian bread in the bottom of the soup bowl.

MAKES ENOUGH FOR 4 BOWLS

Tomatoes
1½ pounds

Olive oil
about 1½ cups

Garlic
17 cloves, peeled

Onion
1 cup cut into ½-inch dice

Firm white fish
4 skinless fillets, each about
5 ounces and 2 inches thick

Salt
1½ teaspoons

Kalamata olives
¾ cup pitted and quartered
lengthwise

**Pickled Calabrian
chile peppers**
8, stems removed and discarded

Capers
1 tablespoon rinsed

**Crusty country white or
sourdough bread**
4 thick slices

Fresh flat-leaf parsley
2 tablespoons coarsely chopped

Lemon
1

Finishing-quality olive oil
about 2 tablespoons

1. Preheat the oven to 375°F. Bring a large pot of water to a rapid boil. Fill a large bowl with ice water to make an ice bath.

2. Using a paring knife, remove the core from the stem end of the tomatoes and score a small X on the bud end. Gently drop the tomatoes into the boiling water for 20 seconds and, using a spider strainer or slotted spoon, transfer the tomatoes to the ice bath to stop the cooking. This method is called score, blanch, and shock. Swirl the tomatoes in the ice bath for 1 minute and transfer to a cutting board. Using a paring knife and starting at the X in the bud end, peel off and discard the skins from the tomatoes. Coarsely chop the tomatoes into 1-inch cubes to measure 3 cups.

3. Heat a 4-quart Dutch oven over medium-high heat and add ½ inch of the oil to the pan. Add 15 cloves of the garlic to the pan, cut the heat down to medium, and cook until golden brown on all sides, 8 to 10 minutes, turning and stirring the garlic pretty often to keep it from burning. Use a slotted spoon or tongs to transfer the browned garlic

to a bowl. Add the onions to the oil, shake to mix with the oil, then remove the pot from the heat. After 10 minutes, pour the oil and onions through a small strainer into a small bowl. Reserve the oil in the bowl. Transfer the onions to the bowl with the garlic.

4. Pour about ¼ cup of the reserved oil into the Dutch oven. Pat the fish dry and season with ¼ teaspoon of the salt. Arrange the fish in a single layer over the oil in the Dutch oven.

5. Evenly spread the onions and garlic, tomatoes, olives, peppers, and capers over the fish. Sprinkle with the remaining 1¼ teaspoons of salt and toss gently to combine; the salt will help the vegetables release their juices. Drizzle about ⅓ cup of the reserved oil over the vegetables. Cover the pot, transfer it to the oven, and bake for 20 minutes. Crank the heat up to 400°F, uncover the pot, and roast uncovered for another 10 minutes.

6. Cut the remaining 2 cloves of garlic in half lengthwise. Heat a grill pan over medium-high heat and grill the bread on both sides until lightly charred, about 2 minutes per side. Right when the toast comes off the grill, rub with the cut side of the garlic cloves.

7. In a small bowl, toss the parsley with ¼ teaspoon lemon zest and 2 tablespoons lemon juice.

8. For each serving, set a piece of the garlic toast in the bottom of a shallow serving bowl. Gently place a piece of fish and a couple of spoonfuls of the tomato mixture on top of the toast. Garnish with a spoonful of the parsley mixture, a squeeze of lemon juice, and a generous amount of the finishing oil.

WILD STRIPED BASS WITH WARM BLACK-EYED PEA SALAD

Striped bass swim all the way up the Atlantic coast. They're very prolific, so they have good numbers in the ocean, and they're usually harvested by day boats that deliver fresh fish without a big environmental impact. All that makes wild striped bass a very sustainable seafood choice. My favorite part of this fish is the skin. It's so thin that it crisps up amazingly well. The smell of crispy fish skin reminds me of growing up in the South. I pair it here with another Southern staple, black-eyed peas. The peas are traditionally cooked it a pot with ham, but I wanted to do something lighter. I took a salad approach, like an Italian might take with chickpeas or cannellini beans. Perfectly cut vegetables are very important for the salad. Food processors chop unevenly and tend to liquefy vegetables, which would ruin this dish. Take care to cut the celery, carrot, onion, and peppers into a perfect 1/8-inch dice, known as a brunoise cut.

SHOULD BE ENOUGH FOR 4 PEOPLE

Wild striped bass
4 skin-on fillets, each about 5 ounces and 2 inches thick

Salt

Grapeseed oil
about 2 tablespoons + 2 teaspoons

Onion
1/4 cup + 2 tablespoons cut into 1/8-inch dice

Piquillo chile peppers
1/4 cup cut into 1/8-inch dice

Carrot
3 tablespoons cut into 1/8-inch dice

Celery
3 tablespoons cut into 1/8-inch dice

Black-eyed peas
1 1/2 cups cooked and drained

Sherry vinegar
3 tablespoons

Finishing-quality olive oil
3 tablespoons + 2 teaspoons

Sweet herb mix (page 6)
1/2 cup

Fresh chives
1/4 cup chopped

1. Preheat the oven to 475°F. Line a plate with a double layer of paper towels.

2. Generously season the fish with salt on both sides, then heat a 12-inch ovenproof skillet over high heat. Add 2 tablespoons of the grapeseed oil and swirl to coat the bottom of the pan. The oil should be smokin' hot. Blot dry the fish dry so it is very dry all over, then gently slide the fish skin side down into the pan, being careful not to splash the hot oil. Press and leave a 10-inch flat lid or grill press on top of the fillets so they get a good sear on them. Cook until the fish is nicely browned, about 2 minutes. Remove the lid or press, flip the fillets, and transfer the skillet to the oven. Bake until the fish is firm and no longer translucent, 5 to 7 minutes. Transfer the fish to the paper towels to drain and rest.

3. Heat a 10-inch skillet on high heat, again until smokin' hot. Add the remaining 2 teaspoons grapeseed oil and swirl to coat the bottom of the pan. Add the onions, peppers, carrots, and celery and shake the pan to distribute the vegetables. The pan should be so hot that the vegetables ignite when you tip the pan toward a gas flame; this will add a subtle smoky quality to the dish. Cook for 1 minute, tossing occasionally. Add the black-eyed peas and continue tossing and cooking until the liquid is gone, another minute or so. Add 1 teaspoon salt and the vinegar, stirring the bottom of the pan and scraping all of the browned bits into the sauce. Cook and stir for another minute and then remove from the heat. Drizzle with 3 tablespoons of the finishing oil and toss in all of the fresh herbs.

4. Divide the black-eyed pea salad between serving plates and top with a piece of fish. Finish each dish with a drizzle of the remaining olive oil.

COOKING BLACK-EYED PEAS / To get 1½ cups of cooked black-eyed peas, you'll need to start with about ¾ cup dried. Cover them with plenty of cold unsalted water or vegetable stock and bring to a boil. Cut the heat down to low and simmer the beans, uncovered, until they feel tender but still a little chewy when you bite into one, about 1½ hours. Give them a stir now and then, skimming off any scum or adding more liquid to keep the beans completely covered while cooking. Drain and they're ready to go.

PIQUILLO **MEANS "LITTLE BEAK"** / Piquillo peppers are mild red chile peppers from Spain. Here in the United States we get them roasted and peeled in jars. If you can't find them, use jarred roasted red peppers plus a little ancho or other powdered pure mild chile for some heat.

HALIBUT EN PAPILLOTE

I learned how to cook fish *en papillote,* which means "in parchment," in culinary school. At that age, I was still a little leery in the fish department. Northern Georgia doesn't always have the freshest finfish, and steaming fish in a paper bag didn't seem like it would help. This method doesn't use a lot of fat; it doesn't use a lot of spice; and you don't roast or caramelize the fish. You don't use any of the traditional techniques that amplify flavor. But I was absolutely floored by how delicious this fish tasted. The key is using super fresh fish (don't even think about using frozen) and sealing the parchment very tightly so that the flavors, aromas, and juices get trapped inside. I line the bottom of the parchment with farro, a type of wheat berry, and then top it with carrots, turnips, cabbage, and snap peas, plus a little jalapeño for heat. The fish goes on top with a little lemon zest, and then you seal the parchment and bake the whole thing. It's about as easy as it gets. You serve each guest his or her own parchment bag of beautifully steamed fish and vegetables. Just remember that you only get one shot at seasoning the farro and vegetables as you assemble the dish. I like to sprinkle a little salt on each component right out of the gate as it gets layered onto the parchment.

MAKES ENOUGH FOR 4 PEOPLE

Farro
¾ cup

Water
1½ cups

Cabbage
1 cup thinly sliced on a mandoline

Sugar snap peas
½ cup, ends trimmed and strings removed

Turnip
⅓ cup peeled and cut into matchsticks

Carrot
¼ cup peeled and cut into matchsticks

Jalapeño chile pepper
¼ cup finely diced, seeds and ribs removed

Shallot
¼ cup sliced in thin rings

Garlic
2 cloves, sliced paper-thin on a mandoline

Lemon
1

Salt

Halibut
4 skinless fillets, each about 3 ounces and trimmed to an even thickness

Finishing-quality olive oil
¼ cup

Scallions
2, green and white parts thinly sliced on the diagonal

---

1. Preheat the oven to 400°F.

2. Soak the farro in a bowl with the water for 30 minutes. Drain off the water and rinse with fresh water. Put the farro in a 2-quart saucepan and cover with fresh, cold water. Bring to a boil, then cut the heat down to low, cover, and simmer until the farro is tender yet chewy, about 20 minutes. Drain off any excess liquid and spread the farro on a baking sheet to cool.

3. Meanwhile, in a medium bowl, toss the cabbage, snap peas, turnip, carrot, jalapeño, shallot, garlic, and ½ teaspoon lemon zest. Add 1½ cups of the cooled farro and toss to combine (reserve any remaining farro for another use).

4. Cut four 12-inch squares of parchment paper and evenly divide the farro mixture among the centers of each; sprinkle the farro with salt. Pat the halibut dry, set on top of the farro, and sprinkle with salt and a pinch of lemon zest. Bring two sides of the parchment up over the halibut, align the edges, and fold down the parchment tightly over the fish. Turn the packet and fold the ends of the parchment under the fish to create a tight packet.

5. Set the packets on a baking sheet and bake for 12 minutes. Pull the pan from the oven, transfer the packets to a rack, and let rest for 3 minutes. Set the packets on plates and carefully cut each packet open, drizzling the fish with 1 tablespoon oil. Squeeze some lemon juice on each one, sprinkle with the scallions, and serve.

Sustainable Fish

All of the seafood called for in this book is deemed to be safe for the environment and safe for the species itself as determined by the Monterey Bay Aquarium (MBA). Based in Monterey, California, the MBA is both an active, working aquarium and a research institute. A great deal of funding for the institute comes from the Hewlett-Packard family. Julie Packard is the president of the aquarium, and her family has a long history of conservationism. Years ago, they developed the Seafood Watch program to help ensure that our oceans could continue to provide plenty of healthy fish for generations to come. It was a thorough undertaking. The Seafood Watch program can tell you on any given day in any given part of the country the best fish choices for consumers and chefs to ensure that the environment is not unduly harmed and that the fish species will remain continually available. It's an ever-growing, ever-changing list. Go online to the Monterey Bay Aquarium website and you can see a list of Best Choices, Good Alternatives, and Fish to Avoid in each region of the United States (see Sources, page 326). You can even print a little pocket guide to carry in your wallet to help you make good choices when you're shopping or dining out. I use the Seafood Watch pocket guides for everything I cook in my restaurant and at home, as well as for what I eat when I'm dining out.

The important thing to remember about fish sustainability is that it's not simply about farmed versus wild fish. Some farmed fish like catfish make the Best Choices list while other farmed fish like salmon don't. Some wild fish like swordfish don't make the Best Choices list but other wild fish like striped bass do. Overfishing, environmental destruction, and industrialized farming methods are just a few of the factors that determine where any given fish ends up on the list. This book isn't big enough to delve too deeply into the subject, which is why I recommend Seafood Watch. It's a convenient resource to help you understand what fish is good to use in your area at any given time of the year. Keep in mind that, like every other food, seafood is seasonal. I love Georges Bank diver scallops from Cape Cod, but I can only get them when it starts to get cool outside. The number-one rule of buying fish is freshness, freshness, freshness. If I call for a certain fish in a recipe but that variety is not fresh at your market, by all means use a fresher variety. Talk to the people at the fish counter. Ask them what has come in that day or maybe the night before. They will tell you what is freshest. If it's a Best Choice or Good Alternative on the Seafood Watch list, you're in business.

RIGHT:
Wild striped bass on ice

GRILLED STURGEON OVER SMOKED POTATOES WITH PICKLED GARLIC AND HERB SALAD

Although this is a seafood dish, it approximates a meat dish as closely as possible. When sturgeon is grilled, its density and intramuscular fat take on this quality that's more like a pork chop than a piece of fish. I love this dish because the whole thing is done on one piece of equipment—a grill. Give yourself plenty of grill space to cook the sliced potatoes in a single layer. If you have a small grill, smoke the potatoes in batches. It shouldn't take but a few beers' worth of time.

PLENTY FOR 4 HUNGRY CAMPERS

Red potatoes
4 Hacky Sack–size, about 1 pound

Olive oil
about ¾ cup

Salt

Sturgeon
4 skinless fillets, each about 7 ounces

Sweet herb mix (page 6)
1 cup

Pickled garlic (page 321)
about ¼ cup

Lemon
1 fat one

1. Heat a grill for indirect medium-high heat. If you have a wood or charcoal grill, rake the coals to one side, leaving a space to cook the potatoes with low, indirect heat. Or use the upper rack of your grill.

2. Slice the potatoes into rounds about ¼ inch thick and toss with ¼ cup of the olive oil. Scrape the grill grate and coat it with oil. Arrange the potatoes in a single layer over the unheated part or upper rack of the grill. Cook until the potatoes begin to bead up with juices, about 20 minutes. Sprinkle the potatoes with salt, flip them, and cook until they are fork-tender, another 20 minutes or so. Transfer the potatoes to a plate and tent with foil.

3. Line a plate with a double layer of paper towels.

4. Pat the sturgeon dry with a paper towel and season both sides with salt. Scrape the grill clean and coat it with oil. Coat the fish lightly with oil and set the fish presentation side down (flesh side down) on the grill directly over medium-high heat, positioning it at a 45-degree angle to the grates. Cover with a domed lid or large aluminum pan and grill for 3 minutes to create a steamy environment and help the fish cook faster while retaining moisture. Rotate the fish 90 degrees, cover, and grill for another 3 minutes. Sliding a thin fish spatula in the same direction as the grates, carefully flip each fillet onto a new, hot part of the grill. Cover again and grill to an internal temperature of 150°F, 4 to 5 minutes. Transfer the fish to the paper towels and let rest for 5 minutes.

5. Combine the herb mix with the garlic and its pickling liquid, ¼ teaspoon lemon zest, and ½ teaspoon lemon juice. Add a Kevin pinch of salt and stir in the remaining ½ cup olive oil.

6. For each plate, shingle one-quarter of the potatoes in a circle in the center. Top with a piece of fish and spoon one-quarter of the pickled garlic and herb salad over the fish. Serve.

WILD SALMON CRUDO

If you want to show off the natural flavors of an ingredient, serve it raw. This easy appetizer cuts to the chase about why salmon is so delicious. It's about balancing the key tastes of salt, fat, and acid. There is no cooking and very little technique. You thinly slice the fish, marinate it in vinegar and citrus juices, and then serve it with thinly sliced cucumber marinated the same way. It makes an ideal light starter course.

---

1. Peel a small piece of the cucumber and taste the skin; if it's tender and sweet, leave it on. If the skin is bitter, peel the cucumber and discard the skin. Slice the cucumber on a mandoline into ⅛-inch-thick slices (about 12 rounds). Tightly stretch plastic wrap across a large plate or over the top of a small rimmed baking sheet. This will give you a taut, flat layer of wrap. Evenly spread a single layer of cucumber rounds over the wrap and spoon on ¼ cup of the citrus vinegar. Stretch another piece of plastic wrap directly over the cucumbers and seal the edges to trap the vinegar and quickly infuse the flavors. The tight plastic wrap will create a sort of vacuum effect and speed up the marinating. Give the cucumbers about 15 minutes to completely infuse.

2. Cut the salmon kind of like you cut the cucumber. You'll need a very sharp thin-bladed slicing knife; use it to slice along the natural grain of the fish on a slight diagonal, cutting it into ⅛-inch-thick slices (about 12 slices). Use the same infusion technique as for the cucumbers: Stretch plastic wrap across another large plate or small rimmed baking sheet; spread the salmon slices in a single layer on the plastic wrap, sprinkle with salt, drizzle with the remaining citrus vinegar, and stretch another sheet of plastic wrap over the top. In about a minute, the salmon will turn from translucent pink or orange to a more dull, opaque color. When it does, remove the salmon from the marinade, place on a paper towel, and pat dry.

3. For each plate, arrange 3 slices of salmon in the center. Shingle 3 marinated cucumbers over the salmon, then drizzle with ¼ teaspoon lemon olive oil and generously sprinkle with coarse salt. Garnish with fennel fronds and serve.

MAKES ENOUGH FOR 4 SMALL PLATES

Kirby cucumber
1 plump

Citrus vinegar (see Sources page 327)
¾ cup

Wild sockeye salmon
1 Copper River or Columbia River center-cut fillet, 4 ounces, skinned and trimmed to an even thickness

Lemon olive oil (see Sources, page 327)
1 teaspoon

Coarse salt

Fennel fronds for garnish

SHAWARMA <u>WITH TAHINI SAUCE</u>

━━━━━━━━━━━━━━━━━━━━

This is the grab-and-go sandwich of the Middle East. It's like the Lebanese version of a dirty water dog. But shawarma is infinitely healthier. It's fresh meat that's slow-roasted on a vertical spit, sliced paper-thin, and served in flatbread with vegetables. Lamb is traditional, but chicken is popular too. I use turkey to switch things up. I marinate the turkey breast in lemon zest, herbs, and olive oil and then grill it on a hot grate. The add-ons are what really make the sandwich sing. Tahini sauce, made from Lebanese sesame seed paste, adds a little bitterness. Lemon juice and pickled beets add a plucky quality along with some earthiness. Richness comes in the form of tarragon aioli. You end up with a sandwich that has very balanced flavor. You could swap out the tarragon aioli for spicy raita (page 75) if you like. You could also replace the turkey with just about any meat, from shredded oven-roasted chicken (page 137) to grilled flank steak (page 204) or London broil (page 208).

─────────────────────────

1. In a small bowl, combine the parsley, cornichons, and chives and gently toss with about 1 tablespoon lemon juice.

2. Heat the pita directly over an open flame or under the broiler just enough to heat through, soften, and take the chill off, about 30 seconds. Spread the center of each bread with tarragon aioli, and then layer on the meat and beets. Drizzle with about 1 tablespoon of the tahini sauce and top with the herb mixture. This sandwich has the perfect balance of sweet, sour, bitter, and salty components. Fold your shawarma in half and enjoy the taste sensation.

━━━━━━━━━━━━━━━━━━━━

PREP AHEAD / The beauty of this sandwich is that almost all of the components are prepared ahead of time. That's how street vendors can whip up shawarma in no time. Marinate the turkey and make the pickled beets, tahini sauce, tarragon aioli, and the herb mixture up to a day ahead. Keep them all refrigerated until serving time. Then all you have to do is grill and slice the turkey and warm up the pitas.

ENOUGH FOR 4 PEOPLE

Fresh flat-leaf parsley leaves
1/4 cup coarsely chopped

Cornichons
2 tablespoons coarsely chopped

Fresh chives
1 tablespoon thinly sliced

Lemon
1

Pita or flatbread
4 rounds

Tarragon aioli (page 298)
about 1/3 cup

**Grilled turkey breast
(recipe follows)**
2 cups sliced very thin

Pickled beets (page 320)
1/4 cup finely shredded

Tahini sauce (page 307)
about 1/3 cup

GRILLED **TURKEY** BREAST

ENOUGH FOR 6 PEOPLE

Turkey breasts
2 pounds boneless and skinless

Celery leaves
⅓ cup chopped

Fresh tarragon
⅔ cup chopped

Fresh basil
⅓ cup chopped

Lemon
1

Olive oil
1 cup

Salt and ground black pepper

1. Pound or trim the turkey breasts to an even thickness. In a large zip-top bag, combine the celery leaves, tarragon, basil, all of the zest from the lemon, and the olive oil. Add the turkey breasts and lightly massage the marinade into the meat. Squeeze the air out of the bag and seal. Let the turkey marinate in the refrigerator for at least 4 hours or overnight.

2. Heat a grill for direct high heat.

3. Remove the turkey from the marinade, pat dry, and season both sides with salt and pepper. Scrape the grill clean and coat it with grapeseed oil. Set the turkey on the grill, shiny side down (where the skin used to be), at a 45-degree angle to the grates. Cook for 5 minutes, then rotate the meat 90 degrees and continue grilling for another 3 minutes. The meat will start turning opaque on the sides. Flip the turkey over and again place it at a 45-degree angle to the grates; cook until the internal temperature reaches 150°F, about 5 more minutes. Transfer the meat to a plate and let rest for 10 minutes. Slice paper-thin while still warm.

BRÛLÉED GRAPEFRUIT WITH GREEK YOGURT

I developed this dish as a dessert. But it could also be breakfast in the way that sweet pancakes can also be dessert. Or it could be a classy way to start brunch. Regardless, it's health in a bowl. Grapefruit and yogurt are both supergood for you. You might think that they'd be too bitter and acidic together, but honey and brown sugar add enough sweetness to soften everything out. I use Greek yogurt because it's strained and has a thicker, richer texture than regular yogurt. I also add some chopped figs to amplify the floral sweetness of the whole dish. Some savory flavor comes when you scatter turbinado sugar on the grapefruit and brûlée it, which means you melt the sugar with a kitchen torch or under the broiler until it melts and caramelizes. As sugar caramelizes, it becomes increasingly brown and savory and decreasingly sweet. That savory-sweet caramelized sugar flavor brings the whole dish into balance.

ENOUGH FOR 4 FOLKS

Grapefruit
2, thoroughly washed

Greek yogurt
1 cup

Tupelo or other flavorful honey
4 teaspoons

Salt

Turbinado sugar
¼ cup

Dried Black Mission figs
4, finely diced

Fresh basil or tarragon
*2 teaspoons chiffonade
(cut into thin strips)*

Hazelnuts (optional)
8, toasted and crushed

Finishing-quality olive oil
1 teaspoon

1. Line a plate with a double layer of paper towels.

2. Using a Microplane zester, remove and collect 1 teaspoon grapefruit zest; set aside.

3. Cut the grapefruit into supremes (see photo on page 156): Cut the ends from the fruit, then stand the grapefruit on one flat end. Following the natural curve of the fruit, remove the outer peel and inner white pith with a sharp knife, taking off as little of the flesh as possible. Working over a bowl, carefully run your knife in a V around each side of each segment to remove the segments from the membranes that separate them. You should end up with about 1 cup of segments and a fair amount of juice; collect the juice in the bowl and reserve. Spread the segments on the paper towels to drain.

4. Whisk the yogurt and honey together in a small bowl. Add a pinch of salt and the reserved grapefruit zest and stir to combine.

5. Line a baking sheet with nonstick aluminum foil, nonstick side up. Spread the grapefruit sections on the foil and sprinkle heavily with the sugar. Using a kitchen torch, melt and brown the sugar, like you would finish a crème brûlée. You could also use a very hot broiler with the grapefruit set a few inches from the heating element.

6. To serve, divide the yogurt mixture among shallow bowls. Sprinkle the figs, basil, and crushed hazelnuts on the yogurt and arrange the grapefruit sections over the top. Drizzle with some of the collected grapefruit juice and a little finishing oil.

PREP TIPS / I love the golden glow and full flavor of tupelo honey. If you can't find it, use another floral honey, like sage or orange blossom. If you have trouble finding turbinado sugar, use light brown sugar pressed through a sieve.

Keep in mind that chopping dried figs tends to clog up your knife blade. Before you start chopping, wipe the blade with a little oil to help reduce stickiness.

Chapter

6

FOOD + FIRE = DELICIOUS

My parents' house is perched on a hill overlooking a tree line in Locust Grove, Georgia. When you stand on the deck, all you see is woods, and you feel like you are the center of the universe. Growing up, I'd sit on the deck, stare into woods, and let the smell of wood smoke from the grill pull me into a trance.

My mom usually cooked on weeknights, but on weekends Dad liked to grill. Building a fire, taming it, and managing the heat seemed appealing to my father. I always took it for granted until the day my mom had to grill. I was in fourth grade at the time, and we were spending the weekend at my grandparents' house. My dad was away, yet my mother's mind was set that we were going to have grilled pork chops that Saturday. I was stoked, because I loved pork chops. That afternoon, she started prepping the food, but usually she just handed it off to my father. He would always have the fire ready and have all his grill instruments in place, like a surgeon in an operating room. Not this day.

My mom had no idea how to light a charcoal fire. So she used the gas grill cranked up to high. She finally got the chops on the grill, and the next few minutes were a blur. I'm sure she figured she would simply put the chops over the fire and take them off when they were done. My dad always judged the doneness of food by how many beers it would take. Chicken was six beers. Pork chops were two. He made it seem easy.

Some time elapsed, and I figured two beers were long gone and we should be eating by now. I was upstairs playing and came outside and said, "Mom, when are we gonna eat?" She had a look on her face that was panicked, embarrassed, frustrated, angry, and sad all at once. I asked, "Shouldn't the pork chops be ready by now?" "I'll call you when they're ready!" she snapped. I went upstairs to play some more, and when I came back down, the table was already set. But there were no pork chops. The subtleties of social interaction are lost on a fourth-grader, and I innocently asked, "Where are the pork chops, Mom?" She said, "They didn't come out right." "What's wrong with them?" I asked. I wasn't trying to be a jerk. I just wanted more information. My grandfather was holding back his laughter. My grandmother was looking vacant like she didn't want to get involved. Finally, my mom said, "I burned the pork chops." I said, "It's not a big deal. I'll still eat them." I glanced over to the kitchen and saw what looked like a plate of pork chops. But when I stared at them they looked more like little meteorites. Each one was fully carbonized. They were 100 percent not edible and would probably be instantly carcinogenic if you ate one. I had never before and have never to this day seen a piece of meat so burnt. I turned my head back and there was a pause at the table. Then we all burst out laughing. We laughed for a good two minutes, then passed the green beans and mashed potatoes and had dinner.

That moment made me appreciate the finer points of working a grill. We all thought it was just my dad's

My dad always judged the doneness of food by how many beers it would take. Chicken was six beers. Pork chops were two. He made it seem easy.

excuse to sit outside and drink beer. But it turns out there is actually some skill in it. Since then, I've become completely obsessed with the grill.

At Woodfire Grill, we have a huge open pit where we cook at least half of the dishes for the restaurant. From the day I started working there, that piece of equipment has captured my imagination. It has driven me to cook hundreds of things you wouldn't think could be grilled or smoked. I make braised greens that are incredibly smoky, rich, and satisfying, yet 100 percent vegetarian. Every Southerner that walks through the door can't believe there's no pork in the greens. I've made smoked foie gras, smoked potatoes . . . you name it, I've tried to cook it on that grill. In my mind, grilling is one of the purest and most unadulterated methods of cooking there is. Taking that crude apparatus and creating newness out of it is something I find endlessly inspiring.

I could write a whole book about barbecue, but I'll keep it simple here. The most important thing to remember is that grilling and barbecue are not the same thing. Grilling is cooking small food over high heat for a short time. Barbecue is big food smoked over a low fire for a long time. It's the difference between a grilled steak and smoky pork barbecue. Each technique requires a different kind of heat and in some cases different equipment. For more details on setting up grills and smokers and managing the heat and smoke, see page 10 in the What I Mean When I Say . . . chapter.

GRILLED SCALLOPS WITH TOMATE FRITO

MAKES ENOUGH FOR 4 PLATES

Scallops
12 large day boat or "dry-pack" U10

Salt

Olive oil

Tomate frito (page 312)
about 1 cup

Lemon
1

DAY BOAT SCALLOPS / Scallop boats often stay out at sea for weeks at a time. To keep the scallops fresh during that time, they soak the catch in a solution of sodium tripolyphosphate (STP). The scallops absorb the STP on the way back to shore, and they plump up, which increases the weight and thus the price. The problem is that the soaking water leaks out during cooking, making it difficult to get a good, dark-brown sear on soaked scallops. To avoid the problem, look for day boat scallops or ask for "dry-pack" or "unsoaked" scallops. The dry ones usually remain separate in the seafood case, while the soaked ones tend to clump together and look abnormally shiny. You want nice big scallops for grilling, which means /10 or "under 10" per pound.

I love putting scallops on the grill. Even though they are a seafood, they have a firm, meaty texture and are shaped like mini filet mignons. The only hitch is that scallops are full of water, and water prevents those brown grill stripes you see on grilled food. That kind of browning only happens when the surface of food gets above 250°F. The water has to steam off before the browning can take place. It really helps to blot dry the surface of your scallops. It also helps to buy scallops labeled "dry" or "unsoaked" (explained at left). And a little oil on the scallops doesn't hurt either. It transfers heat fast, creates good grill marks, and helps prevent sticking. Scallops are naturally sweet, so they get nice and caramelized on the grill. To balance those flavors, the sauce here has a sharp and spicy punch. Tomate frito (page 312) is basically fried red tomatoes spiked with vinegar and chile flakes. It's a great sauce to make in bulk and keep in the fridge because it's almost like tomato confit. The tomatoes are cooked and preserved under a top layer of oil, and the sauce lasts refrigerated for months. You could also serve these scallops with skillet-roasted cabbage (page 29).

1. Heat a grill for direct high heat. Pat the scallops dry with a paper towel and season each side first with a little salt and then a drizzle of oil. You want the salt directly on the protein, and just a little oil will keep it in place.

2. Scrape the grill clean and coat it with oil. Using tongs, set the scallops on the hot grill and cook for 7 minutes; flip and cook until the scallops are tender and the sides just start to turn opaque, about 3 minutes more. You can see the doneness of the scallop as the protein cooks around the circumference; gradually, a white ring will close in on the center. Scallops are great to eat medium-rare (in fact; they are one of the safest shellfish to eat raw), so take them off the grill before the white ring completely closes in on the center; they'll continue to cook a little after you remove them from the grill. Let rest for 3 minutes.

3. For each plate, spread some tomate frito in the center. Set 3 scallops over the frito and squeeze a little lemon juice on the top. Sprinkle with another pinch of salt and serve.

GRILLED SALMON WITH RAPINI

Some people think grilling means throwing any and all food over the hottest possible fire. But you can't grill fish that way. It burns, dries out, and falls apart. King salmon is pretty forgiving, but it's such a beautiful, majestic fish that you don't want to overcook it. For this recipe, you want a hot fire but not a blazing inferno. You also want to let the fish cook undisturbed. A hot grate and a little patience will give you deep grill marks and help prevent sticking.

1. Heat a grill for direct medium heat. Trim about 2 inches off the bottom of the rapini to remove the tough lower part of the stalk. Bring a large pot of water to a rolling boil and fill a large bowl with ice water. Drop the rapini in the boiling water and blanch for 1 minute. Using tongs, transfer the rapini to the ice bath to cool and stop the cooking, swirling for about 45 seconds. Fish out the rapini and transfer to paper towels, patting it dry.

2. Put the almonds in a zip-top bag and, using a rolling pin or heavy skillet, coarsely crush them. Set aside.

3. Set the salmon on a flat plate and pat dry with paper towels. Generously season both sides of each fillet with salt and very lightly drizzle with the garlic oil. Avoid brushing on the oil because the brush will remove the salt. Let stand for 5 minutes; the salt will extract some moisture from the fish. Pat each fillet dry with a paper towel and drizzle with a little more garlic oil. The oil adds flavor and helps prevent the fish from sticking to the grill.

4. Scrape the grill clean and coat it with oil. Set the fillets on the grill, presentation side (flesh side) down, at a 45-degree angle to the grates. Grill for 3 minutes, then turn each fillet 90 degrees and grill for 2 minutes more. Slip a spatula straight along the line of the grates beneath the fish to loosen and flip each fillet. Drizzle with a little more garlic oil and grill until the fish is slightly translucent in the center, another 2 to 3 minutes. Line a plate with a double layer of paper towels and transfer the fish to the paper towels, presentation side up, to rest for 3 minutes.

5. Grill the rapini directly over medium heat for 2 minutes, then flip and grill for 1 minute more. You only need to heat the rapini through, since it's already been blanched. Sprinkle the rapini with salt.

6. For each plate, drizzle a 4-inch circle of the sherry vinegar reduction in the center. Set the salmon in the center of the plate and arrange the rapini along the long side of the fillet. Scatter the almonds over the fish and rapini and drizzle the whole dish with a generous amount of finishing oil.

ENOUGH FOR 4 PEOPLE

Rapini (broccoli raab)
4 stalks, about 8 ounces

Marcona almonds
3 tablespoons

Wild king salmon fillets
4, each about 3 ounces, skinned and trimmed to an even thickness

Salt

Confit garlic oil (page 321)
2 tablespoons

Sherry vinegar reduction (page 306)
2 tablespoons

Finishing-quality olive oil
2 tablespoons

GRILLED HONEY-LACQUERED QUAIL

We grill more quail at Woodfire Grill than any restaurant in the world. At least it seems that way. I'm slightly concerned that we may be singlehandedly destroying the world's quail population. But in Georgia, people love quail. I also decided early on that Woodfire Grill would not serve chicken because we couldn't get a steady supply of high-quality birds. Quail has been on our menu for at least 4 years now. One of the techniques we stumbled on was honey-lacquering the birds. I always liked glazing fruit by cooking down honey until it caramelizes and then brushing it over the fruit. The honey takes on a savory flavor and makes a beautiful glossy lacquer. We tried it on quail, and the honey's sweetness and savoriness completely erased any gamy taste in the birds.

Hunters often ask me how to cook quail. The trick is using superhigh heat for a super short time. Quail are like the Thumbelina of poultry. They're tiny. If your quail grills for more than 5 minutes, something has gone wrong. The longer they cook, the gamier they taste. Just give them a quick sear on both sides, take them off the grill, and lacquer them with the caramelized honey. It's my favorite way to cook these birds.

1. Put the honey and garlic confit in an 8-inch sauté pan and set over medium-high heat. When the mixture starts to bubble and foam, cut the heat down to medium. As the honey cooks, take a whiff. After a couple minutes, it will begin to smell like toasted rice, then the aromas of the flowers will start to develop; orange blossom honey will have a citrus aroma, wildflower honey will smell more floral. The flavors will intensify and the honey will start to change color from very pale to slightly golden after about 5 minutes. When the color starts to change, add the vinegar. It will foam up and then deflate, and the mixture will continue to bubble. Cut the heat down so that the mixture simmers very gently and cook for another 15 minutes. The mixture will be crazy hot, so be very careful. Gently pull the pan from the heat and let cool for 5 minutes. Puree the mixture in a blender, then strain the puree and discard the solids.

2. Heat a grill for direct high heat.

3. Pat the quail dry, brush both sides lightly with oil, and season the breast side with salt. Scrape the grill clean and coat it with oil. Set the quail on the grill, breast side down, at a 45-degree angle to the grates. Grill for 1 minute, rotate 90 degrees, then cover with a foil pan or metal bowl and grill for another 2 minutes. Flip the quail over, cover again, and grill for 2 minutes more. Remove the quail from the grill and immediately brush on a thin, even coating of the honey lacquer. Let the quail rest for 2 minutes before serving.

MAKES ENOUGH FOR 4 SMALL PLATES

Honey
1 cup

Confit garlic (page 321)
12 cloves

Red wine vinegar
⅓ cup

Quail
4, with skin on, breast bones removed, leg and wing bones intact (often labeled "semiboneless")

Olive oil

Salt

PREP AHEAD / You can make the honey lacquer ahead and store it covered in the refrigerator for up to 3 days. Just heat it up a little in a pan before using, so it's free-flowing.

BARBECUE CHICKEN WITH ALABAMA WHITE BARBECUE SAUCE

FEEDS 4 HUNGRY FOLKS

Egg yolks
4

Apple cider vinegar
¼ cup

Water
¼ cup

Poultry seasoning
2 tablespoons

Salt
2 tablespoons

Grapeseed oil
1 cup

Chicken leg/thigh pieces
6

Alabama white barbecue sauce (recipe follows)
about 1½ cups

You see barbecue chicken all the time on menus, but chicken is not traditional meat for barbecue. You don't barbecue chicken the same way you barbecue a pig or a brisket. One place that does have barbecue chicken down pat is Cornell University, in Ithaca, New York. Cornell has one of the world's best meat and poultry science programs. Out of that program came one of the best methods for barbecuing chicken. Dr. Robert C. Baker became famous for his "Cornell chicken"—so famous that Baker was inducted into the American Poultry Hall of Fame in 2004 (no joke). He also invented chicken nuggets, chicken hot dogs, and turkey ham. The guy was an avian genius. For "Cornell chicken," you marinate the meat in a mixture of vinegar, oil, herbs, and egg yolks. It sounds strange, but the eggs create a glaze over the chicken and take on this gorgeous ocher color.

Alabama white barbecue sauce also contains egg yolks, so both the marinade and sauce are similar to egg-based mayonnaise. Again, it sounds weird, but both marinade and sauce work phenomenally well with lean meat. This is not the sauce you would turn to for pulled pork or brisket. But for chicken, Alabama white barbecue sauce is absolutely the way to go. Grill master Big Bob Gibson developed it in 1925, and it's since become an Alabama staple. To use the sauce, you flip and baste the chicken every 10 minutes. It takes on this unbelievably golden glow and stays tender and juicy. It's just amazing. If you can, cook this dish on a charcoal or wood grill, because part of the charm is the smoky taste you get from the marinade dripping into the hot grill and sending billows of smoke back up to the chicken.

1. In a food processor fitted with a metal blade, blend the egg yolks, vinegar, water, poultry seasoning, and salt until the yolks fluff a little, about 30 seconds. With the processor running, slowly drizzle in the oil; the mixture will blend, emulsify, and resemble a thick mayonnaise. You will hear the sound change to a whop, whop; it should take about 1 minute. Spoon the marinade into a large zip-top bag, add the chicken pieces, and massage until the chicken is completely covered with the marinade. Zip the top closed, pressing out any air as you seal the bag. Set the bag in a bowl in the refrigerator overnight or for up to 24 hours.

ALABAMA
WHITE BARBECUE SAUCE

MAKES ABOUT 1½ CUPS

Egg yolks
2

Lemon juice
¼ cup

Apple cider vinegar
3 tablespoons

Salt
2 teaspoons

Garlic powder
½ teaspoon

Cayenne pepper
½ teaspoon

Ground black pepper
2 teaspoons

Grapeseed oil
1 cup

1. In a food processor fitted with a metal blade, combine the egg yolks, lemon juice, vinegar, salt, garlic powder, cayenne, and black pepper and process until the yolks fluff a little, about 30 seconds. With the processor running, slowly drizzle in the oil; the mixture will blend and emulsify but won't be as thick as the marinade used for the barbecue chicken. You will again hear the sound change to a whop, whop; it should take about a minute.

2. Pour ¾ cup of the Alabama white barbecue sauce into a bowl to use for basting. Heat a grill for indirect medium-high heat. On a gas grill, just leave one side of the grill unlit. On a wood or charcoal grill, rake the coals to one side. Remove the chicken from the marinade and pat completely dry. Scrape the grill clean and coat with oil. Place the chicken, skin side down, over the unheated part of the grill and cover with an aluminum pan or tent with foil. After 10 minutes, flip the chicken pieces, moving them to a hotter part of the grill, but still over indirect heat. Cover again with the pan or foil. After 10 more minutes, baste the chicken with the sauce, flip so the skin side is down, and baste again. Cover with the pan or foil, cook for another 10 minutes, and then baste, flip, and cover again. Cook, baste, flip, and cover one last time, for a total cooking time of 40 minutes. Discard the basting sauce. Remove the chicken from the grill and rest, tented with foil or a foil pan, for 10 minutes. Serve with the remaining sauce on the side.

CHICKEN SPATCHCOCK

Spatchcock is not only an awesome name, it's an awesome cooking technique. It was created to make it possible to cook a whole chicken directly on a grill. You cut out the bird's backbone, then smash the bird down to make it lay flat. You have to smash with some force because evening the chicken out as much as possible is the key to this technique. With this method, you get both white and dark meat and you grill the meat on the bone. Whenever you cook meat on the bone, it's like riding a bike with training wheels or swimming with water wings. It increases your chances of success. Bones conduct heat within the meat so that it cooks more evenly and is less likely to dry out. Bones also release gelatin, which gives cooked meat a juicy, silky feel in your mouth.

FEEDS ABOUT 4 FOLKS

Chicken
*1 fresh bird,
about 3 pounds*

**Salt and ground
black pepper**

Balsamic vinegar
about ¼ cup

1. Heat a grill for direct medium-high heat. Cover a brick or large grill press with foil.

2. Pat the chicken dry and, using kitchen shears, cut from the tail end up to the neck end on either side of the backbone to remove the backbone. Flip the bird over and flatten it with the heel of your hand; it should splay open so that both sides are relatively flat and will make direct contact with the grill grate. Flip the bird again and pat the inside cavity dry. Season the inside cavity with salt, then flip the bird again so the chicken is breast side up; turn in the legs a bit so they sit flat and season the skin all over the bird aggressively with salt and pepper. Tuck the wings back and under the breast.

3. Scrape the grill clean and coat it with oil. Transfer the chicken, breast side up, to the grill. Firmly press a sizzle platter or small baking sheet on top of the breast (rimmed side down) to flatten the bird, and weigh it down with the brick or grill press. The sizzle platter or baking sheet will catch and hold a little of the heat while keeping the chicken flat. Grill for 20 minutes, leaving the grill uncovered. Using tongs or grill mitts, remove the brick and the platter. Flip the chicken; breast side down; onto the same spot on the grill. Reposition the sizzle platter or baking sheet over the chicken, this time with the rimmed side up, and top with the brick. Again, this will keep the chicken flat. Grill the bird until a meat thermometer inserted into the thigh registers 160°F, another 10 to 12 minutes. Use tongs or grill mitts to remove the brick and the platter. Flip the chicken over and brush the breast side with the balsamic vinegar; return the chicken to the grill, breast side down, and cook until the skin crisps and the vinegar caramelizes, about 3 minutes more. While the chicken skin is crisping, baste the inside cavity with a generous amount of the vinegar. Flip the chicken breast side up, baste one last time with vinegar, and cook for another 2 minutes, uncovered.

4. Remove the chicken from the grill and set breast side up on a cutting board. Tent with foil and let rest for 20 minutes before carving.

GRILLED DUCK BREAST WITH SKILLET-ROASTED CABBAGE

Duck gets a bad rap. As a teenager, I asked my dad, "Have you ever had duck?" He said, "It's greasy." So I always believed that duck was greasy and nasty. Then I tasted it and changed my mind. Yes, duck can be kind of nasty if it's not cooked properly. Just remember that duck is more meat than poultry. You don't need to cook it to 165°F like chicken and turkey. It tastes much better cooked to medium-rare, like steak. I take it off the heat when it's about 125° or 130°F in the center. It's also true that duck has a lot of fat, but it's all on the outside of the bird. The key is to render out that fat so the duck doesn't taste greasy. And one of the grill's strong suits is its ability to render fat. With an open surface, there's somewhere for the grease to go. To get the fat moving quickly, you score the skin and fat of the duck breast in a diamond-shaped pattern, and then put the duck, skin side down, on the grill. The heat reaches into the scored fat and melts it quickly so that it drips away into the grill. Just be careful not to put the duck over a raging hot fire or it will ignite. Medium heat is perfect. If you've never had duck, try this recipe. My dad thinks it's delicious and asks me, "What did you do to it?" The answer: I put salt on it and cooked it. Period. I like to serve the grilled duck with skillet-roasted cabbage (page 29), but you could also serve it alongside farro with Brussels sprouts (page 89).

1. Heat a grill for direct medium heat.

2. Using a sharp boning knife, score a diamond pattern into the skin of the duck: For each breast, cut 4 slits diagonally across the skin and fat layers and 4 more slits in the opposite direction to form a diamond pattern, cutting just down to but not through the meat layer. Scoring the skin and fat helps the fat to easily render out and the skin to shrink as the duck cooks, allowing the breast meat to remain flat instead of curling up with the skin.

3. Pat the duck dry with a paper towel. Generously season the skin side of the breast with salt. Scrape the grill clean and coat it with oil. Set the breasts on the grill, skin side down, at a 45-degree angle to the grates. Grill for 4 minutes. Use tongs to rotate the breasts 90 degrees and move them, still skin side down, to a new hot spot on the grill. (The cold duck will have cooled the grill grate where it was sitting, so it helps to relocate the duck to a hotter spot; the aim here is to crisp the skin and render the fat.) Grill until the skin is brown and crispy, another 3 minutes. Flip the duck over and continue cooking to medium-rare (130°F internal temperature), another 7 minutes. Transfer the duck to a plate and let rest for 5 minutes before slicing.

4. To serve, slice the breasts at an angle across the grain. I usually don't serve the two end pieces because they don't cook evenly, but they make a delicious snack for the cook! Serve with the cabbage.

FEEDS 4 FOLKS

Duck breasts
4 single breasts, trimmed, tenderloin removed, about 7 ounces each

Salt

Skillet-roasted cabbage (page 29)

GRILLED FLANK STEAK WITH CHIMICHURRI

It's almost comical how much I love steak. At Woodfire Grill, we inevitably have little scraps of beef left in the kitchen at the end of the night. Whoever is working the grill knows that they have to grill these scraps and give them to me. I could eat steak every day of the week. You won't see me rushing to buy a filet mignon. I like steak with texture, like flank steak. The more work a muscle does, the more flavorful it gets. The flank or abdomen of a steer does a mountain of work holding up this half-ton animal and helping it walk. Flank has an intensely beefy flavor and a satisfying chew. Plus, it's one of the less expensive steak cuts. But it's critical to remember that flank overcooks really fast. If this cut goes past medium-rare, it's completely inedible.

My favorite complement for grilled steak is chimichurri, a sort of Argentine vinaigrette with lots of herbs. I make mine a little differently than most people do. Argentineans just combine all of the ingredients in a bowl. I like to keep the vinegar away from the herbs until the last minute so that the herbs stay bright green and highly aromatic. I was a little concerned that South Americans wouldn't like it because it's not traditional. But one of my cooks at the restaurant is from South America, and when he tasted it he said, "This is light years better than the classic version." To me, that's a thumbs-up.

SHOULD FEED 4 PEOPLE

Dried porcini mushrooms
¼ cup, about ½ ounce

Carrot
1, peeled and thinly sliced into rounds, about ½ cup

Celery
1 stalk, thinly sliced into half-moons, about ½ cup

Vidalia onion
1 cup thinly sliced strips

Garlic
1 clove, thinly sliced

Ground black pepper
1 tablespoon

Red wine
1 cup (whatever you are drinking with dinner; I prefer Pinot Noir with this recipe)

Flank steak
about 2 pounds, trimmed

Grapeseed oil

Salt

Chimichurri (recipe follows)
about 1 cup

1. Combine the mushrooms, carrots, celery, onion, garlic, black pepper, and red wine in a large zip-top plastic bag. Add the steak, press out all the air, and seal the bag. Refrigerate for 8 hours or overnight.

2. Heat a grill for direct high heat. Pull the meat out of the marinade and brush off any herbs or vegetables. Pat the meat completely dry with paper towels and brush all over with grapeseed oil. Aggressively season both sides of the steak with salt.

3. Scrape the grill clean and coat it with oil. Set the steak over direct heat on the grill with the grain at a 45-degree angle to the grates; grill for 5 minutes. Rotate the steak 90 degrees and grill for 3 minutes. Flip the steak so the grain is again at a 45-degree angle to the grates; grill for 5 minutes more. Rotate 90 degrees and cook to rare (120° to 125°F internal temperature), about 2 minutes longer. Transfer the steak to a plate and let the meat rest for 5 minutes. Slice the steak very thinly across the grain. Serve with the chimichurri sauce.

PREP AHEAD / **You can make the chimichurri up to 8 hours ahead; just refrigerate the oil mixture and vinegar mixture in separate bowls. Combine them just before serving. Chimichurri is amazingly versatile. Try it on any grilled meat, on grilled shrimp, or on roasted oysters (page 42).**

CHIMICHURRI *MAKES ABOUT 1 CUP*

Fresh flat-leaf parsley leaves
¼ cup chopped

Fresh oregano leaves
2 tablespoons chopped

Olive oil
¼ cup

Red wine vinegar
2 tablespoons

Dried oregano
1 tablespoon

Salt
1 teaspoon

Espelette pepper
¼ teaspoon

Red onion
1 tablespoon finely chopped

Roasted red pepper
1 tablespoon finely chopped

Garlic
2 teaspoons minced

Dried red pepper flakes
½ teaspoon

1. Mix the parsley, fresh oregano, and olive oil and set aside. The oil prevents the herbs from oxidizing (turning brown). In a separate bowl, whisk the vinegar, dried oregano, salt, and Espelette pepper until the salt dissolves. Stir in the onion, roasted red pepper, garlic, and red pepper flakes and set aside. Just before serving, mix the oil mixture with the vinegar mixture.

Buying Beef

If you bracket beef into a few categories, the easiest ones to spot are grass-fed, natural, and commodity beef. I never call for commodity beef, but that's the vast majority of what's available in grocery stores. Here's how I choose what to buy.

COMMODITY BEEF. Producing beef is pretty simple. You raise cattle on a farm. The animals stand in grass fields and chew their cud. They eat and get big and eventually get sent for processing. In commodity-beef production, the calves stay on grass just until the time that they are weaned off their mother's milk, and then they are sent to a feedlot—usually less than 6 months. In the feedlot, there can be as many as 100,000 head of cattle eating a diet primarily made up of corn. They put on weight at an insane pace. It's like sitting on a couch and stuffing your face all day. The muscles stay soft and the animals gain weight. It's an efficient system for getting meat to market.

If there's any issue I have with commodity beef, it's the way it's processed. You've heard the term *cattle call*. It's a massive lineup of cows entering the processing plant and being slaughtered as quickly as possible. There's been a lot of bad press about cattle processing plants. There should be a better way to process meat. But the truth of the matter is that we have no one to blame but ourselves. We eat a lot of beef and we don't want to pay a lot for it. The cattle industry has responded to market demands by giving the people what they want: lots of cheap beef. If you have a problem with that, the solution is not to give up eating meat for good. It's to demand higher quality. Go the extra mile and spend the appropriate amount of money on beef that is raised and processed more responsibly and humanely.

NATURAL BEEF. Natural is a vague term. Legally, it only means that the meat is produced without artificial flavors, colors, and chemical preservatives; the meat doesn't include artificial or synthetic ingredients; and it's "minimally processed," which means just enough to get it

Grassfed cows from White Oak
Pastures, Bluffton, Georgia

to market without fundamentally altering the raw product. That doesn't really tell you much about how the animals are raised and processed. For me, it means that the meat comes from a known and reputable breed stock like Black Angus, Red Angus, Limousin, or Texas Longhorn, and the cattle are raised on grass until just a couple weeks before they go to processing. Commodity cattle eat grass for less than 6 months, but natural cattle eat grass for 16 or more months. That is a much longer time commitment for ranchers. It costs more to raise cattle on grass for that long, which is one reason why natural beef costs more. The industry also calls this kind of beef "grain finished" because the animals do eat corn or other grains during the last 2 to 4 weeks before processing. I prefer it to be 2 because just 2 weeks of grain finishing increases the marbling in the meat and "cleans up" the flavor of the beef. It makes the meat taste less grassy, more tender, beefier, and closer to what we as Americans have grown accustomed to enjoying. Natural beef is also significantly higher in beneficial omega-3 fatty acids than commodity beef.

GRASS-FED BEEF.
Beef that's 100 percent grass-fed is a tricky thing. When an animal eats only grass, the quality of the grass itself has an enormous impact on the taste, tenderness, and fat content of the meat. Not every grass-feeding farm produces beef that you want to eat. There is no arguing the health benefits. Grass-fed beef is leaner and higher in beneficial nutrients than any other type. It is usually processed humanely. Yet, some grass-feeding operations produce beef that is so tough that you can't grill it. It turns into a brick. If you are committed to buying and eating 100 percent grass-fed beef, it is critical to find a producer you trust and make sure you like the taste of the beef.

WHAT I BUY.
I use grass-fed beef for braising, brisket, short ribs, and grinding into hamburger. These tougher cuts have more fat and connective tissue that improves flavor, and if I'm grinding the meat, it negates any question of whether or not the beef will be tender enough. I also use grass-fed beef for raw

preparations like tartare and carpaccio because it has a more assertive flavor. But for steak or preparations where the meat will be quickly cooked, I prefer natural beef. The flavor is a little cleaner and there is a tremendous difference in tenderness.

WHERE I BUY.
I get grass-fed beef from White Oak Pastures, in Bluffton, Georgia. In the mid 1990s, the owner, Will Harris, converted his traditional commodity cattle farm to a grass-feeding operation. But then he thought, "Are we going to ship these grass-fed cattle off to a processor that might be inhumane?" Will didn't want to do that. So he built his own processing plant right on the farm. It was a massive undertaking but one that I totally support because processing is such an important piece of the puzzle for me. White Oak Pastures grass-fed beef is available in Publix and Whole Foods grocery stores throughout the South. You can also buy it online (see Sources, page 326).

For natural beef, I buy from Country Natural Beef in Oregon. It's a co-op of ranchers throughout the Northwest United States who produce to the same standards. The ranchers grow a mixture of Black and Red Angus crossbreeds without any growth hormones or antibiotics. I also buy from Painted Hills Natural Beef, named for the Painted Hills of Oregon. It's a similar network of ranchers raising Angus crossbreeds. You can buy from both producers at Whole Foods and other retailers scattered throughout the United States (see Sources, page 326).

I recommend finding good purveyors in your area. Almost every co-op I've been to around the country has their own farm or network of farms that raise their own beef, pork, and chicken. Do a little research about who's producing meat in your area. You can go to the website Eatwild (see Sources, page 326) to find a map of natural and grass-fed beef ranchers in every region of the country. Taste some of the beef products sold near you, then buy from someone you trust.

GRILLED LONDON BROIL WITH GINGER AND WHITE SOY

I don't usually put spice rubs on steak, but I love the Japanese spice blend, togarashi. With orange peels, crushed seaweed, sesame seeds, and red pepper flakes, the flavor just pops. It's awesome on steak, but it's very spicy. There's no getting around that. If you don't like spicy food, try one of the other steak recipes in the book. Here I like to use London broil, a lean, flat rectangular cut of beef meant for broiling or grilling. London broil is more a method of cutting and cooking beef than it is a particular cut from a specific muscle group. In the United States, London broil is usually a top round steak. You might see flank labeled as London broil, but top round steak is what's called for in this recipe. It's the perfect cut for feeding 6 or 8 people. It doesn't have a lot of fat, which is great from a health standpoint, but there is absolutely no room for overcooking this cut of beef. I cook it to rare and I don't recommend going past medium-rare. The white soy and ginger sauce makes the perfect complement to the spicy togarashi. Traditional soy sauce is fermented from about 80 percent soybeans and 20 percent wheat. White soy is the opposite: It's fermented from 20 percent soybeans and 80 percent wheat. The greater amount of wheat gives it a lighter color and sweeter flavor. White soy sauce has a lot of subtlety and is incredibly flavorful on beef. Look for it in the Asian section of your grocery store, or see the Sources on page 327.

SHOULD BE ENOUGH FOR 8 PEOPLE

Togarashi spice blend (see tip)
3 tablespoons

London broil or top round steak
1½ pounds, about 1¾-inches thick

Salt

Lime, white soy, and ginger sauce (recipe follows)
about ⅔ cup

1. Grind the togarashi as directed. Grinding will break down some of the spices and sesame seeds and allow the flavors to seep into the steak and form a nice crust. Trim any excess fat from the steak and pat the meat dry. Generously coat both sides with the spice blend.

2. Heat a grill for direct high heat.

3. Shake any excess spice blend off the steak, so you have a nice dusting left. Season both sides of the steak with salt. Scrape the grill clean and coat it with oil. Set the steak at a 45-degree angle to the grates. Grill for 4 minutes, then rotate it 90 degrees to a new hot part of the grill. Grill for another 3 minutes. Flip the steak over and place on a new hot part of the grill. Grill until the steak is rare (125°F internal temperature), 3 to 5 more minutes. When you press your finger on the steak, a little juice should rise to the surface. Transfer the steak to a cutting board and let rest for at least 5 minutes and up to 10 minutes.

4. Thinly slice the meat across the grain at a slight diagonal. For each plate, set 4 or 5 slices in the center and drizzle with about 2 tablespoons of the ginger sauce.

LIME, WHITE SOY, AND **GINGER** SAUCE

MAKES ABOUT ⅔ CUP

Lime juice
⅓ cup

Fresh ginger
2 tablespoons peeled and minced

White soy sauce
2 tablespoons

Garlic
2 teaspoons minced

Light brown sugar
1 teaspoon packed

Xanthan gum
¼ teaspoon

Grapeseed oil
3 tablespoons

Salt

Scallions
¼ cup thinly sliced on the diagonal

London Broil

1. Combine the lime juice, ginger, white soy, garlic, and light brown sugar in a blender and blend until smooth. Add the xanthan gum and pulse to combine. With the blender running, slowly drizzle in the oil. Add a pinch of salt and give it a final pulse in the blender. Pour the sauce into a bowl and stir in the sliced scallions.

TOGARASHI / Japan's go-to spice blend combines dried citrus zest, seaweed, sesame seeds, and chiles. Look for it in the Asian foods section of your grocery store and grind it at home if it isn't already ground. Or make a basic version at home. For about ¼ cup, grate 1 tablespoon zest from an orange into a large skillet and toast over low heat just until dried, about 5 minutes. Remove, then toast 1 tablespoon sesame seeds in the pan until fragrant, a few minutes. Remove, then toast 1 sheet of dried nori seaweed in the pan, a few minutes per side. Tear the nori into pieces small enough to fit in a spice grinder, clean coffee grinder, or mortar and pestle. Add the sesame seeds, dried orange peel, and 1 teaspoon dried red pepper flakes. Grind until the nori is powdered and you have a coarse spice blend.

WHAT IS XANTHAN GUM? / You'll see this stabilizer listed on commercial ice creams and other food products. It's used to stabilize, thicken, and emulsify liquid mixtures. Here, it does the same for the sauce, giving it a nice texture that's thick but not too thick. Bob's Red Mill is a widely available brand of xanthan gum that's found in the natural foods section of the grocery store, near the flours, grains, and baking mixes. If you can't find xanthan gum, the sauce tastes fine without it; it's just a little thin.

GRILLED STRIP LOIN WITH BALSAMIC ONIONS AND HORSERADISH POTATOES

FEEDS 4 PEOPLE

Beef strip loin
1 piece, about 2 pounds and 8 inches long

Sweet herb mix (page 6)
¼ cup

Grapeseed oil
½ cup + 3 tablespoons

Fingerling potatoes
12 ounces, sliced into ¼-inch rounds

Vidalia onion
1 baseball-size, cut crosswise into ½-inch rings

Balsamic vinegar
¼ cup

Salt and ground black pepper

Fresh chives
½ cup finely chopped

Parmesan cheese
⅓ cup finely grated

Garlic
2 teaspoons minced

Prepared horseradish
2 tablespoons

Arugula
3 cups

Olive oil
2 teaspoons

This dish doesn't step too far away from classic American steakhouse fare. Beef, onions, potatoes—it's all here but with a subtle twist. When I worked at Fife restaurant in Portland, Oregon, we got potatoes and horseradish fresh-dug right after the first frost. The potatoes were great for roasting. We took them straight from the oven and tossed them in a bowl with freshly grated horseradish. The heat opened up the horseradish aromas and flavors, which got absorbed back into the potatoes. It was fantastic. The same method is used here with prepared horseradish (which includes vinegar). If you have fresh horseradish, by all means use it, but the prepared stuff works well too. For the onions, I cut them into rings, toss them in balsamic vinegar, grill them, and mix them with arugula and oil for a quick salad. The beef itself is marinated in herbs. You slice the grilled beef, serve it with the horseradish potatoes, and top it all with the arugula-onion salad.

---

1. Using a sharp knife, trim the fat layer from the meat. Set the strip loin on the cutting board with the (former) fat side up. Cut the strip loin in half both widthwise and lengthwise, then trim the meat so you end up with four perfect 2 by 2 by 4-inch block-like pieces.

2. In a gallon-size zip-top plastic bag, combine the sweet herb mix with ½ cup of the grapeseed oil and massage to combine. Drop in the meat, press out any excess air, and zip the top closed. Massage the bag to coat all sides of the meat with the marinade, then refrigerate for at least 8 hours or overnight.

3. Preheat the oven to 425°F.

4. Drizzle the remaining 3 tablespoons grapeseed oil over a baking sheet and transfer to the oven for 5 minutes. Pull the pan from the oven, shake it to coat the bottom of the pan with the hot oil, and spread the potatoes in a single layer on the oil. Return the pan to the oven and roast the potatoes for 15 minutes. Pull the pan from the oven, stir and turn the potatoes, and return the pan to the oven, cooking until the potatoes start to brown around the edges, about 10 more minutes.

5. While the potatoes are cooking, heat a grill for direct high heat.

6. Separate the onions into rings and toss in a large bowl with the balsamic vinegar. Scrape the grill clean and coat it with oil. Use tongs to transfer the onions to the grill grate and grill until the onions are nicely charred, about 3 minutes. Turn and grill for another 2 minutes. Transfer the onions back to the vinegar bowl and toss with the vinegar. Immediately cover the bowl with plastic wrap to trap the heat and "wilt" the onions. Set aside.

7. Remove the meat from the marinade and pat dry with paper towels. Season all sides of the meat with a little salt and pepper and transfer to the grill, setting it at a 45-degree angle to the grates. Grill for 2 minutes, rotate 90 degrees, and grill for another 2 minutes on the same side. Flip the meat to a new hot part of the grill, again at a 45-degree angle to the grates, and cook for 2 minutes. Repeat for the remaining two sides, grilling the meat for a total of 10 minutes. Transfer to a platter to rest for 5 minutes.

8. Combine the chives, Parmesan, garlic, and horseradish in a large mixing bowl.

9. Line a plate with a double layer of paper towels. Using a slotted spatula, transfer the potatoes to the paper towels to drain. Season with salt and pepper and immediately transfer the potatoes to the bowl with the herbs and horseradish and toss to combine.

10. Using tongs or a slotted spoon, pull the onions from the vinegar, discard the vinegar, and cut the onions on the diagonal into 1-inch pieces. Return the onions to the bowl and toss with the arugula, a Kevin pinch of salt, a few grinds of pepper, and the olive oil.

11. To serve, divide the potatoes among the plates. Slice each steak across the grain into ½-inch-thick slices and shingle them across one side of the potatoes. Using tongs, mound the arugula salad on top of the steak and potatoes.

GRILLED PORK STEAK WITH KC-STYLE BARBECUE SAUCE

The first time I met my wife's parents, in Missouri, we made steak. "Great!" I said, "I love steak!" We went out and bought these huge slabs of pork. I said to Valerie, "What the hell? This isn't steak." But I wasn't going to fuss the first time I met her parents. We got back to the house, grilled the pork, and when it was all said and done, it was incredible! I was so impressed that I cooked the same cut again and again after we got home. Pork steak is basically a bisected shoulder blade that still has the bones. It has a ton of different muscle groups, and they're all connected by little pieces of fat and connective tissue. The fat and connective tissue melt as the steak cooks, so a pork steak is essentially self-basting. It's one of the most idiot-proof cuts you could ever throw over a fire. You can leave it on the grill for a half hour and it still comes out moist and juicy. The longer it cooks, the softer the meat gets. If you want a firmer texture like beef steak, shoot for medium. If you want a more flake-apart texture like pork barbecue, go for well-done over a lower fire. At medium doneness, you'll see liquid beading up between all those muscle groups but the meat itself will feel kind of firm when you press on it. At well-done, the liquid will mostly stop flowing but the meat will flake apart in shreds. The exact cooking time is somewhere between two and ten beers. I like it steaky—four or five beers. Kansas City-style barbecue sauce is a natural here. I slather it over the steak during the last half of cooking. My version of the sauce has less sugar than your typical bottled barbecue sauce, so if you're using the sweet stuff, only baste during the last 10 minutes to prevent burning.

FEEDS 4 FOLKS

Pork shoulder steaks
2 bone-in steaks, each about 2 pounds and 2 inches thick

Salt and ground black pepper

KC-style barbecue sauce (recipe follows)
2 cups

1. Heat a grill for direct high heat.

2. Generously season the pork steaks on both sides with salt and pepper. Scrape the grill clean and coat it with oil. Grill the steaks directly over high heat for 5 minutes. Flip and cook for another 5 minutes. Baste with a thick coating of sauce, then flip and cook for 5 minutes. Continue basting and flipping at 5-minute intervals until the steak reaches an internal temperature of 160°F, 3 or 4 more turns. Brushing the steaks with the sauce midway helps create a rich-tasting mahogany glaze. Pull the steaks from the grill and let rest for at least 10 minutes before serving.

3. To serve, thinly slice the steaks and serve with more barbecue sauce on the side.

KC-STYLE **BARBECUE** SAUCE

MAKES ABOUT 2 CUPS

Apple cider vinegar
1 cup

Yellow mustard
½ cup

Dark brown sugar
¼ cup packed

Ketchup
¼ cup

Worcestershire sauce
¼ cup

Tomato paste
3 tablespoons

Sweet paprika
2 tablespoons

Salt
1 tablespoon

Celery seeds
2 teaspoons, finely ground

Ground black pepper
½ teaspoon

Cayenne pepper
½ teaspoon

Garlic powder
½ teaspoon

Onion powder
½ teaspoon

Ground cinnamon
¼ teaspoon

Ground allspice
⅛ teaspoon

Ground cloves
⅛ teaspoon

PREP AHEAD / The barbecue sauce can be made ahead and kept in the refrigerator for up to 2 weeks. It's modeled after the sauce served at Arthur Bryant's in Kansas City. It's dead easy to make, but if you'd rather buy Arthur Bryant's, you can order it online, (see Sources, page 327).

1. Combine all of the ingredients in a 2-quart saucepan and bring to a boil over medium-high heat. Cut the heat down so that the mixture simmers, and simmer until thick and terra cotta–colored, about 45 minutes.

SLOW-COOKED RIBS WITH CHILE-LIME BUTTER

You see pork ribs eaten all over the South. Everybody's got their favorite recipe, but the ribs are always slow-smoked and basted in sweet sauce. I wanted some different flavors here. I got to thinking about a Cuban pig roast . . . the garlic, the citrus, the smoke aroma, the moist and tender meat . . . I just love everything about it. But it's a hell of an undertaking to roast a whole pig in the ground. So I took the Cuban mojo seasoning as inspiration and added some hot chile paste to the citrus and garlic to make a chile-lime butter sauce. I also wanted the recipe to be easy to make, so there's no braising, steaming, or precooking here. The ribs are slow-smoked and then seared at the very end for some crispy char on the meat. That's it. Just be sure to keep the temperature consistent as you smoke the ribs. That will make them tender without the need for braising or steaming. A rib rack helps keep the ribs upright on the smoker. It's a cheap wire contraption that resembles a desktop file holder, with slots for the ribs. But if you don't have a rib rack, you can also just lay the ribs on your smoker rack, away from the heat.

FEEDS 4 HUNGRY FOLKS

St. Louis-cut pork ribs
2 slabs, about 4 pounds total

Salt
1 teaspoon + plus more for the ribs

Black pepper
a few coarse grinds

Honey
¼ cup

Beer
¼ cup lager style

Garlic
6 large cloves, coarsely chopped, about ⅓ cup

Limes
4 fat ones, juice and zest

Scallions
4, cut into 1-inch pieces, about 1 cup

Fresh cilantro
1 cup loosely packed leaves

Sambal olek (chile paste)
2 tablespoons

Butter
¾ cup, melted

LET'S GET STARTED →

SLOW-COOKED RIBS WITH CHILE-LIME BUTTER

1. Heat a smoker to 290°F. Or set up a covered charcoal or wood grill with indirect heat and wood chips (see page 10).

2. Remove and discard the sheer white membrane from the underside of the ribs. The membrane will be slippery, so grab it with a kitchen towel to pull it off. Pat the ribs dry, then generously season both sides with salt and coarsely ground black pepper, patting the seasoning into the meat. Slide the ribs into a wire rib rack and put the rack in the smoker or on the grill away from the heat. Or lay the ribs on the smoker or grill rack away from the heat. Smoke the ribs until tender, about 3½ hours total, maintaining a consistent temperature of 290°F.

3. While the ribs are smoking, whisk the honey and beer in a small bowl until blended. After about 1 hour of cooking the ribs, when juices start to bead up on the surface, brush the ribs with the honey mixture and rotate the slabs for even cooking. After the second hour of cooking, flip the ribs over and baste with the honey mixture again. Continue turning and basting every 30 minutes until the meat is tender, takes on a reddish tint, and starts to pull away from the bones. The total cooking time will be 3½ to 4 hours. Remove the ribs from the smoker or grill and let them rest at room temperature until warm, at least 20 minutes. Add wood or charcoal to the fire to bring the temperature up to medium; you will finish the ribs over direct medium heat.

4. To make the chile-lime butter, put the garlic, lime zest and juice, scallions, cilantro, sambal olek, melted butter, and the 1 teaspoon salt in a blender and blend until there are no big chunks left, about 2 minutes.

5. Cut and separate the ribs into single-bone pieces and toss the pieces in the chile-lime butter. Grill the ribs over the hot side of the grill just until they start to char, about 4 minutes per side. Toss again in the chile-lime butter and serve hot.

WHY ST. LOUIS–CUT RIBS? /

A slab of pork ribs has a piece of tough brisket (chest) meat attached to the wide end, and it tapers down to the shorter ribs at the narrow end. When the brisket and shorter ribs are trimmed off to make the whole slab more rectangular, it's called a St. Louis cut, which is easier to work with because the meat on the entire slab cooks more evenly. Ask any butcher for St. Louis–cut ribs, and he or she will know what you mean. Or trim up the ribs yourself.

GRILLED LAMB BLADE STEAKS WITH MINT JULEP SYRUP

Lamb chop prices have gone through the roof. But lamb blade steaks are one-fifth the cost. They're also more flavorful and stand up better to grilling. Here, I scatter some ground cardamom, garlic, pepper, and salt on the steaks and let them marinate. The traditional mint comes in from an unexpected direction. I'm totally on board with lamb and mint as a flavor combination, because it works. This mint julep sauce just puts a new twist on it. I started making the sauce with chef Marco Shaw in Portland, Oregon. Marco created it, and this is my version. The sauce turns the South's favorite cocktail into a type of sweet-and-sour sauce or French gastrique by boiling down cider vinegar, onions, and sugar to a syrup, and then stirring in bourbon and mint. The sweetness of the sauce and the vanilla aromas in the whiskey completely erase any hint of gaminess that might be in the lamb.

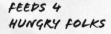

FEEDS 4 HUNGRY FOLKS

Salt
1 tablespoon

Ground black pepper
2 teaspoons

Garlic powder
1 teaspoon

Ground cardamom
½ teaspoon

Lamb blade steaks
4, each about 10 ounces and 1½ inches thick

Grapeseed oil
about 2 tablespoons

**Mint julep syrup
(recipe follows)**
about ½ cup

Fresh mint leaves
a few nice-looking ones for garnish

1. In a small bowl, whisk together the salt, pepper, garlic powder, and cardamom. Pat the lamb steaks dry and generously season both sides of the steaks with the spice mixture, using all of it. Set the steaks on a platter, cover, and refrigerate for at least 30 minutes and up to 3 hours.

2. Heat a grill for direct medium heat.

3. Scrape the grill clean and coat it with oil. Brush the lamb steaks with the grapeseed oil and set the steaks at a 45-degree angle to the grill grates. Grill for 3 minutes, then rotate 90 degrees and grill for another 3 minutes. Flip the steaks over onto a new hot part of the grill and grill to rare (125°F internal temperature), about 7 minutes more. Transfer the steaks to a clean platter and let rest for 10 minutes.

4. Serve the steaks drizzled with the mint julep syrup and garnished with fresh mint leaves.

MINT JULEP SYRUP

MAKES ABOUT ½ CUP

Apple cider vinegar
¾ cup

Sugar
¾ cup

Vidalia onion
2 tablespoons finely minced

Fresh mint leaves
1 cup gently packed + 4 nice whole leaves

Bourbon
2 tablespoons

1. In an 8-inch skillet, combine the vinegar, sugar, and onion, gently swirling with a wooden spoon. Bring the mixture to a boil over high heat, gently swirling but not stirring. Crush and roll the mint leaves between your fingers, then drop them into the sauce. Cut the heat down to medium-high so that the liquid simmers aggressively, and cook for 4 minutes. Keep an eye on the mixture and stir only if it starts to foam up to the top of the skillet. Swirl in the bourbon and return the mixture to a boil for a minute more. Pull the pan from the heat, strain the sauce, and discard the solids. Stir 4 fresh whole mint leaves into the sauce and pour into a smal heat-proof bowl or jar.

GROUND VENISON KABOBS WITH TOMATO JAM

I get a lot of hunters asking me how to cook deer meat. Most hunters have the entire animal ground into hamburger because they don't know what else to do with the meat. Here's a recipe for all that ground venison you have in cold storage. The venison stands in for lamb in a classic Middle Eastern preparation. You season the ground meat and pack it into a cylinder on a long metal skewer, then grill it. Remember that venison is extremely lean, so you only want to cook these to medium. Otherwise they will get very dry. Gamey meats love the sweet stuff, and the tomato jam pairs perfectly with all the herbs and spices in the venison. It's like a different look at hamburgers with ketchup—a venison burger on a stick with tomato jam.

FEEDS 5 FOLKS

Venison
2 pounds ground, 90% lean

Water
2 tablespoons ice-cold

Fresh flat-leaf parsley
2 cups finely chopped

Fresh mint
1 cup finely chopped

Fresh cilantro
½ cup finely chopped

Onion
½ cup finely minced

Za'atar
2 tablespoons

Salt
1 tablespoon + 1 teaspoon

Garlic
2 teaspoons finely minced

Grapeseed oil
about 2 tablespoons

Tomato jam (page 313)
about ½ cup

1. Heat a grill for direct high heat.

2. In a large bowl, crumble the venison and pour the ice water over the top. With gloved hands, gently mix in the parsley, mint, cilantro, onion, za'atar, salt, and garlic to combine. Divide into 4-ounce portions (about 10 portions) and shape each portion into a log around a long metal skewer, pressing gently.

3. Scrape the grill clean and coat it with oil. Brush the skewers all over with the oil and grill for 2 minutes. Turn and grill for another 2 minutes, then turn one final time and grill for 2 minutes more. The 6-minute cooking time is for medium-rare kabobs—the perfect temperature to serve venison. Transfer the kabobs to a platter and let rest for 5 minutes before serving.

4. For each plate, spread a generous spoonful of tomato jam on the plate and top with 2 kabobs.

ABOUT ZA'ATAR / Most countries have a go-to spice blend for meats, vegetables, dips . . . you name it. Za'atar is the blend in the Middle East. The key ingredient is dried sumac (don't worry; not the poisonous kind). You can buy za'atar online at various retailers (see Sources, page 327), or you can mix it up yourself. To make 2 tablespoons, combine 4 teaspoons dried thyme, 1½ teaspoons dried sumac, 1 teaspoon toasted sesame seeds, and ¼ teaspoon salt in a mortar and pestle or spice grinder and briefly grind to a coarse texture.

I apparently was born with an innate desire to eat spicy food. I'm not sure where it came from. There's nothing in Southern food culture that's over-the-top spicy. But I love it hot and I can't stop.

When I was young, eating spicy food was one of my bonding experiences with my dad. He and his brothers were always playing practical jokes and one-upping each other. They had chile-eating contests to see who was man enough to eat the hottest pepper. My uncle lived up the street, and he grew jalapeños one year. The next year, my dad grew habaneros. In an attempt to be part of the gang, I decided to get in on the action. I was about 12, and the peppers my dad grew looked like miniature bell peppers. They were just these squatty little green things. They hadn't turned orange yet, and I had no idea how spicy they were. I bit off half the habanero clear through the middle and chewed it up.

Within seconds, I dropped to my knees, screaming and crying in agony. It was like getting hit in the face with a sledgehammer.

I vowed never again to eat anything that spicy.

Years later, I was on a road trip with my friends. I must have been about twenty at the time. We were getting hungry and pulled into this hot wing place. Their wing categories were Mild, Medium, Hot, Extra-Hot, Nuclear, Three Mile Island, and Insane. You got your name on the "Wall of Flame" if you could eat twelve of the Insane wings. I knew how hot food could be, so I only ordered two of them. When they got to the table, the person next to us leaned over and asked, "Are those the Insane wings?" "Yes," I said, "did you ever eat these?" "Yeah," he replied. "I ate half of one once. I vomited and shit myself." Then he turned back to his dinner. I should've learned my lesson. I got the first one down and was halfway through the second when I went into a time machine. I was back to being twelve years old. There was this intense, beyond delicious burn, and I face-planted into the table, doubled over in pain.

I vowed, again, never to do that again.

In 2008, I went to an Indian restaurant in Portland, Oregon, called the Bombay Cricket Club. Everything at the Cricket Club is served mild. If you request medium a couple of times and clean your plate, they will allow you to order medium-hot. Only after you work your way through these heat levels will they finally serve you hot. It was my first time at the restaurant. I lied. "I can't believe you don't remember me," I said. "You served me medium-hot last week." The waitress turned to face me and gave me a hard look. "I absolutely want the hot," I said. The chef came out of the kitchen. He didn't come to the table; he just looked at me from the kitchen door. I gave him a smile and a nod. Why? Because I am apparently a glutton for punishment.

Within seconds, I dropped to my knees, screaming and crying in agony. It was like getting hit in the face with a sledgehammer.

He sent out the hot. This was the most crippling, mind-bendingly hot thing I have ever put in my mouth. It was dizzying, nauseating, and anything but pleasant. I couldn't taste a damn thing except maybe the taste of blood. It quickly became clear to the waitress and the chef that I had never eaten the medium-hot. I paid for all of my food—even the food I hadn't eaten. I slinked out the door and screamed profanities that shall never be repeated.

That was the last time I ate something superhot. I vowed right then and there to never eat something that painfully spicy again. And to this day I can honestly say that I have not broken that vow.

CRISPY GREEN BEANS WITH SALSA BRAVA

I don't remember where I was, but a group of people took me to an Italian restaurant and someone ordered *fritto misto* as an appetizer to share. It was like every other *fritto misto* with bits of fried vegetables, fish, and meat. But it had green beans in it. It never occurred to me to fry green beans. I loved it. The green beans changed the texture of the whole dish. They still had snap, like raw green beans. As soon as I got back to the kitchen, I fried some green beans. I prefer a light tempura-style batter for these because it leaves the snappy texture of the green beans intact. *Salsa brava* is the dipping sauce. When I was in Spain, *patatas bravas* (fried potatoes with spicy tomato sauce) were served at every tapas place. I thought the sauce would make a great dip for fried green beans. It's one of those sauces that goes with just about everything. But it packs some heat!

ENOUGH FOR 4

AS A SIDE DISH

Canola oil for frying

Cornstarch
½ cup

All-purpose flour
½ cup

Club soda or seltzer water
1 cup cold

Young green beans
8 ounces, trimmed

Salt

Salsa brava (page 308)
¼ cup

1. Heat the oil in a deep fryer to 350°F. Place a cooling rack over a baking sheet and set aside.

2. In a large bowl, whisk the cornstarch and flour until combined. Add a few ice cubes to the club soda and swirl to chill it through. Remove the ice cubes and whisk the club soda into the cornstarch mixture to form a smooth batter. One at a time, dip and swirl the green beans in the batter to completely coat them. Allow excess batter to drip off, then drop the beans, one by one, into the fryer and fry until crispy, about 1 minute. The crust won't brown, but you'll have a crispy, light coating on your beans. Using a spider strainer or tongs, transfer the green beans to the cooling rack and immediately sprinkle with salt.

3. For each plate, swoosh a tablespoon of salsa brava down the side of the plate and mound one-quarter of the beans in the center. Or for a more casual presentation, serve the crispy green beans on absorbent paper and the salsa brava in a small bowl.

SPICY CHANTERELLES

Only a handful of ingredients fare well with mushrooms. Green chiles are one of them. The grassy, herbaceous aroma of green chiles makes the perfect top note for earthy-tasting mushrooms. Chanterelles also have a floral scent that softens the flavor combination. Here, the mushrooms and chiles are quickly roasted and sautéed along with some corn kernels for sweetness and cream for richness. This makes the perfect side dish for grilled meat. Try it with grilled turkey breast (page 189) or grilled flank steak (page 204). It also makes an amazing filling for vegetarian lasagna or enchiladas. Or just spoon some over crispy tortillas or a toasted baguette. If you need to sub out the chanterelles, oyster mushrooms or hen of the woods would work too. But don't use something bland and watery like cremini or button mushrooms. You need more flavor than those mushrooms will provide.

MAKES ABOUT 1½ CUPS AS A FILLING OR FEEDS 4 TO 6 AS A SIDE DISH

Corn
1 ear, shucked

Poblano chile peppers
2

Garlic
1 clove, shaved into thin slices

Chanterelle mushrooms
8 ounces, trimmed, about 2 cups

Butter
1 tablespoon

New Mexico green chile powder (see Sources, page 327)
1 tablespoon

Heavy cream
1 cup

Lime
1

Salt
1 teaspoon

Sugar
¼ teaspoon

PREP AHEAD / This dish tastes best eaten right after it's made, but if you need to make it ahead as a filling, let it cool down, then cover it and refrigerate for up to 2 days. Reheat gently in a medium skillet over low heat until warmed through, 3 to 4 minutes, stirring now and then.

1. Char the corn and chile peppers over an open flame, 3 to 4 minutes. You can use a grill or kitchen torch or just sit them over a gas burner. The peppers should be blackened on all sides and the corn should be evenly charred. Transfer the peppers to a small bowl and cover tightly with plastic wrap so they can steam and soften. Transfer the corn to a cutting board and cut the kernels off the cob. When the peppers are cool enough to handle, after about 10 minutes, slip off and discard the charred skins. Cut the peppers in half and remove and discard the stem, core, seeds, and ribs. Dice the roasted peppers into ¼-inch pieces and place in a small bowl. Mix in the corn and garlic.

2. If the mushrooms are huge, cut them into 1½-inch pieces. You want to maintain the integrity of the mushroom but also want to create a dish that's easy to eat.

3. Melt the butter in a 10-inch skillet over medium-high heat. When the butter is foamy, add the mushrooms, shaking the pan to evenly distribute. Cook, undisturbed, until they start to caramelize, about 2 minutes. Add the pepper mixture and chile powder. Toss everything together and cook for 1 minute to toast the chile powder; toasting the chile powder brings out the natural oils so more flavor can be released into the cream. Add the cream and cook until the mixture begins to get a ring of fat around the edge, about 1 minute. Pull the pan from the heat and stir in about 2 teaspoons lime juice, the salt, and the sugar. The acid from the lime juice balances the richness of the cream and the heat of the peppers.

GRILLED CORN WITH COTIJA CHEESE

Every summer, I look forward to corn. I could skip the sweltering heat, but not the corn. My favorite way to cook it is to roast it over an open fire. When you get a little caramelization on the kernels and they steam and soften inside, it's one of the most delicious things in the world. There are lots of methods for grilling corn. Here's mine: Peel down the husk from the cob and pull out as much of the silk as possible. Pull the husk back up over the corn, tear off a rogue piece of husk, and tie it around the top to secure the husk around the kernels. If you can keep the corn completely enclosed in the husk, it steams as it cooks. You get the best of all possible worlds—gently steamed sweet kernels with a savory caramelized surface. In Mexico, you see street vendors selling roasted corn in stalls. If you're ever there, do yourself a favor and buy it. It's usually roasted really dark, then slathered in mayonnaise and rolled in a thick coating of cotija cheese. It's called *elotes* in Spanish and it's unbelievably delicious. This recipe doesn't stray too far from the classic street food preparation. I use chile-lime butter instead of mayo. The dish is not about finesse. Roast the hell out of your corn and coat it in as much cheese as it can hold. My favorite corn is Silver Queen. The sweeter the corn, the more you'll notice the savoriness of the cheese. If you can't find cotija at your market, use an aged Asiago instead.

1. For each ear of corn, slowly and carefully peel down the husk, leaving the husk attached to the cob. Pull off and discard the silks. Trim 1 inch off the tip of the corn cob and pull the husk back up over the corn. Tear off a piece of husk and tie it around the top to secure the husk around the kernels. Soak the corn, completely submerged, in water for 2 or more hours.

2. Heat a grill for direct medium-high heat.

3. Scrape the grill clean and coat with oil. Grill the corn in the husk until charred all over, about 30 minutes. Transfer the corn to a platter and let rest for 5 minutes. Untie, peel back, and discard the husks. Slather the corn with the jalapeño-lime butter and sprinkle with a generous amount of cheese.

MAKES 4 EARS

Corn
4 super-fresh ears in the husk

Jalapeño-lime butter
(page 295)
½ cup

Cotija cheese
¼ cup grated

GRILLED OYSTER MUSHROOMS ON MASCARPONE TOAST WITH
HOT GIARDINIERA

The last time I went to Chicago, I gorged myself on hot beef sandwiches slathered with giardiniera sauce. Giardiniera is an Italian pickled vegetable mixture; it's often eaten with appetizers for a sour punch. The sandwiches in Chicago had a thick sauce with spicy, puckery pickled vegetables as the base. When I got home, I could still remember that taste in my mouth. I thought it would be perfect with meaty oyster mushrooms. For the giardiniera, I use pickled Calabrian chiles, the short red peppers you sometimes see in Neapolitan pizzerias for nibbling. These are usually labeled "pickled red chile peppers." They're hot as balls for three seconds, then twenty seconds later the heat is gone. Mascarpone is the critical ingredient that pulls the dish together. Without it, the giardiniera would burn with every bite, but the mascarpone mellows the heat. It's spread like an open-faced sandwich on grilled Italian bread; the mushrooms go on the bread, and you spoon on a generous helping of the spicy giardiniera.

1. Combine the peppers, garlic, and grapeseed oil in a blender and puree until the mixture is almost smooth but still a little chunky. Spoon the pepper mixture into a small skillet and stir in the celery, onion, vinegar, and a pinch of salt. Heat over medium heat just until the mixture warms through, about 3 minutes.

2. Heat a grill for direct medium heat.

3. Trim and discard the hard stem/core of the mushrooms. Cut each cluster in half, then drizzle with olive oil and sprinkle with salt. Scrape the grill clean and coat it with oil. Set the mushrooms on the grill and cook for 2 minutes; then flip and cook for 2 more minutes. Continue flipping every 2 minutes just until the mushrooms are soft, about 8 minutes total. Right before removing the mushrooms from the grill, squeeze a little lemon juice over the top.

4. While the mushrooms are grilling, brush the olive oil on both sides of the bread. Grill the bread until it is nicely marked, about 2 minutes on each side. Smear 1 tablespoon mascarpone cheese onto each slice of bread while it's still hot. Transfer the mushrooms directly to the bread and set a piece on each plate. Generously spoon the giardiniera over the top and serve warm. This is a knife-and-fork appetizer—a little messy, but really tasty.

ENOUGH FOR 4 AS AN APPETIZER

Pickled Calabrian chile peppers
10-ounce jar, drained and stems removed (see Sources, page 326)

Garlic
1 tablespoon chopped

Grapeseed oil
¼ cup

Celery
1 stalk, cut very thinly on the diagonal, about ⅓ cup

Vidalia onion
⅓ cup finely diced

Red wine vinegar
1 tablespoon + 1 teaspoon

Salt

Oyster mushroom clusters
4 handfuls, about 6 ounces

Olive oil
about ¼ cup

Lemon
1 plump

Focaccia or other hearty rustic bread
4 slices, each about the size of your hand

Mascarpone cheese
¼ cup

TOMATO SALAD WITH SMOKY MELON AND SPICY SALAMI

For die-hard tomato fans like myself, a raw sliced heirloom tomato with a little salt is all you need. This salad has that fresh tomato flavor, along with a few other flavors for contrast. Cantaloupe adds sweetness to help you taste the tomato as a fruit. But a little smoked paprika keeps the melon from tasting too sweet. Salami Calabrese adds the heat. I like to slice it paper-thin and fry it for just a split second. Quick frying softens the heat but brings the pork flavor forward. It also gives the edges some crispness. If you don't have salami Calabrese, another spicy salami or even hot coppa will do. To calm the flavors down, the salad includes mozzarella marinated in herbed oil. Fresh celery leaves add a nice grassiness, and fried croutons bring the crunch. I like to fry the croutons in the same oil as the salami so the bread picks up a whiff of heat. It's a tossed salad, but all of the flavors remain distinct.

1. Cut the mozzarella into bite-size pieces. In a small bowl, combine the sweet herb mix with ¼ cup of the olive oil. Add the mozzarella and toss to coat. Let the mozzarella mixture marinate at room temperature for 1 hour. You can make this part ahead and store it covered in the refrigerator for up to 4 days. Bring the mixture back to room temperature before using.

2. Core the tomatoes, cut them into wedges, and set in a shallow bowl. Sprinkle with salt and pepper and let rest until they start releasing their juices, about 10 minutes.

3. Line a plate with a double layer of paper towels. Heat a large skillet over medium-high heat and add the remaining 2 tablespoons oil, swirling to coat the bottom of the pan. Let the oil get very hot. Test the heat of the oil by dropping in one slice of salami; it should immediately sizzle and crisp. Drop the salami into the hot oil one piece at a time and, using tongs, quickly transfer the pieces to the paper towels.

4. Set the cantaloupe in a large bowl and sprinkle with the smoked paprika. Drain the mozzarella and discard the oil. Add the mozzarella to the cantaloupe along with the tomatoes and their juice and the salami. Stir gently to combine. Divide the salad among serving plates and drizzle with the vinegar. Garnish with the croutons and celery leaves.

SHOULD BE ENOUGH FOR 6 FOLKS

Buffalo mozzarella
6 ounces

Sweet herb mix (page 6)
2 tablespoons

Olive oil
¼ cup + 2 tablespoons

Heirloom beefsteak tomatoes
3 ripe

Salt and ground black pepper

Salami Calabres
4 ounces, very thinly sliced

Cantaloupe
1 cup cut into ½-inch dice

Smoked paprika
¼ teaspoon

Noble XO sherry vinegar (see page 237)
1 tablespoon

Fried croutons (page 314)
¾ cup

Celery leaves or micro celery
¼ cup

PICKLED CHILE PEPPERS / From India to Mexico, most cultures have some form of pickled peppers. In Asia, they tend to grind the chile peppers with garlic, vinegar, and sometimes other seasonings. Usually the peppers are red, but sometimes they're green. I call for specific types of pickled chile peppers throughout the recipes.

NOBLE VINEGAR / I only call for a few special ingredients in this book, and Noble vinegar is one of them. Noble Tonic 05 XO vinegar has a syrupy viscosity like extra-aged balsamic vinegar, but it's actually sherry vinegar aged in charred oak barrels that were once used for bourbon. The flavors of this vinegar are deep, mellow, complex, and completely delicious. Mikuni, a company in Seattle, makes it, and you can buy the vinegar online (see Sources, page 327). Trust me, it's worth it.

NOT YOUR EVERYDAY BUTTERNUT SQUASH SOUP

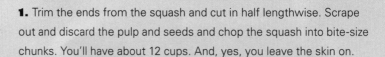

This is a chunky, stick-to-your ribs vegetable soup that's perfect for a cold winter day. It's not chile pepper hot, just loaded with spices. I start by dicing butternut squash with the skin on, which adds a rustic texture to the soup and keeps the squash from completely falling apart. I use lard to sauté the squash, onion, celery, and carrot so you get a little pork flavor. You could use bacon fat instead. The fat helps to caramelize the vegetables in the pan, creating a deep, savory flavor. The spices are basically warm Indian spices along with some Espelette pepper for heat and pomegranate molasses adds some acidity and sweetness. Look for it in Middle Eastern grocery stores and online. Or make it at home by juicing some pomegranates and boiling down the juice until it's syrupy, like thin honey.

FEEDS 8 TO 10 HUNGRY FOLKS

Butternut squash
2 tall boy–sized, about 3½ pounds total

Lard or bacon grease
¼ cup

Onion
1 softball-size, cut into ¾-inch dice

Celery
3 ribs, cut into ¾-inch dice

Salt
2 tablespoons

Carrot
1 huge one, peeled and cut into ¾-inch dice

Masala punjabi chole curry
2 tablespoons

Sumatra ground cinnamon
1 teaspoon

No-salt chicken stock
5½ cups

Sherry vinegar
1 tablespoon

Lemon juice
2 teaspoons

Pomegranate molasses
2 tablespoons

1. Trim the ends from the squash and cut in half lengthwise. Scrape out and discard the pulp and seeds and chop the squash into bite-size chunks. You'll have about 12 cups. And, yes, you leave the skin on.

2. Melt the lard in a 4-quart Dutch oven over medium-high heat. Layer the vegetables and salt in the pot in the following order: onion first, then celery, then 1 tablespoon of the salt, then the squash, and finally the carrot. Let the mixture cook until the vegetables on the bottom start to brown, about 5 minutes. Then vigorously stir with a wooden spoon, scraping up all the browned bits and stirring them into the mixture. Let cook undisturbed for another 5 minutes, then scrape up the brown bits and stir them into the mixture. Continue cooking and scraping up the brown bits every 5 minutes until the squash is tender, about 15 minutes total. This process creates deep flavor. Don't rush it!

3. Stir in the curry and cinnamon to coat the vegetables. Add 4 cups of the stock and bring the mixture to a boil. Cut the heat down so that the liquid simmers and let simmer for 20 minutes, stirring now and then. Stir in the vinegar, lemon juice, the remaining 1 tablespoon salt, and the remaining 1½ cups stock; simmer for another 10 minutes.

4. Serve in warm bowls and drizzle with some pomegranate molasses.

MASALA PUNJABI CHOLE CURRY / This is one of my favorite spice blends from the Dekalb Farmers Market in Atlanta, Georgia. If you can't get your hands on this particular blend, substitute 1 tablespoon + 2 teaspoons Madras curry powder mixed with another ½ teaspoon of Sumatra cinnamon.

HATCH CHILE <u>STEW</u>

████████

I buy locally in the South with the exception of iconic American foods from other places. Hatch chiles come from Hatch, New Mexico, and I absolutely adore them. Every time I'm in New Mexico, that's all I want to eat. But the chiles have a very defined season, from late August to mid October. I've been known to buy them frozen and have them shipped here—they're that good. Hatch chiles are spicy but not bitter or tannic. They have a savory, almost herbal taste that's accentuated by roasting, which is the first step to making this stew. I use green Hatch chiles in the stew, but tomatoes give it a deep red color. The chicken also falls to shreds because it's braised like in traditional Mexican *tinga*. This is a hearty, mildly spicy stew for a chilly day. It's absolutely fantastic with warm tortillas or on top of fried eggs. And it makes out-of-this-world chicken nachos.

---

1. Char the chiles over an open flame. You want them blackened all over; a wood fire lends a little smoke aroma, but you can also just set them over a gas burner or blast them with a kitchen torch, turning them a few times until charred all over, 4 to 5 minutes total. Transfer to a metal bowl and cover tightly with plastic wrap. Let the chiles steam for 10 minutes, then remove them from the bowl and slip off the charred skins (gloves help here so you don't end up with chile-hot fingertips!). Cut the chiles—ribs, seeds, and all—into a ½-inch dice and set aside; you should have about 2½ cups.

2. Heat a Dutch oven over medium-high heat. Add 2 tablespoons of the oil and swirl to coat the bottom of the pot. Add the onions, carrot, celery, garlic, and 2 teaspoons of the salt and cook until the onions are soft and translucent, about 10 minutes, shaking the pot now and then. Add the remaining 1 tablespoon oil and stir in the potatoes; cook until the potatoes are fork-tender, about 10 minutes more.

3. Stir the coriander, cumin, and oregano into the vegetables. Cook for 5 minutes to heat up and toast the spices and herbs, which helps the flavors release into the stew. Add the tomatoes with their juice, breaking them up slightly, and the chicken stock. Crank the heat up to high and bring the mixture to a boil. Cut the heat down to low and simmer for 15 minutes.

4. Separately, cut the chicken thighs and breast meat into 1-inch cubes. Add the thigh meat and chiles to the stew, cover, and simmer for 20 minutes. Add the breast meat and remaining 1 tablespoon salt and simmer, uncovered, for 15 minutes more, stirring now and then. Pull the pot from the heat and stir in the cilantro and 1 tablespoon lime juice.

MAKES ENOUGH FOR 12 TO 14 BOWLFULS, ABOUT 4 QUARTS

Green Hatch chiles
8

Grapeseed oil
3 tablespoons

Onion
1, cut into ½-inch dice, about 2 cups

Carrot
2, peeled and cut into ½-inch dice, about 1 cup

Celery
3 stalks, cut into ½-inch dice, about 1 cup

Garlic
6 cloves, peeled and halved

Salt
1 tablespoon + 2 teaspoons

Baking potatoes
1¼ pounds, cut into ½-inch dice, about 2 cups

Coriander
2 tablespoons, freshly ground

Cumin
1 tablespoon, freshly ground

Oregano
1 tablespoon dried

San Marzano whole tomatoes
2 cans, 28 ounces each

Chicken stock
4 cups

Chicken thighs
6 boneless and skinless, about 1 pound

Chicken breasts
3 boneless and skinless, about 1 ½ pounds

Fresh cilantro
¼ cup coarsely chopped

Lime
1

A Few Chiles I Like

POBLANOS. These are a total crapshoot. More often than not, they fall into the mild category. But that is not a constant. I have certainly been the victim of more than one really hot poblano pepper. It depends on how the peppers are grown. Bees pollinate the plants, and if the bees cross-pollinate between jalapeño plants and poblano plants, you're likely to end up with a hot poblano. Either way, they're perfect for stuffing because they're big and have a low seed count. Plus, they're not as tannic as most green peppers. They make a good substitute for jalapeños when you don't want quite that much heat.

PADRÓN PEPPERS. Here's another Russian roulette chile pepper. Most people consider it a sweet pepper and not a chile pepper. But for whatever reason—natural genetics, I suppose—Padrón peppers fluctuate drastically in spiciness. You could get 20 Padróns that are sweet and mild, and then you bite into pepper number 21 and it's kick-you-in-the-face hot. Padrón peppers are popular in Spain. For tapas, you get a bowl of them fried and you ask, "Who's gonna get the hot one?" But Padróns are little, and the burn doesn't last long. That's one thing you won't learn from the popular Scoville scale that rates chile peppers according to heat level. The Scoville scale will tell you that a habanero is 75 times hotter than a jalapeño, but it neglects to tell you about the length of the burn. Jalapeños have a burn that goes on and on and on. A Padrón's heat is short. It hits you, then it's over and done.

JALAPEÑOS. Markedly spicier than a poblano, a jalapeño is still not that hot in the grand spectrum of chiles. Some people eat them out of hand. The skin is thin, so they roast well, but they have very thick walls. Seeding them requires splitting the peppers open and physically cutting away the seedpod and white pith or ribs. There's a lot of heat in the white seeds and pith. Classic Indian white coconut chutney is stark white but ludicrously hot. They grind up the seeds and pith with fresh coconut so you can't tell that there are chiles in the chutney. Just remember that jalapeños can be tannic, bitter, and overwhelming. I use them sparingly because they are something of a show-stealer.

CALABRIAN CHILES. We're moving up the heat scale. Calabrian chiles are hotter than jalapeños, but only for a minute. They're little red peppers from Calabria, Italy, that are shaped like jalapeños but shorter. And they have practically no flesh. You can buy Calabrian chiles dried, but the dried ones tend to be longer and skinnier. When I call for Calabrian chiles, I'm calling for the plump red chiles brined in vinegar and stored in olive oil infused with garlic and herbs. They have tons of flavor, they're acidic from pickling, and the oil turns bright red. Pickled Calabrian chiles are brutally hot, but only for a few seconds. That's what makes them addictive. They're worth keeping on hand because they keep in the fridge for weeks. Tutto Calabria is my favorite brand (see Sources, page 326).

THAI CHILES. Bird peppers, Thai bird peppers, Vietnamese superhots . . . they're all teeny-tiny chiles that pack a wallop. Turn to Thai chiles when you're not interested in having any flavor from a chile, but you just want some heat. You can take a Thai chile, slice it thin, and add it to a sauce or soup and it will bring a nice amount of heat without drastically altering the flavor of everything else in the dish.

HABANEROS. Everybody knows that habaneros are blazingly hot. But many people don't know that they actually have fantastic flavor. Habaneros are fruity and sweet. It's no mistake that habaneros show up in tropical dishes paired with sweet ingredients like mangos. If you like the flavor and aroma of habaneros but can't stand the heat, you have two options. 1. Remove all the seeds, which cuts the heat quite a bit. 2. Roast them. You will have to peel them (wear gloves!), but roasting concentrates the sugars and makes the heat more manageable.

GHOST PEPPERS. Also known as Bhut Jolokia or Naga peppers, these chiles arrived on the scene from India several years ago and blew the habanero pepper off the top of the Scoville scale. Ghost peppers are 5 times hotter than habaneros and 400 times hotter than Tabasco sauce. They are agonizingly, brutally hot. I don't recommend ever dealing with these peppers without wearing gloves and goggles. I will warn you: If you dice up ghost peppers and toss them into a hot skillet, you will be hit with a wave of pain like mustard gas that will rip right through the pores of your skin. What do they taste like? They're so fucking hot it doesn't matter. But sometimes I want that intensity of heat. It just doesn't exist in any other form. I buy a puree of ghost peppers from Dave's Gourmet, the makers of Dave's Insanity Sauce (see Sources, page 327). I blend it with cayenne and Vietnamese superhots to make a house hot sauce at Woodfire Grill. The recipe is not in this book. I don't think anyone should ever make this sauce. We keep it on hand for the smart-asses who come into the restaurant and get upset with me for not making super spicy food. I remind them that Woodfire is a regular restaurant, not a temple for hotheads. Then I deliver to their table a small ramekin of our house elixir. That usually fixes their little red wagon.

ગરવી ગુજરાતી™

GARVI GUJARAT

From the heart of Gujarat

હળદર અથાણું
Fresh Turmeric Pickle

NET Wt. 25 oz (720g)

BOK CHOY AND PORK BELLY

MAKES ENOUGH FOR 4 SMALL PLATES

Canola oil for frying
about 3 cups

Baby bok choy
4 heads, about 4 ounces

Scallions
2, thinly sliced on the diagonal, about ¼ cup

Jalapeño chile pepper
1, shaved into coins on a mandoline

Fresh ginger
2 teaspoons finely minced

Black bean sauce
½ teaspoon

Toasted sesame oil
⅛ teaspoon

Salt
¼ teaspoon

Dried arbol chile pepper
2 whole

Slow-roasted pork belly (page 305)
12 ounces, cooked and cut into 3 by ½-inch blocks

Cornstarch
about 2 tablespoons

Spicy salt rub (recipe follows)
about 1 tablespoon

Lemon
1

Sugar
a pinch

Finishing-quality olive oil

In the suburbs just north of Atlanta, I get a dish like this at Tasty China. It's a Szechuan restaurant. Sometimes the dish is nice and spicy, but other times it's so blisteringly hot that I think I won't make it out of there alive. I created this version 100 percent from flavor memory. It's like a marinated bok choy salad with spicy slabs of pork belly on top. The key for the spice rub is grinding all the ingredients superfine. It almost looks like powdered sugar when it's all said and done. You toss the pork belly slabs in the spice rub right when they come out of the fryer. One of the signature flavors comes from Szechuan peppercorns in the Chinese five-spice powder. They have a little heat, a flowery aroma, and a tongue-numbing tingle that no other ingredient quite matches. If your five-spice powder doesn't include Szechuan peppercorns (some cheaper blends don't), add ¼ to ½ teaspoon Szechuan peppercorns to the salt rub and grind along with the other ingredients. The bok choy brings a soft cabbage flavor and some sweetness that helps mellow the heat of the dish.

---

1. Heat the oil in a deep fryer to 375°F. Or heat 2 inches of oil to 375°F in a cast-iron skillet over medium-high heat.

2. Using a sharp knife, separate the green leaves from the stems of the bok choy, and reserve the leaves. Trim off and discard the tough ends from the stems, then slice the stems into 1-inch pieces. In a large bowl, combine the scallions, jalapeño, ginger, black bean sauce, sesame oil, and salt. Finely crush the dried arbol chiles and stir into the mix, along with the bok choy stems. Set aside for 15 minutes to marinate.

3. Line a plate with a double layer of paper towels. Lightly toss the pork belly pieces with the cornstarch and shake off any excess. Drop the pieces in the fryer, one by one, and fry until GBD, about 3 minutes. If pan-frying, place the pieces in a single layer in the pan without crowding and fry for 3 minutes; then flip and fry until GBD, another minute. Using tongs, transfer the pork belly to the paper towels and immediately dust both sides with the spicy salt rub.

4. Stack the bok choy leaves and slice crosswise into very thin strips (chiffonade). Add the bok choy chiffonade to the scallion mixture, along with 1 teaspoon lemon juice and a teeny pinch of sugar, tossing to combine.

5. For each plate, mound a small handful of the bok choy salad in the center. Top with the pork belly and drizzle with the finishing oil.

SPICY SALT RUB

MAKES ABOUT 1/4 CUP

Salt
2 tablespoons

Black peppercorns
1 tablespoon

Chinese five-spice powder
2 teaspoons

Dried arbol chile pepper
1 whole

---

1. Combine the salt, black peppercorns, five-spice powder, and chile in a spice grinder, and grind to a very fine powder. Sift the powder and discard any large pieces.

BLACK BEAN SAUCE / A workhorse in Asian kitchens, black bean sauce is made by fermenting soybeans, which turns them black. They're often mixed with garlic or spices like star anise and served with beef, pork, and chicken on many a Chinese menu. Look for black bean sauce in the Asian section of your market. Lee Kum Kee is a popular brand. If you can't find black bean sauce, you use an equal amount of fermented black beans.

SPICY CHORIZO

I started developing this recipe years ago when I worked with Michael Tuohy at Woodfire Grill. It's based on both traditional styles of chorizo, Spanish and Mexican. The two styles are completely different. Spanish chorizo is dry-cured and firm like salami. It has a satisfying chew, but the flavor profile is one-dimensional and heavy on the *pimentón* (Spanish smoked paprika). Mexican chorizo is fresh and spicier, but the texture is too wet and crumbly for my taste. This recipe pulls together the strengths of both styles into one adaptable chorizo. It's aggressively seasoned with cumin, smoked paprika, red pepper flakes, onion, and garlic, but you can make it fresh or dried. If you want fresh Mexican-style chorizo, you can cook the sausage loose or pack it into casings and cook it as links. If you want dry-cured Spanish-style chorizo, you can replace the curing salt #1 (a pink salt used to make fresh and cooked sausages) with curing salt #2 (a white salt used to make uncooked, dry-cured sausage). Then you make links and hang them in a refrigerator as directed until they are firm, dry, and slightly shrunken. After 2 to 3 months of hanging, they will be "cured" like salami and firm enough to slice and eat without cooking.

The main recipe is written for fresh Mexican-style chorizo, and I included metric weight measurements in case you fall in love with the recipe and want to double or triple it; weights scale up much more accurately than volumes. Either way, the sausage makes an absurdly good addition to almost any recipe. I chop the firm, dry-cured chorizo to spice up cooked black beans and black-eyed peas. I cook the loose, fresh version with vegetables like sautéed green beans, roasted asparagus, and shaved corn. I also use it as a stuffing for one of my favorite late-night drunken munchies, chorizo hash–stuffed potatoes (page 270).

SHOULD MAKE ABOUT
3 POUNDS BULK
(SIXTEEN 5-INCH LINKS,
EACH WEIGHING ABOUT
3 OUNCES)

Natural hog casings
at least 7 feet

Cumin seeds
*2 tablespoons + 2 teaspoons,
or 20 grams*

Hot smoked paprika
(*pimentón picante*)
3 tablespoons, or 20 grams

Sweet smoked paprika
(*pimentón dulce*)
2 tablespoons, or 12 grams

Dried red pepper flakes
1 tablespoon, or 6 grams

Ground cinnamon
½ teaspoon, or 1.5 grams

Ground cloves
⅛ teaspoon, or 0.3 gram

Grapeseed oil
*2 teaspoons, or 8 grams,
for the pan*

Yellow onion
*2 tablespoons + 1½ teaspoons
minced, or 25 grams*

Garlic
*3 tablespoons minced,
or 30 grams*

Sherry vinegar
2¼ teaspoons, or 18 grams

Boneless pork shoulder
3 pounds, or 1.36 kg, ground

Kosher salt
*1 tablespoon + 2 teaspoons,
or 25 grams*

Curing salt #1
(**pink curing salt**)
¾ teaspoon, or 5 grams

1. Soak the hog casings in water overnight, changing the water one or two times. This will make them more malleable and less prone to splitting when you stuff them. It also ensures they are clean.

2. Finely grind the cumin seeds in a spice grinder, then pour them into a small bowl. Stir in the hot paprika, sweet paprika, pepper flakes, cinnamon, and cloves.

3. Heat a medium skillet over medium heat. Add the oil and swirl to coat the bottom of the pan. Add the onion and garlic and cook until very soft but not browned, 6 to 8 minutes depending on how juicy your onions are. Add the spice mixture and sherry vinegar to the pan and cut the heat down to medium-low. Stir together to form a paste. Spread the paste in the pan and stir a few times, cooking for another 2 minutes. The mixture will become very aromatic and will darken a little. Remove the pan from the heat, spread the mixture on a small baking sheet, and let cool completely.

4. Make sure you are working in a cool, very clean environment while mixing and stuffing your sausage. Put the ground pork in a large chilled bowl and add the cooled onion-spice mixture, the kosher salt, and the curing salt. (If you intend to make dry-cured Spanish-style chorizo, replace the curing salt #1 with curing salt #2.) Wearing sterile food-handling gloves, mix the sausage with your hands until it comes together and feels sticky, somewhat like bread dough. If it's loose or crumbly, mix a little longer. Remove a large pinch of sausage, pat it into a small patty, and fry it in a skillet. Taste to test the seasoning, and then adjust the seasonings in the bowl as needed. Chorizo should taste spicy and a little on the salty side. Chill the pork while you set up the sausage stuffer.

5. Hold open the soaked casings under cold running water and rinse the insides. Using butcher's twine, tie a secure double knot at one end of the casing. Thoroughly clean and dry your sausage stuffer, and coat the stuffer tube with nonstick spray or a little oil. Spray a baking sheet with nonstick spray.

CONTINUED →

6. Again working with sterile gloves and cold equipment, stuff the sausage into the casings. This process is much easier with two people: one to feed the meat into the stuffer and one to hold the casings. Turn on or crank the stuffer and begin slowly feeding in meat just until the meat pokes out the end of the stuffer tube, then stop. This eliminates air from the system. You don't want any air inside your sausage because that's where mold could grow. Stretch the open end of the rinsed and tied casing over the end of the stuffer tube. Gather the casing straight onto the stuffer tube without twisting, like bunching up a sock on your foot, until the tied end of the casing reaches the meat that's poking out the stuffer tube. Turn the stuffer on low speed or crank slowly and feed in the remaining meat. Keep gentle pressure against the stuffer tube so that the casing fills evenly but not too tightly. The sausage should be packed loosely enough so that you can twist it into links when the casing is full. As the casing fills with meat, coil it like a garden hose onto the prepared baking sheet. When all the meat is stuffed into the casing, tie off the open end with a double knot of butcher's twine. Sight-measure about 5 inches of length from one end of the sausage, then pick it up and twist it there several times, going in one direction, to make a link. Again measure about 5 inches down the sausage and twist several times in the opposite direction to create another link. Continue twisting up links, making sure that you twist in alternate directions each time, which tightens the previous link and helps ensure that the links won't unravel when you hang them. Before you hang the sausage, inspect it thoroughly for air bubbles. When you see a bubble, pop the bubble with the tip of a sharp knife and press gently to ease out the air.

7. Clear out a shelf in your refrigerator and use butcher's twine to hang the sausages in the refrigerator. There should be plenty of air circulation around the sausages and they should not touch each other. You can cook the sausage immediately, let it hang in the refrigerator for up to 1 week, or freeze it for up to 3 months. If you have replaced the curing salt #1 with curing salt #2 to make Spanish-style dry-cured chorizo, let the sausage hang in the refrigerator until firm and slightly shrunken, 2 to 3 months.

SAFE SAUSAGE AND EQUIPMENT /
There are two keys to safe sausage making: 1. Keep everything clean. Wash and sanitize your work area, sausage stuffer, and any and all equipment that will come in contact with the meat. Also wash your hands with hot, soapy water and wear sterile, food-safe gloves. 2. Keep everything cold. Put all of the ingredients and the sausage stuffer parts and other equipment in the freezer for 20 to 30 minutes so they are very cold before you start working. It also helps to work in a cold room and stick your hands in ice water. Keeping everything clean and cold minimizes the risk of bacterial contamination.

As for buying ingredients and equipment, you can get the curing salt, hog casings, sausage stuffer, and anything else you might need online from the Sausage Maker (see Sources, page 326). Or if you already have a stuffer, pick up some natural hog casings from your butcher. They come packed in salt and should be soaked and rinsed as directed in the recipe. If you have a KitchenAid stand mixer, you can get a meat grinding and sausage stuffing attachment for it. I like to grind meat myself and, for this recipe, I grind the meat coarse with the large cutting die on the grinder. Again, just be sure to keep everything clean and cold during grinding to minimize bacterial growth.

COUNTRY SAUSAGE

This recipe is based on the sack sausages I grew up eating in the South. They come in a cloth sack like a sock, and you just squeeze out what you need. It's a traditional Southern preparation that dates back to when people processed hogs in the late fall and made the pork scraps into fresh sausage. Whether you make it sweet or hot is up to you. Adjust the pitch of the heat by adding more or less red pepper flakes. As the recipe stands now, it's hot but won't blow your head off. I use both fresh and dried sage, too, for a deeper flavor. This is an almost universal sausage. You can scramble it up with eggs, mix it into sauces, or stuff quail with it. I also like to fill fresh cabbage leaves with it to make cabbage dumplings (page 92).

1. If you're starting with whole pork shoulder, cut it into cubes and refrigerate until cold, at least 1 hour. Chill the fine die and other metal parts of a meat grinder, then grind the cold pork with the fine die. Return the pork to the refrigerator until you are ready to make the sausage. It's important to keep everything cold when making sausage (even your hands!) so that the grinder cuts the cold fat into little chunks rather than smearing it into a sloppy mess. Combine the fresh sage, salt, garlic, black pepper, rubbed sage, red pepper, ginger, cloves, nutmeg, and ice water in a large bowl and mix thoroughly. Add the cold ground pork to the bowl and, using gloved hands, mix together.

2. Heat a small skillet over medium-high heat. Pinch a small piece of sausage from the bowl, thoroughly cook it in the skillet, then taste it. Adjust the seasoning in the bowl as necessary.

PREP AHEAD / **This sausage works best when made at least a day ahead. You can cover it tightly in plastic wrap and refrigerate it for 2 to 3 days. For longer storage, vacuum-seal it, then refrigerate it for up to 5 days or freeze it for up to 1 month.**

MAKES ABOUT 1¾ POUNDS

Pork shoulder
1¾ pounds whole or 70% lean ground

Fresh sage
1 tablespoon + ½ teaspoon

Salt
2 teaspoons

Garlic
1 teaspoon finely minced

Ground black pepper
¾ teaspoon

Rubbed sage
¾ teaspoon

Dried red pepper flakes
½ teaspoon

Fresh ginger
about ½ teaspoon peeled and finely grated

Ground cloves
a pinch

Freshly grated nutmeg
a pinch

Ice water
½ cup

GRILLED PEACHES WITH PEPPER JELLY

Is this a dessert or an appetizer? I don't know. But it's a fun dish. I travel a lot on Delta Air Lines, and they give away Biscoff cookies. I'm always coming across them in my pockets and backpack. When I get home, I just throw the packets in the kitchen drawer. This recipe puts them to good use. It starts with super-ripe grilled peaches. The best way to tell whether peaches are ripe is by smelling them: They should smell like a bottle of peach perfume. You don't put anything on them; you just cut them in half and get them on the grill. You put some dark grill marks on the peaches, just shy of charred, then cover them in red pepper jelly, which is spicy and sweet and very traditional in the South. The crowning touch is to crush those Biscoff cookies over the top. Or if you really want to amp up the peach flavor, use Italian amaretti cookies, since almonds and peaches are in the same flavor family. Either way, if you're set on doing a heat-freak dinner with chile peppers in every course, this would make a bad-ass dessert. Serve it with a scoop of vanilla ice cream and you're in business.

1. Heat a grill for direct medium heat.

2. Cut the peaches from north pole to south pole and down to the pit. Twist to separate the halves, and remove the pits. Scrape the grill clean and coat it with oil. Brush the cut sides and outsides of the peaches with the grapeseed oil and, using tongs, set them cut side down on the grill. Grill for 2 minutes, turn the peaches 90 degrees, and grill for 2 minutes more. Flip the fruit and grill for another minute. Remove the peaches from the grill.

3. For each plate, shingle 2 peach halves in the center. Fill the hollow centers of each peach half with 1 teaspoon pepper jelly and sprinkle with the cookie crumbs.

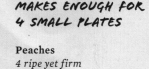

MAKES ENOUGH FOR 4 SMALL PLATES

Peaches
4 ripe yet firm

Grapeseed oil
about 1 tablespoon

Red pepper jelly
8 teaspoons

Biscoff cookies
4 plain (2 packets containing 2 cookies each), crumbled

Chapter

8

JUNK FOOD

For as long as I can remember, my family has gone to the Annual Highland Games festival in Stone Mountain Park, Georgia. Yes, we're Scottish. One look at my red beard tells you that. It's like a Gaelic birth certificate.

I love everything about the Highland Games: the hammer throw, the sheaf toss, the bagpipes and drums, the smooth-stepping, ghillie-wearing Highland dancers, and the deep-fried Mars bars.

Okay. At least I thought I'd like the fried Mars bar.

I love candy.

I love deep-fried food.

I love stuff that melts.

What could go wrong? Standing in line for one, I could almost taste the light, crackling crust. The sweet milk chocolate ... the soft, warm caramel ... the melty nougat stretching away from my lips like a hot fried mozzarella stick. After one bite, I realized I actually had a soggy sponge-bomb of grease in my mouth. There was no crust. The batter was thick, soft, and saturated with over-used fryer oil. The candy melted into a gob of goo. It was a total train wreck.

I don't find too many things disgusting. When I was 9, I demanded that my dad let me watch *Platoon*. That desensitized me to violence. For years, I saw freshly shot animals skinned and eviscerated at the end of my driveway. As a teen-ager, I made it a point to see all the gory movies ... *Evil Dead*, *Evil Dead II*, *Night of the Living Dead*, *Dawn of the Dead*, plus all the good slasher movies. Blood, guts, gore, and more. I saw it all.

But this lame-ass Mars bar was the most revolting thing I'd ever come across. My mouth instantly rejected it into the trash bin.

Of course, it then became my mission to create the best deep-fried Mars bar ever. I mean, it's good in theory, right? Fried crust. Barely melted chocolate. Warm, stretchy caramel and nougat. It should work. As soon as I got home from the Highland Games, I enlisted a corps of teenagers to help create The Greatest Deep-Fried Candy Bar on Earth. I roped in my friends Anthony Garcia, Brian Kilbern, Ronnie McCord, and Brent Edmonson. Brent was the one with the money. He had a job. We all pitched in to buy a deep fryer and every kind of fun-size candy at the store: Snickers. Zero. Milky Way (regular and dark). Three Musketeers. Kit Kat. Twix. Caramello. We even bought M&Ms.

This project was kind of a big deal for me. As a been-there-done-that teenager, I didn't get excited about much of anything in life. But frying candy bars? And frying them well? This was something an aspiring 16-year-old chef could get behind.

We set up the fryer on Anthony's porch so we wouldn't burn down the house. I had no idea how to make the batter. Maybe pancake batter? We tried that on a Caramello and threw it in the fryer. It exploded like a volcano. Attempt #1: Fail. We had to dump out the oil and start over. Okay, I thought, how about tempura batter? We tried that on a Zero bar. The batter was too thin and crispy, and the filling melted through the batter. Attempt #2: Fail. Maybe it should be more like the batter for fish and chips? At the time, my grandfather had gone on a fishing trip in Alaska and we were eating a lot of fried fish. I was used to dipping fish in wet batter and then frying it. We tried it and it was the best yet, but the batter still didn't taste quite right. So we opened one of Anthony's dad's beers to make beer batter. That was the breakthrough; the frothiness made all the difference.

At this point, Andy's house was a mess. There was fryer oil on the deck. Flour scattered around the kitchen. Candy wrappers everywhere. And we were jumping out of our skin. Six teenagers hopped up on every candy imaginable! But we still had half the candy bars left. We'd spent all our savings on the fryer, the oil, and the candy; I'd be damned if we were gonna waste it all. We battered and fried everything we had. That was our dinner. The Caramellos still turned to molten lava. The Three Musketeers got a little too mushy. Snickers turned out second best. But we all agreed that the Milky Way won hands down.

It was about 9 p.m. when we finally finished. Thank God we didn't have to eat any more. No one threw up, but everyone looked like they'd been hit by a truck. It was the look I had seen on adult faces when they had too much to drink and they started sobering up sooner than expected. We had a fried candy hangover.

I found out later that deep-fried Mars bars originated in chip shops in Scotland. That made me feel pretty good, like I was participating in Scottish food history. I didn't care that it was junk food. What mattered was that we worked out this culinary problem. We pushed through to meet the goal. It was a formative moment for me as a chef. Out of the blue, I had come into my own, laying out a plan, doling out tasks, and getting the job done.

It all started with one little craving. All I wanted was to eat a properly deep-fried candy bar (page 287). I've learned that when a craving hits, it needs instant gratification. Nothing else will do. Junk food is, by definition, not about getting your recommended daily allowance of fruits and vegetables. It is about satisfaction. Every dish in this chapter has the same origin point. I get cravings in midafternoon, after work, at midnight, and the morning after. When a craving hits, a taste pops into my mouth, and I say, "Damn, that sounds good!" The end result might be junk food, but it's the best junk food you've ever had. This is bad-for-you food that's too good to be bad for you.

CHEDDAR WAFFLES WITH PORK SCHNITZEL, COUNTRY HAM, AND SUNNY-SIDE-UP EGG

I'm fanatical about waffles. They are far superior to pancakes, French toast, and the other breakfast sweets of the world. If you don't have a good waffle iron, spend a few bucks on a heavy-gauge, nonstick model. The reason is, we're tempting the waffle gods by adding so much cheddar cheese here. You don't want the waffles to stick. The cheese is inspired by Italian *frico*, which is just fried cheese in a pan. You get a similar effect here with a layer of cheddar sprinkled on the waffle batter that melts, browns, and crisps. Fried pork makes the perfect accompaniment. The trick to schnitzel is pounding the meat nice and thin—no thicker than ¼ inch. That way, it isn't too chewy. Panko bread crumbs give the schnitzel awesome crunch. But one piece of pork is never enough for breakfast! I add a slice of country ham to each plate along with some fried eggs . . . and rivers of maple syrup, of course.

---

1. Pour 2 inches of oil into a large cast-iron skillet and heat it to 375°F.

2. Place the pork loin slices between two sheets of plastic wrap and gently and evenly pound them to a ¼-inch thickness. Pat the pork dry with a paper towel and season with salt. Bread the pork using the 3-step fry prep with flour, 2 of the eggs, and the panko (see page 7). Fry the pork in the hot oil until golden brown, about 2 minutes on the first side and 1 minute on the other. Line a plate with a double layer of paper towels. Transfer the pork schnitzel to the paper towels to drain.

3. In a small skillet over low heat, bring the maple syrup to a low simmer. Pull the pan from the heat and whisk in 2 tablespoons of the butter until melted. Set to the side but keep warm.

4. Melt the remaining 2 tablespoons butter in a 12-inch skillet over medium-low heat and swirl to coat the bottom of the pan. Crack 1 egg into a small bowl and gently slide the egg into one side of the warmed skillet; repeat the process with the remaining eggs, gently sliding each egg into its own section of the skillet. Season the eggs with a pinch of salt and cover the skillet. Reduce the heat to low and cook until the whites are fully cooked and opaque, about 4 minutes.

5. For each plate, set a waffle in the center and generously spoon some syrup over the waffle. Add a slice of schnitzel and spoon on a little more syrup. Top with a slice of ham, and crown with a sunny-side-up egg and, yes, a little more syrup.

CONTINUED →

FEEDS 4 HUNGRY FOLKS

Canola oil for frying
about ½ cup

Pork loin
4 trimmed slices, about 1½ ounces each

Salt

All-purpose flour
1 cup

Eggs
6 large

Panko bread crumbs
1 cup finely ground

Best-quality pure maple syrup, such as BLiS (see next page)
½ cup

Butter
4 tablespoons

Cheddar waffles (recipe follows)
4 single waffles

Country ham
4 very thin slices, about 2 ounces total

CHEDDAR WAFFLES

**MAKES
3 DOUBLE WAFFLES
(SIX 4½-INCH
SQUARE WAFFLES)**

All-purpose flour
⅔ cup

Salt
⅛ teaspoon

Baking powder
1 teaspoon

Eggs
2 large

Whole milk
1 cup

Egg whites
2

Sugar
1 tablespoon + 1 teaspoon

Butter
5 tablespoons + 1 teaspoon,
melted and kept warm

Cheddar cheese
⅔ cup grated, 3 ounces

1. Heat an electric Belgian-style waffle maker on the medium setting. I like to preheat the waffle iron for at least 10 minutes to make sure it's nice and hot.

2. In a large bowl, whisk together the flour, salt, and baking powder. In a separate bowl, whisk the eggs and milk. In a third, deep bowl, using a handheld mixer, beat the egg whites until frothy. With the mixer running, gradually add the sugar to the whites and continue beating until the whites form soft peaks when the mixer is lifted. Pour the milk mixture into the dry ingredients and stir with a large spoon just until no giant flour clumps remain; there will still be some small lumps. Start whisking and slowly add the melted butter, whisking gently yet nonstop until incorporated. Gently fold the egg whites into the batter; you'll have a few small clumps of whites remaining—that's okay.

3. Generously coat the waffle maker with nonstick spray. Ladle about ½ cup batter onto the center of the waffle maker and sprinkle with a generous amount of the cheese. Close the top and cook according to the manufacturer's instructions. For most waffle makers, the waffles are golden brown when you no longer see steam escaping and you can see the edges browning, 4 to 5 minutes after closing the lid. The cook's rule is that the first waffle is always a forfeit; it won't come out cleanly. Enjoy it as a snack, then spray the waffle iron again and repeat until all the waffles are cooked. When you remove the waffles, set them on a cooling rack so they don't steam or get soggy.

BLiS MAPLE SYRUP / I love BLiS maple syrups. How could you not love anything aged in charred oak bourbon barrels? In the barrel, the syrup picks up a deeply caramelized, smoky flavor that's bang-on perfect with the cheddar waffles and schnitzel. Look for it online (see Sources, page 327). And if you need a waffle iron, the All-Clad four-square Belgian-style waffle maker turns out really nice, crispy, light waffles. You can find that at The Cook's Warehouse (see Sources, page 327).

BREAKFAST FÜD

I'm always at Woodfire Grill at the ass-crack of dawn. Usually I don't eat anything before I show up. By 9 a.m. my chef de cuisine, E.J. Hodgkinson, and I are completely starving. We make breakfast by raiding all the other cooks' bins. There's usually some leftover pork belly. On one particular morning, there were some diced potatoes, and I said to E.J., "We should make pork belly hash." A little stock and butter brought the whole thing together in a pan. Topped with sunny-side-up eggs, it's completely delicious. I like it with cheddar cheese too. It's rich as all hell, so you won't need a giant portion. If you have leftover pork belly from the bok choy and pork belly (page 244), this is the perfect use for it.

ENOUGH FOR 4 HUNGRY PEOPLE

Slow-roasted pork belly (page 305)
8 ounces cut into ½-inch dice, about 1½ cups

New potatoes
4 golf ball–sized, cut into ¼-inch dice, about 1½ cups

Onion
1 cut into ¼-inch dice, about 1 cup

Garlic
2 cloves minced, about 1 tablespoon

New Mexico green chile powder (see Sources, page 327)
1 teaspoon

Chicken stock
½ cup

Butter
3 tablespoons

Scallions
4 sliced on the diagonal, about ½ cup

Salt and ground black pepper

Eggs
8 large

1. Heat a 10-inch skillet over medium-high heat. Add the pork belly and cook until golden brown, about 3 minutes, stirring now and then. Add the potatoes and cook for another 5 minutes. Stir in the onion and garlic and cook until tender, about 3 minutes. Stir in the chile powder and cook for another minute. Crank the heat up to high, add the chicken stock, and scrape up all the browned bits, stirring them into the sauce. Cook until almost all of the chicken stock evaporates, about 2 minutes. Pull the pan from the heat, add 1 tablespoon of the butter, the scallions, 1 teaspoon salt, and ½ teaspoon pepper, and toss until the butter melts.

2. Melt another tablespoon of the butter in a 12-inch skillet over medium-low heat and swirl to coat the bottom of the pan. Crack 1 egg into a small bowl and gently slide the egg into the warmed skillet; repeat the process, gently sliding 3 more of the eggs, one by one, each into its own section of the pan. Season the eggs with a pinch of salt and cover the skillet. Reduce the heat to low and cook until the whites are fully cooked and turn opaque, about 4 minutes. The yolks will still be runny. Gently slide the eggs onto a plate and tent with foil to keep warm. Repeat the process for the second batch of 4 eggs, using the remaining butter.

3. For each plate, mound one-quarter of the hash mixture in the center and top with 2 sunny-side-up eggs. Season lightly with salt and pepper.

PIZZA ROLLS

My dad's favorite midnight snack is Totino's pizza rolls. When I was little, he would let me stay up late, watch movies with him, and nibble on those little pillows of cheesy red sauce. When I grew up, I realized they weren't all that great. But I still had fond memories of them and thought, "How hard could it be to make a decent pizza roll?" Turns out, pretty damn hard! It took hours and hours to get the flavor and texture right. I knew exactly what the end result should be. Everything had to be finely diced and cooked until very soft. The crust had to be crispy yet tender. Small wonton wrappers are the secret. They have the perfect texture. I tried deep-frying the filled rolls, but it didn't work. It's critical to bake these to get the texture right. When you bite into one, it should be boiling-lava hot—the sign of a properly made pizza roll.

---

1. Heat a Dutch oven over medium-high heat. Add the oil and swirl to coat the bottom of the pot. Squeeze the sausage from the casings, crumbling it into the pot, and cook until brown, about 3 minutes, stirring to break up the clumps. Line a plate with a double layer of paper towels. Using a slotted spoon, transfer the sausage to the plate and let cool. Add the mushrooms, bell peppers, onion, and garlic to the pot and cook for 2 minutes. Stir like hell and add the pepperoni, sausage, and oregano. Cook for another 2 minutes, stirring a few times. Stir in the vinegar and cook until the mixture is almost dry. Stir in the olives, red pepper flakes, and tomato paste. Pull the pot from the heat and stir in the mozzarella and basil until the cheese is completely melted, about a minute. Spread the mixture on a baking sheet to cool.

2. Preheat the oven to 375°F.

3. In a small bowl, whisk the egg with about a tablespoon of water to make an egg wash. This mixture will act as the glue to seal the pizza rolls.

4. Line up the wonton wrappers in a single layer on a work surface with one corner facing you, about 6 wrappers at a time. Brush each wrapper with egg wash and spoon a scant tablespoon of the filling into the bottom third of each wrapper. Fold the corner nearest you up and over the filling, then fold in the sides over the filling; continue rolling the packet away from you into a tight bundle, like a burrito. Repeat to use up the filling and wonton wrappers.

5. Line a baking sheet with a silicone baking mat, parchment paper, or nonstick aluminum foil. Arrange the rolls evenly on the sheet and bake for 8 minutes; pull the pan from the oven and flip the rolls over so they get nice and crispy on the second side too, about 7 minutes more in the oven.

MAKES ABOUT 40

Olive oil
1 teaspoon

Mild Italian sausage
4 ounces

Button mushrooms
4 ounces finely diced, about 1¾ cups

Green bell pepper
1 finely diced, ribs and seeds removed, about 1 cup

Onion
1 minced, about ¾ cup

Garlic
2 cloves minced, about 1 tablespoon

Pepperoni
4 ounces sliced then finely diced, about 1 cup

Dried oregano
2 teaspoons

Red wine vinegar
¼ cup

Kalamata olives
1 tablespoon pitted and chopped

Dried red pepper flakes
¾ teaspoon

Tomato paste
2 tablespoons

Mozzarella cheese
1 cup grated, about 4 ounces

Fresh basil
¼ cup chopped

Egg
1 large

Wonton wrappers
40 squares, about two-thirds of a 1-pound package

Cured Pork

These ingredients are near and dear to my heart. One of the misconceptions about Southern food is that it's loaded with meat. The reality is, Southerners don't eat a ton of meat because they never had a ton of meat. Meat is more often than not a garnish or seasoning. Ham, bacon, and fatback add oomph, but they're not the stars of the show. When I want porky flavor and salty punch, these are the cured meats I usually turn to. But use a gentle hand. Sometimes less is more.

BACON. The consensus is that bacon has its origins in Britain, but when it came to the United States it hit its stride. Americans tend to like an aggressive cure and intense smoke in their bacon. Mass-market American bacon is usually plunged into brine. But moisture dilutes flavor. In my opinion, the superior American bacons are dry-cured. As for smoke, you'll find everything from apple and cherry to hickory and mesquite. In Georgia, hickory grows everywhere, so that's what we use. In North Carolina and Alabama, they have more oak. In Wisconsin and North Dakota, you find apple trees. That's where applewood-smoked bacon got its start, from meat suppliers like Nueske's. Whatever brand you buy, make sure the pork belly has actually been smoked over burning wood. God forbid you purchase bacon that has been smoke-flavored with "liquid smoke" infused into the brine (smoke is not a liquid!). That stuff is crap, but it accounts for 90 percent of the commercial bacon available in supermarkets. Look for reputable bacon. A telltale sign is that the bacon doesn't need to be refrigerated. It shouldn't need to be if it's been cured properly. I buy almost exclusively from Benton's, in Madisonville, Tennessee. Allan

Benton sells his bacon wrapped in paper in a cardboard box. He dry-cures it the old-fashioned way in salt, sugar, and spices, then smokes it for 2 days over hickory wood. It's incredible, and you can buy it online (see Sources, page 326).

PANCETTA. Italian bacon is also made from pork belly, but it's not smoked. It looks different because they roll the pork belly like a jelly roll instead of leaving the belly flat like Americans do. The big flavor difference is the lack of smoke. You'll taste that right away. Pancetta also has more seasonings in the cure, like cloves, allspice, juniper, and garlic. There are as many variations as there are people who make it. I like to use pancetta when I'm making a traditional Italian dish or when I don't want the smokiness of American bacon to dominate. In root vegetable soup (page 165), pancetta adds richness without stealing the show.

FATBACK. Italians call this *lardo*. It's cured fat that comes from the back of a pig directly above the loin (the pork chop area) but below the skin. This particular cap of fat is not spongy or wet. It's just a perfect block of fat. Italians cure it in salt, cinnamon, and other spices and then eat it raw. In the U.S., fatback is almost always cooked. American fatback is typically cured in salt alone to get it as dry as possible. Southerners leave the salt intact until the last minute; you dust off the salt right before cooking. Fatback is extremely salty, so if you put a piece of fatback in a pot of beans, for example, you'll hardly need to add any extra salt. But mostly it adds a luxurious texture. The fat melts and adds a velvety luster to beans, greens, soups, stews . . . you name it. Salt pork is similar, but it's usually made with a fatty piece of pork belly instead of back fat.

SALUMI. This is a huge category of cured pork that includes everything from sopressata to fennel salami to chorizo. They are all made by grinding pork, seasoning it with salt and spices, and hang-

"LARDO"
(ITALIAN
FOR FATBACK)

ing it to dry. Salumi can be salty, sweet, savory, and everything in between. It's like cheese. You choose varieties based on what you're making. Salumi can be tricky to make at home, but you can buy whatever you need from a local butcher. The small shops tend to make salumi that tastes better than the shrink-wrapped stuff in supermarkets. Just remember that salumi does not need to be cooked, because it has been cured. You just slice it and eat it. I do include a recipe here for spicy chorizo (page 246) because I was never fully on board with either the dry-cured Spanish style or the fresh Mexican style. My version allows you to take it in either direction. If you've never made sausage, give it a try. It's pretty easy.

HAM. Prosciutto, Serrano, Westphalian, country ham . . . every culture makes ham and believes its ham is the best in the world. The truth is, all ham is made from a pig's back leg cured in salt. The flavors vary, but the basic method is the same. The idea is to make the meat safe to eat at a later time. When you slaughter a whole animal, it's nearly impossible to eat all the meat right away. Before refrigeration, curing was the way to make food last. In the U.S., country ham is more often than not dry-cured in salt and sugar and then smoked. Americans brought their ham-making skills from Europe, then took a shine to the Native American tradition of smoking food to preserve it. In Italy and Spain, they generally prefer unsmoked ham. Prosciutto and Serrano hams have a straight-to-the-point savory flavor. The taste has less to do with how it's cured and more to do with the breed of the pig, what it ate, and where it was raised. The sky-high price of Spanish Jamón Ibérico tells you how much time and money it took to get these purebred, acorn-fed blackfoot Iberian pigs ready to be cured. I use all kinds of ham in my cooking, but most often I call for country ham, the dry-cured, smoked specialty of the American South. Make sure you buy dry-cured ham, not the wet-cured or "city" ham found shrink-wrapped in super-markets all over the country. There are dozens of great Southern ham makers. Again, Benton's makes some of my favorite country hams (see Sources, page 326).

BAKED HOT WINGS

It's no secret that my all-time favorite junk food is hot wings. I am completely obsessed to the point of absurdity. If I go to a restaurant and wings are on the menu, I feel it's imperative to order them. Even if I don't plan on it and have just finished placing my order, out of nowhere, the words will come out of my mouth: "And I gotta get the wings." It's a sickness. I usually don't make wings at home because who wants to pull out the deep fryer for a quick snack? I thought there had to be a way to make respectable baked wings. "Absolutely not," all my cooks told me. "Baked wings suck." Game on. I was going to make baked wings and make them delicious. Most baked wings taste soggy because the chicken skin isn't crisp enough. So I sear the wings in a smokin' hot pan, then put the pan in the oven. The sauce is sriracha and soy sauce, which gives the wings an Asian flavor. But you could use any sauce you like. The key is not to drown the wings in sauce or they'll lose their crispness. A thin glaze is all you need. My wife, Valerie, was at the photo shoot for this recipe, and she's not a fan of chicken wings. However, I had to practically slap her hand to keep her from eating these before the photographer could get a shot of them.

1. Preheat the oven to 500°F.

2. Pat the wings very dry with a paper towel. Heat a large (14-inch) cast-iron skillet or two smaller cast-iron skillets over high heat until smokin' hot. Add just enough of the oil to coat the bottom of the pan. Using tongs, set the wings in the pan in a single layer with the meatiest side down. This will help render the fat. Cook the wings for 2 minutes, then transfer the skillet to the oven for 5 minutes. Carefully remove the skillet from the oven and, using tongs, flip the wings over. Continue baking until the wings are cooked through and the juices run clear, another 10 minutes.

3. Combine the sriracha, vinegar, soy sauce, sugar, and garlic in a small saucepan. Bring to a boil over high heat, then cut the heat down to medium-low and simmer for 5 minutes. Pour the sauce into a large bowl and toss in 1 tablespoon of the scallions.

4. Carefully remove the skillet from the oven and, using tongs, transfer the wings to the bowl and toss with the sauce. Transfer to a platter and garnish with the remaining 3 tablespoons scallions.

FEEDS 2 FOLKS (OR 1 HUNGRY NIBBLER)

Chicken wings
24, a mix of drums and flats, about 2 pounds

Grapeseed oil
1 tablespoon

Sriracha chile sauce
⅓ cup

Malt vinegar
¼ cup

Soy sauce
¼ cup

Sugar
2 tablespoons

Garlic
2 cloves, very thinly sliced

Scallions
¼ cup thinly sliced on the diagonal

CHORIZO HASH-STUFFED POTATO

If you like twice-baked potatoes, you'll love this. You scoop out a baked potato, then mash the innards into sautéed chorizo to make a hash. Then you mix in an absolutely epic amount of cheddar cheese. It's comical how much cheese goes into this. And there's some chopped jalapeño and cilantro too. Then you stuff the potato shells and bake them until the cheese melts into a nice and brown bubbly blanket. If you were to eat this at 2 o'clock in the morning, it would set you straight. You might not sleep worth a damn, but you'd be a pretty happy camper.

ENOUGH FOR 2 RAVENOUS SNACKERS

Baking potato
1 big one, about 1 pound

Lime
1 fat one

Crème fraîche
¼ cup

Spicy chorizo (page 246)
6 ounces, or two 5-inch links

Cheddar cheese
1 cup grated, about 4 ounces

Fresh cilantro
1 tablespoon coarsely chopped

Jalapeño chile pepper
2 tablespoons finely diced, seeds and ribs removed

1. Preheat the oven to 400°F.

2. Bake the potato directly on the oven rack until fork-tender, about 1 hour.

3. In a small bowl, whisk 1 teaspoon lime zest and 1 tablespoon lime juice into the crème fraîche. Set aside.

4. Heat a 10-inch skillet over medium-high heat. Squeeze the sausage out of the casing and crumble the meat into the skillet. Using a wooden spoon, break up the chorizo as it cooks through, about 5 minutes.

5. Split the potato lengthwise into two halves and use a large spoon to scrape out the flesh, leaving a ½-inch layer of potato in the shell. Finely chop the potato flesh and mash it into the chorizo until combined. Pull the pan from the heat and stir in the cheese, cilantro, and jalapeño.

6. Line a baking sheet with a silicone baking mat, parchment paper, or nonstick aluminum foil. Divide the mixture between the potato shells and set on the baking sheet. Bake until bubbly and starting to brown on the surface, 10 to 12 minutes.

7. Transfer each potato to a plate and top with about 3 tablespoons of the lime crème fraîche.

CHILI SLAW DAWGS

When my mom was pregnant with me, she craved hot dogs from The Varsity, a fast-food institution in Atlanta. She ate Varsity dogs for nine months straight. My aunt Pat even brought her a Varsity dog at the hospital right after I was born. Those chili dogs are in my blood. As I grew older, my love of eating them also grew, but my stomach's tolerance for chili dogs didn't quite keep pace. My goal: to make a chili dog that wouldn't send you to the thunder bucket for hours. First, you need great chili that sits well on a hot dog. You see, meat wants to clump up in big pieces when it cooks, but that's not what you want in a chili dog. You want a fine texture. So I came up with this method of cooking the raw meat, water, and onions together to keep the meat from clumping up. Second, the hot dog has to be skinny, preferably with a natural casing. I like to cook the dogs on a smokin' hot griddle so they get that awesome snap, which is on my list of all-time incredibly good things in food. Finally, you need a soft, top-loading bun that's cut down the center—not the side. That's absolutely imperative. For the slaw, use the tender inner green leaves from a head of cabbage. Pull off the dark outer leaves and reserve those for another use, like cabbage dumplings (page 92).

1. Heat a 10-inch cast-iron skillet over high heat and wipe the pan with a paper towel dipped in the canola oil. You only want enough oil to shine up the skillet. When the pan is smokin' hot, pat the dogs dry and add them to the pan. Cut the heat down to medium and cook just until the dogs are lightly charred, about 4 minutes per side. Slice the buns lengthwise through the top (if not already sliced for top loading). Slip in the dogs, spoon a generous amount of chili onto each dog, and squeeze a generous amount of mustard down the length of the chili. Top with about ¼ cup slaw, then garnish with a thick layer of onions. The order of ingredients matters: You want to enclose the mustard in the chili and slaw so it's almost a surprise within the bite.

MAKES 8

Hot dogs
*8 of your favorite brand
(I like the long, skinny
Sabrett-style dogs)*

Canola oil
1 teaspoon

Hot dog buns
8 top-loading

**Hot dog chili
(recipe follows)**
4 cups

Yellow mustard

Slaw (recipe follows)
2 cups

Vidalia onion
½ cup finely diced

CONTINUED →

HOT DOG CHILI

MAKES ABOUT 4 CUPS

Grass-fed ground beef
1 pound, 85% lean

Vidalia onion
*1 baseball-size cut into ¼-inch dice,
about 2 cups*

Water
1 cup

Garlic
*5 cloves peeled and sliced
really thin, about ¼ cup*

Tomato paste
3 tablespoons

**New Mexico pure red chile
powder (see Sources, page 327)**
3 tablespoons

Salt
1 tablespoon

Beer
1 cup

---

1. In a heavy saucepan, combine the beef, onion, water, garlic, tomato paste, chile powder, and salt and stir. The mixture will be thick and pasty. Cook over medium-high heat until most of the liquid evaporates, about 10 minutes. Add the beer and return the chili to a simmer. Cut the heat down to medium-low and simmer for another 20 minutes. Pull the pan from the heat and let the chili cool in the pan. This is a weird technique because there is no caramelization or browning of the meat, but it achieves the perfect texture and consistency for hot dog chili with no big chunks of meat.

SLAW

MAKES ABOUT 2 CUPS

Green cabbage
*½ small head,
dark outer leaves removed,
about 1 pound*

Sugar
3 tablespoons

Salt
1½ teaspoons

Mayonnaise
2 tablespoons

---

1. Cut the cabbage into coarse chunks and drop into a food processor fitted with the metal blade. Give it about 20 quick pulses; you want a very fine chop, but be careful that you don't end up with mush. You should have a little more than 2½ cups chopped cabbage. Scrape the cabbage into a bowl and mix in the sugar and salt. Press and pack the mixture down to compact it, then cover and refrigerate for about 1 hour so the sugar and salt dissolve and start to draw the liquid out of the cabbage. Press the mixture through a fine-mesh strainer and discard the liquid. Stir the mayonnaise into the cabbage until combined.

FRIED BANANAS **WITH CILANTRO AND LIME**

For Lent, I usually give up meat, sugar, fun . . . all the good stuff. Even though I'm in my thirties, I can eat sugar like a seven-year-old. I can't get enough. This is my cheater dessert for when I'm not supposed to be eating sugar. I take completely ripened, black-skinned bananas, dust them in cornstarch, and deep-fry them. Ripe bananas are already sweet, but when you fry them, the sugar concentrates and goes through the roof. You're not eating any processed sugar—just the natural sugar in the fruit. But this dessert tastes as sweet as any sugar-based candy. I eat the fried bananas plain, but they're also good with lime and cilantro. The acidity of the lime and the bitterness of the cilantro balance the sweetness.

SHOULD BE ENOUGH FOR 4 PEOPLE

Canola oil for frying

Cornstarch
about 2 tablespoons

Bananas
4 ripe

Fresh cilantro leaves
¼ cup minced

Limes
2

Olive oil
1 tablespoon + 1 teaspoon

Salt

1. Heat the oil in a deep fryer to 375°F, or heat 1 inch of oil to 400°F in a large cast-iron skillet.

2. Line a plate with a double layer of paper towels. Spoon the cornstarch into a shallow bowl. Peel the bananas, split them in half lengthwise, and then cut them in half crosswise. Each banana will end up in 4 pieces. Dredge the banana pieces in the cornstarch, patting to remove any excess; then dredge and pat again. You should have an even dusting of cornstarch completely covering the bananas.

3. Deep-fry the bananas until they are GBD, about 2 minutes. If you are pan-frying, fry for 2 minutes, then turn and fry for another 1 minute, until GBD on all sides. Using a spider strainer or slotted spoon, transfer the bananas to the paper towels to drain.

4. In a small bowl, whisk together the cilantro, ½ teaspoon lime zest, ¼ cup lime juice, and the olive oil.

5. For each plate, set 4 banana pieces in the center, overlapping the pieces as you like. Sprinkle with a little salt and drizzle with a couple of spoonfuls of the cilantro-lime sauce.

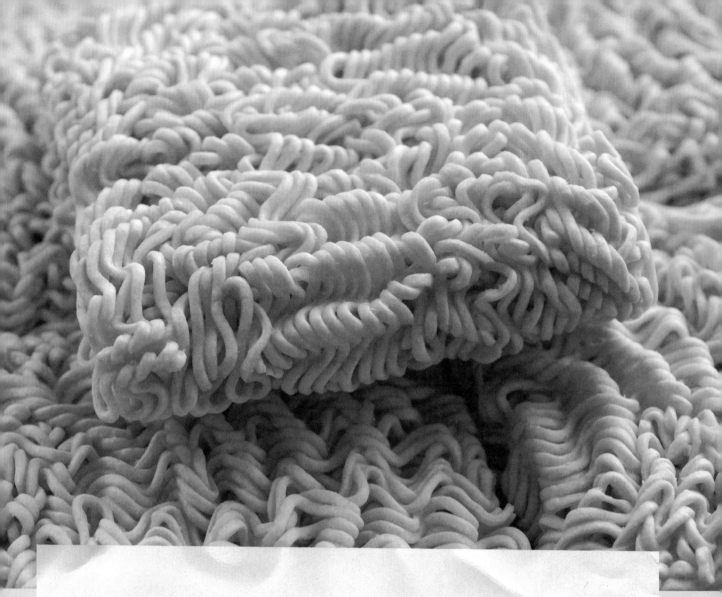

NOODLES RAMEN OFF

I'll admit it. I've always liked ramen noodles. I know they're total crap, but I like them. One day in the kitchen, I thought it would be fun to make ramen a little fancier, a bit more adult. I bought four packets of Maruchan ramen—two chicken and two beef. I kept the beef and gave the chicken to my chef de cuisine, E.J. We set a timer for 30 minutes and had a ramen-off. Who could make the better-tasting ramen dish? E.J. stir-fried his noodles like a Hong Kong crispy noodle cake, adding mushrooms, garlic, scallions, sriracha, and sesame oil. I was more focused on the broth, adding stock, soy sauce, fish sauce, lime juice, and herbs . . . almost like making Vietnamese pho with slices of beef poached in the broth. His noodles were better than mine. My broth was better than his. But they were both fantastic. The point is that you can make ramen however you like. They're just noodles! You don't have to follow the recipe on the packet.

CONTINUED →

VERSION 1

by E.J. Hodgkinson

SERVES 2 DRUNK CHEFS AFTER WORK

Shiitake mushrooms
6

Ramen noodles with chicken seasoning packet
2 packages, 3 ounces each

Olive oil
about 5 teaspoons

Dry mustard
1 tablespoon

Sriracha chile sauce
1¼ teaspoons

Lime
1 fat one

Onion
8 very thin slices

Garlic
2 cloves, minced

Scallions
4, thinly sliced on the diagonal

Sesame oil
a dash

Fresh mint leaves
a small handful torn into pieces

Fresh cilantro leaves
a small handful

1. Fill a 3-quart pot three-quarters full with water and bring to a boil.

2. Remove the stems from the mushrooms and add the stems to the boiling water. Cut the mushroom caps into thin slices and set aside. Add both packages of noodles to the mushroom water (reserve the seasoning packets) and cook until tender yet chewy, about 2 minutes, stirring to break up the noodles. Drain the noodles, and remove and discard the shiitake stems. Toss 1 teaspoon of the olive oil with the noodles so they don't stick together.

3. Return the pot to high heat and add 4 cups water. Bring to a boil and whisk in the 2 seasoning packets and the mustard. Remove the broth from the heat.

4. In a small bowl, combine the sriracha, 1½ teaspoons lime juice, and 2 teaspoons water. Set aside.

5. Heat a 10-inch sauté pan over high heat until smokin' hot. Add 2 teaspoons of the olive oil and swirl to coat the bottom of the pan. Add the mushroom caps and toss nonstop until they get crispy, 2 to 3 minutes. Add the onion and garlic and toss nonstop until they soften, about 2 more minutes. Add half the scallions and cook until they crisp up, another minute. Transfer the mushroom mixture to a small plate and set aside.

6. Keeping the pan superhot, add the remaining 2 teaspoons olive oil and swirl to coat the bottom of the pan. Add the noodles and cook undisturbed until they crisp up, about 2 minutes. Drizzle a tiny bit of sesame oil over the top and, using tongs, break the noodle cake up and cook for another minute. Add the sriracha mixture to the pan and toss to combine. Cook for another minute.

7. Return the seasoned broth to a boil.

8. Divide the noodles between large serving bowls, divide the onion mixture between the bowls, and pour about 1 cup of the broth into each bowl. Garnish with the remaining scallions, the mint, cilantro, a big squeeze of lime juice, and a big wedge of lime.

1. Place the beef in the freezer for about 20 minutes. You want to partially freeze it, just until it starts to firm up, so that it's easier to slice. Remove the beef from the freezer and slice it across the grain into pieces as thin as you can get them with a knife.

2. Bring the stock, beef seasoning packets, ginger, black bean paste, tamari, and white soy sauce to a boil in a medium saucepan.

3. Fill a second pan three-quarters full with water and bring to a rolling boil. Add the noodles and cook for 2 minutes, stirring to break up the noodles. Drain the noodles and set aside.

4. Add the fish sauce, sambal olek, salt, cinnamon, cloves, garlic, and about 2 tablespoons lime juice to the stock mixture, whisk, and return to a boil. Crack 1 egg into a small bowl. Pull the pan from the heat and, using a whisk, create a fast-spinning whirlpool in the center of the stock; pour the egg into the center of the whirlpool, then stop whisking. Return to the heat and cook for 4 minutes; then use a slotted spoon to transfer the egg to a small plate. Bring the sauce back to a boil and repeat the whirlpool process for the second egg. Return the pan to the heat and bring to a boil.

5. Divide the noodles between large serving bowls. Layer on the mushrooms, red onion, a few cracks of black pepper, the cilantro, scallion, and just a small drizzle of sesame oil. Tear the Thai basil leaves into a few pieces and add to the bowls. Divide the beef between the bowls and spread in a single layer on top of the vegetables. Top the beef with the eggs and ladle just enough of the broth into each bowl to completely cover the meat. The meat will cook in about 1 minute. Serve piping hot.

SRIRACHA / It seems like everybody knows about sriracha, but if you're late to the party, it's a can't-miss chile sauce from Vietnam that looks blood red from the ground chiles inside. Look for it in the Asian section of the grocery store or in an Asian market, where you'll find the sambal olek and white soy sauce, too. It's in a clear, green-topped bottle with a rooster on it.

VERSION 2

by Kevin Gillespie

Beef top round
4 ounces

Chicken stock
2 cups

Ramen noodles with beef seasoning packet
2 packages, 3 ounces each

Fresh ginger
10 paper-thin slices peeled and shaved on a mandoline

Black bean paste
1 teaspoon

Tamari
1 teaspoon

White soy sauce
1 teaspoon

Asian fish sauce
½ teaspoon

Sambal olek chile paste
½ teaspoon

Salt
¼ teaspoon

Ground cinnamon
a tiny pinch

Ground cloves
a tiny pinch

Garlic
1 clove, sliced paper-thin on a mandoline

Lime
1

Eggs
2 large

Shiitake mushrooms
4 nice ones, stems removed, caps sliced very thin

Red onion
½ cup sliced paper-thin on a mandoline

Ground black pepper

Fresh cilantro leaves
2 tablespoons

Scallion
1, sliced very thin on the diagonal

Sesame oil
¼ teaspoon

Fresh Thai basil leaves
2 tablespoons

CLOSED-ON-SUNDAY CHICKEN SANDWICH

The fast-food chain Chik-fil-A is based here in Atlanta. They're closed on Sunday for religious reasons. I respect that. But why is it that I crave a Chik-fil-A chicken sandwich almost exclusively on Sundays? It's like clockwork. I wake up on Sunday morning and think, "You know what would be really good right now? A Chick-fil-A sandwich." Like most food companies, they guard their secret recipe. But it's a breaded fried chicken breast on a bun with pickles. I figured I could come up with something pretty close. First, it's important to buy a pasture-raised bird. Start with the most flavorful chicken you can. Here's my proprietary recipe: I brine the chicken in pickle juice along with Hidden Valley Ranch salad dressing packets. Not the Hidden Valley prepared wet dressing or dip, but the dry mix they sell in a blister pack. It sounds strange, but the spice blend in that mix is really intense. I also add a little of it to the breading. You fry the chicken, toast the buns in honey butter, slather on some spicy pickle mayo, and then slap on the breaded chicken. For buns, I use King's Hawaiian sandwich buns, which are pretty widely available in the bakery or deli department of grocery stores (see Sources, page 326). They have the perfect soft texture and sweet taste.

FEEDS 4 HUNGRY FOLKS
(ESPECIALLY AFTER LATE-SUNDAY-MORNING CHURCH SERVICE)

Chicken breasts *4, boneless and skinless*	**All-purpose flour** *1 cup*
Dill pickle chips, preferably Mt. Olive *1 jar, 16 ounces*	**Espelette pepper** *1 tablespoon*
Water *2 cups*	**Ground black pepper** *1 teaspoon*
Hidden Valley Ranch Original dry salad dressing mix *5 packets, 1 ounce each*	**Butter** *4 tablespoons*
Sugar *¼ cup*	**Honey** *2 tablespoons*
Salt *3 tablespoons*	**King's Hawaiian sandwich buns or brioche rolls** *8*
Canola oil for frying	**Spicy pickle mayonnaise** **(page 299)** *about 1 cup*

1. Trim the connective tissue from the chicken breasts. Lightly pound the thickest end of the breast to match the rest of breast in thickness; it's important that the chicken be evenly thick for even cooking. Don't worry if the pounded breasts seem a little thin and larger than the buns; the chicken will shrink and puff up during cooking.

2. Strain the pickles over a large bowl, reserving the pickles and juice separately; you should have about 1 cup juice. Whisk the water, 4 packets of the salad dressing mix, the sugar, and 1 tablespoon of the salt into the pickle juice to make a brine. Pour the brine into a large zip-top bag and add the chicken; press out the air, seal, and refrigerate for at least 1 hour or up to 3 hours. Don't go past 3 hours, though; too much time in the brine will toughen the chicken.

3. Heat the oil in a deep fryer to 330°F. The somewhat low frying temperature is important so that the chicken will cook through completely before the crust gets too dark.

4. Line a baking sheet with paper towels and top with a cooling rack.

5. In a medium bowl, whisk together the flour, the remaining packet of salad dressing mix, the remaining 2 tablespoons salt, the Espelette pepper, and the black pepper.

6. One at a time, pull the chicken breasts from the brine and, while still wet, dredge in the flour mixture. Shake off the excess flour, set the chicken on the rack, and repeat until all the chicken is coated. Let the chicken rest until the flour has absorbed the brine and the breading sets and gets a little sticky, about 5 minutes. One by one, toss the chicken pieces back into the flour mixture and shake off the excess.

7. Deep-fry the breasts until cooked through and GBD, about 8 minutes. Meanwhile, thoroughly wash and dry the cooling rack and place over a clean baking sheet. Transfer the cooked chicken to the rack to drain.

8. Heat a large skillet or flattop griddle over medium heat.

9. Melt the butter in a small saucepan and whisk in the honey. Bring the mixture to a simmer and remove from the heat. Split open the rolls and brush both cut sides with the honey butter. Toast the rolls in the skillet or on the griddle, cut side down, until golden brown, about 1 minute.

10. Spread a thin layer of spicy pickle mayonnaise on the bottom half of the cut side of the roll and top with a chicken breast. Spread a little more mayonnaise on the chicken and close the sandwich with the top of the roll.

CINCINNATI CHILI FIVE-WAY

Whenever I go somewhere I've never been, I do a little restaurant research. The first time I researched Cincinnati, I found myself inundated with chili parlors. I knew about Cincinnati chili, but I had no idea it was so deeply woven into the local culture. I picked out four places to try. If you told me you were going to take spaghetti noodles and dump cinnamon and chocolate-spiked chili on them, I'd say "What are you talking about?" When the first plate was placed in front of me, I thought, "This is the craziest food I've ever seen!" But I liked it enough to eat it four times in one day. It's now one of my favorite got-a-craving foods. This recipe combines the elements I loved from all four places: It includes the heavy spicing of Skyline, the thin consistency of Pleasant Ridge, the finely grated cheese of Camp Washington, and the topping ratio of Gold Star. This might infuriate some people from Cincinnati, but it's actually meant to honor their city's signature dish. Oh, and if you've never had it, *five-way* means it includes chili, spaghetti, onions, beans, and cheese. Two-way is just chili and spaghetti, and you can figure out the numbers in between.

---

1. Heat a 4-quart Dutch oven over high heat and add enough grapeseed oil to coat the bottom of the pot. Add the bison and beef, stirring with a sturdy wooden spoon to break up the clumps; the meat will brown and crumble after about 5 minutes. Add 2 cups of the onion, which will stick a bit; that's okay. Cook the onion until it softens and starts to brown, about 5 minutes. Stir in 1 cup of the chicken stock, and scrape all the brown bits from the pot bottom into the sauce. Bring the mixture to a boil and cook until almost all of the liquid evaporates and the meat starts to brown again, about 3 minutes. Cut the heat down to medium and stir in the tomato paste, warm seasoning blend, chile powder, salt, sugar, cocoa powder, and cinnamon. Stir in 2 more cups of the chicken stock, and again scrape all the browned bits into the sauce. Now you can stir in the garlic; you want to wait until all of the caramelizing is finished before adding the garlic so that it doesn't burn and taste bitter. When added late in the game, the garlic brings a subtle garlic flavor with the heat and sharpness of raw garlic. Cover the pot, cut the heat down so that the liquid simmers gently, and cook for 45 minutes. After the chili is good and flavorful, add the hot sauce.

2. While the chili cooks, prepare the pasta. Pour the remaining chicken broth into a pot and bring to a rolling boil. Add the pasta and cook until tender. Make sure to *fully* cook the pasta—you want it very tender. I really like to cook the pasta in broth instead of water; it adds so much flavor and makes a big difference in the body of the final dish.

3. The five way comes now: For each shallow bowl, layer in the pasta noodles, chili, remaining onions, kidney beans, and finally the cheese.

NEW MEXICO CHILE POWDER / I'm not talking about chili powder here—the blended kind used to flavor ground meat stews you eat while watching the Super Bowl. I'm talking about pure New Mexican red or green chiles that are dried and ground to a powder. If you're buying something in a bottle, read the ingredients to make sure it's just dried ground New Mexican chiles. If you can't find New Mexican ground red chile powder, use ground ancho chile powder instead. Either way, look for pure chile powder, not blended chili powder made with oregano, cumin, and who the hell knows what else.

GUSSIED-UP MAC-N-CHEESE

Thanksgiving in my family is a potluck. I have a big family, so there are always at least seven versions of macaroni and cheese. When I was a kid, my mom would stand at the potluck table and say, "You can't eat just one thing. Try a little of everything." So I took a small spoonful of each variety of macaroni and cheese. My love of mac and cheese was forged at a very young age. I came to like the crunchy topping of the baked version but the creamy sauce of the stovetop version. This recipe combines the two. When I first started making mac and cheese, I made a béchamel with flour and milk, then added cheese. But it never tasted right. The cheese sauce was too grainy. I knew you couldn't just melt the cheese straight because it would separate. The flour stabilizes it and keeps it from separating. Then one day, I was rolling down the aisle of a grocery store and saw Velveeta. I did a double take. "Shouldn't that be refrigerated in the cheese section?" I wondered. I picked up the package and read the ingredient list. It had a stabilizer in it. Perfect! I know Velveeta is not a staple ingredient for professional chefs, but I thought, "I don't give a damn. I'm going to make the same sauce I was making before and use Velveeta instead of flour." It worked like a charm. Velveeta makes the creamiest, cheesiest mac and cheese you've ever tasted. I add sautéed andouille sausage and top the whole thing with crumbled potato chips, because that's just badass.

---

1. Preheat the oven to 375°F. Butter a 3-quart baking dish and set aside.

2. Bring a large pot of water to a rapid boil. Add the salt and stir to dissolve. Add the pasta and cook just until tender yet still quite chewy in the center (a little under the al dente stage). Drain the pasta in a colander and set aside.

3. While the pasta cooks, line a plate with a double layer of paper towels. Squeeze the sausage from the casing, then quarter it lengthwise and cut it crosswise into ¼-inch pieces. Heat an 8-inch skillet over medium-high heat, add the sausage pieces, and cook until browned around the edges, about 3 minutes. Using a slotted spoon, transfer the sausage to the paper towels to drain.

4. In a Dutch oven, heat the cream to a simmer over medium-high heat. Cut the heat down to low, add the Velveeta, and stir until it melts. Add the sausage, cheddar, and Parrano, stirring until the cheese is completely melted. Pull the pot from the heat and fold in the cooked pasta. Pour the pasta into the baking dish and top with the crumbled potato chips.

5. Bake until bubbly and browned around the edges, about 20 minutes. Pull the dish from the oven and let the sauce set up for at least 5 minutes before serving.

ENOUGH FOR 8 HUNGRY FOLKS

Butter
about 1 tablespoon

Salt
about 2 tablespoons

Dried cavatappi
1 pound

Andouille sausage
8 ounces diced, about 1 cup

Heavy cream
4 cups

Velveeta
1 pound, cut into 1-inch cubes

Smoked cheddar cheese
2 cups grated, about 8 ounces

Parrano cheese
1 cup grated, about 4 ounces

Utz potato chips
4 ounces unsalted, crumbled

THE FINE PRINT / If you can't get Parrano cheese, replace it with 2 ounces aged Gouda and 2 ounces Parmigiano-Reggiano.

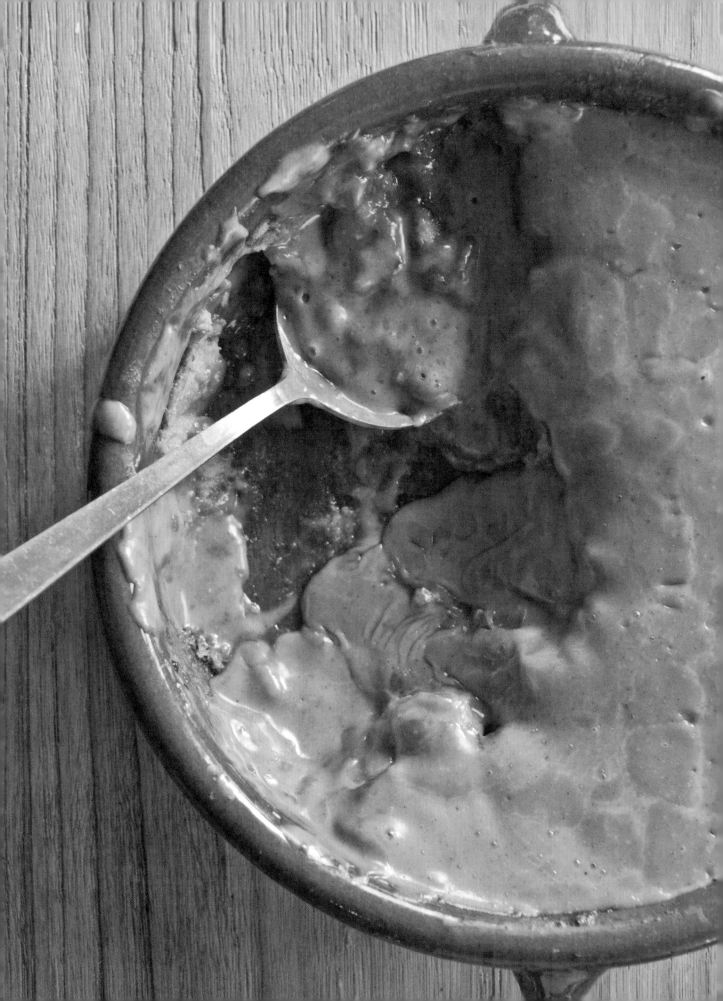

HONEY BUN BREAD PUDDING WITH PEANUT BUTTER–WHISKEY SAUCE

At a gas station one night, a friend of mine made a stupid statement: "You can't cook anything good from ingredients you buy at a gas station." "Bullshit!" I bought a package of honey buns, a jar of peanut butter, and a bottle of whiskey (this wasn't in Georgia, by the way; we don't sell liquor in gas stations). We were staying at my friend's place, and when we got back to the kitchen, I made this dish as over-the-top as I possibly could. It's sickeningly sweet and rich. But that's what makes it awesome plus a thousand.

---

1. Preheat the oven to 325°F. Generously butter a 2-quart baking dish.

2. In a very large bowl, whisk the eggs until frothy. Whisk in the cream, salt, and cinnamon to combine. Break the honey buns into 1-inch pieces and add to the egg mixture. Add the butterscotch chips and stir gently to combine. Pour the honey bun mixture into the baking dish and bake until puffed, golden, and bubbly, 40 to 45 minutes. The custard will be set around the edges and the center will still be a little jiggly. Remove and let rest on a rack for 15 minutes before serving.

3. Serve with the peanut butter–whiskey sauce. You could serve the bread pudding without the sauce, but if you're going to splurge, splurge! For a different flavor, try the citrus butter sauce from the crepes Suzette (page 154).

MAKES ONE 2-QUART CASSEROLE, ENOUGH FOR ABOUT 8 SANE PEOPLE

Eggs
3 large

Heavy cream
1½ cups

Salt
¼ teaspoon

Ground cinnamon
⅛ teaspoon

Little Debbie brand honey buns
9

Butterscotch chips
½ cup

Peanut butter–whiskey sauce (recipe follows)
about 1 cup

PEANUT BUTTER–
WHISKEY SAUCE

MAKES ABOUT 1 CUP

Heavy cream
½ cup

Creamy peanut butter
⅓ cup

Bourbon
3 tablespoons high-alcohol, such as Noah's Mill or Old Rip Van Winkle 10-year

1. Heat the cream in a small heavy pot over medium heat until it starts to simmer. Whisk in the peanut butter until well blended and smooth. The peanut butter is too fatty to melt on its own; the cream stabilizes it so it won't separate or seize. Slowly whisk in the bourbon. Simple, right?

DEEP-FRIED CANDY BARS

It doesn't get much junkier than this. It took a while to get the recipe right, but I think I nailed it. I started out using frozen candy bars on the theory that freezing would keep the candy's filling from melting and leaking out—sort of like fried ice cream. But it didn't work. The candy bars fry so quickly that a frozen filling never even melts. Bamboo skewers turned out to be my big breakthrough in testing. The candy bars were so heavy with batter that they sank to the bottom of the fryer and stuck there. Long skewers allow you to hold the candy bars right in the middle of the hot oil so that they cook evenly and quickly (only 30 seconds!). The fried candy is hot as hell when it comes out of the fryer, but it cools and sets up in just a couple of minutes, so don't wait too long to eat these. The skewers act like handles and make the candy easier to eat. I've fried all kinds of candy bars, from Snickers and Twix to Milky Way and Three Musketeers. The nougat-filled ones work best. Anything with nuts or a lot of caramel doesn't work. And candy bars with a crispy cookie center, like Twix, just get soggy in the middle. Dark chocolate Milky Ways were hands down the best. Seltzer is the secret ingredient in the batter. The bubbles create a fluffy batter that crisps up perfectly in the hot oil.

---

1. Heat the oil in a deep fryer to 375°F.

2. Set a cooling rack over a baking sheet and spray with nonstick cooking spray; set aside.

3. In a large bowl, whisk 1 cup of the flour with the cornstarch and salt. Add a few ice cubes to the seltzer and swirl to chill it. Remove the ice cubes from the water and whisk the water into the cornstarch mixture to form a smooth batter.

4. Spoon the remaining ½ cup flour into a shallow bowl, shaking to spread it. Using eighteen 10-inch wooden skewers, skewer each candy bar lengthwise through a short end so you have one candy bar on the end of each long skewer. Dust the bars with flour and shake off any excess. One at a time, dip and swirl the candy bars in the batter to completely coat. Allow excess batter to drip back into the bowl, then dip the skewers, one by one, into the fryer and fry until crispy, holding them there for 30 to 35 seconds. The crust won't get super dark brown, but you'll get a nice, crisp, light tan coating on each bar. Transfer the skewers to the cooling rack and try to wait for a minute before eating so that you don't burn the shit out of your mouth!

SERVES 6 RAVENOUS SNACKERS

Canola oil for frying

All-purpose flour
1½ cups

Cornstarch
1 tablespoon

Fine sea salt
¼ teaspoon

Seltzer or soda water
1½ cups cold

Dark chocolate Milky Way candy bars
18 fun-size

Chapter

9

NUTS & BOLTS

I am completely unhandy. I can't build or fix a damn thing around the house. On the other hand, my father is brilliant at building, constructing, and fixing just about anything. His basement is like a handyman's dream. The zoning laws were very clear in my parent's house: The upstairs belonged to my mother, and the basement belonged to my father. My dad is a research and development engineer, so I guess it makes sense that his man cave is well stocked with tools and machines. As kid, I thought it was a comical amount of hardware. Is it really necessary that we possess an arc welder at home? I never realized how critical it was to have a set of pneumatic hand tools in one's basement. My father has the ability to sandblast in his home. He also built himself a painting booth so that he could pneumatically paint in a closed environment.

A massive metal chest of drawers lines an entire wall of the basement. It's like the card catalog at the New York Public Library. At least a hundred tiny drawers hold assorted nuts, bolts, screws, fasteners, washers, nails, brads, pins, tacks, spikes, rivets, and brackets collected over a lifetime of building and fixing things. Does this man really need to have all these little bits and pieces at his beck and call at any given time?

It turns out that the answer is yes. Once I started cooking professionally, I understood. Cooks do the same thing. We have a kitchen pantry filled with stocks, broths, sauces, marinades, herb blends, flavored butters, condiments, jams, fillings, and glazes ready at any given time to pull together a dish at a moment's notice. When you're in the middle of constructing a plate of food, these are the little bits that hold it all together. I also realized that I am just as fanatical as my father about outfitting my man cave with cleavers, chef's knives, boning knives, paring knives, frying pans, sizzle pans, roasting pans, saucepans, stock pots, blenders, food processors, ovens, convection ovens, combi-ovens, grills, smokers, tongs, whisks, strainers, graters, zesters, funnels, and spatulas. These are basic kitchen tools that help me assemble something good to eat.

Look at the recipes in this chapter like my dad's wall of nuts and bolts. I admit, this is a much smaller shelf of tidbits, but the recipes here will come in handy whenever you are cooking. I use them all the time. Salsa brava (page 308) turns crispy green beans into something special. Bacon jam (page 309) brings together a basic appetizer of smoked trout puffs (page 130). Tomate frito (page 312) anchors a simple dish of grilled scallops (page 196). You may not cook a single one of my recipes, but these essential preparations should prove helpful beyond the borders of this book. If you're building a sandwich or cooking a Thanksgiving turkey, homemade mayonnaise (page 297) or compound butter (page 295) may be just what you need to pull it together. They don't call it "fixing supper" for nothing.

STOCK AND BROTH

I learned to make stock from every chef I ever worked for. Most chefs roast bones and simmer them with vegetables for seven or eight hours. I always thought stock should be made more simply—with just whole chicken and water—so the flavor would have laser focus and the stock could be used in any dish. You can always add carrots, onions, and celery later on, but you can't take those flavors out once they're in the stock. I wasn't in a position to argue until I became an executive chef. Then I said, "Screw it. I'm using whole birds." Later, I was reading a Michel Roux cookbook that had all kinds of crazy sauces, but I noted that his chicken stock was made with whole birds and cooked for a short period of time. There it was, from a three-star Michelin chef, no less. So I stuck with my method. Technically, this is referred to as white stock because nothing is roasted. Some chefs call it broth. I call it both. I make chicken stock by cutting up a whole bird and simmering it gently for 2 hours, as opposed to 7 or 8 hours. This method gives you a clear, gelatinous stock with a pure unadulterated chicken flavor that works well in a huge range of dishes. You can also just warm it up and drink it as soup.

I make smoked pork broth the same way. Pork bones like knuckles and shins provide the gelatin and smoked ham hocks add a rich, smoky aroma. The pork broth has awesome viscosity. With all that gelatin, you could bounce it like a basketball when it is set and cold. I don't make veal stock at the restaurant, so my pork broth does the job of adding a velvety finish. I use it in a lot of Southern dishes. I get my smoked ham hocks dirt cheap from Benton's (see Sources, page 326). The quantity here is based on Benton's heavily smoked hocks. If you use another brand, you'll probably need to use more to get the same level of smoke flavor.

CHICKEN stock

MAKES ABOUT 10 CUPS

Chicken
1 bird, about 3 pounds

---

1. Cut down along one side of the bird's breastbone, then run the knife along the contour of the rib cage and around the wishbone to remove the breast meat; repeat on the other side and reserve the breast meat. Using kitchen shears, cut from the tail end up to the neck end on either side of the backbone to remove the backbone; place the backbone in an 8-quart stock pot. Cut the chicken wings from the body and put in the stockpot. Bend the leg away from the body, cut down to the joint, then bend the joint to break it; cut between the ball and socket and then down around the carcass to remove the entire leg/thigh portion. Separate the drumsticks and thighs into separate pieces and cut each in half to expose additional bone. Put all of the drumstick and thigh pieces into the pot. Cut the remaining carcass in half and put in the pot. Fill the pot with enough water to completely cover all the bones.

2. Set the pot over high heat and bring to a boil. Cut the heat down so that the liquid simmers very gently; you only want a few bubbles coming up now and then. Using a ladle, skim and discard any foam and fat from the pot. Drop the chicken breasts into the water and poach just until no longer pink (165°F internal temperature), about 15 minutes. Remove the breasts and reserve for another use. Simmer the stock gently for 2 hours, skimming the surface now and then. Pull the pot from the heat and let cool for 1 hour.

3. Using tongs, remove and discard the bones. Strain the stock through a fine-mesh strainer and then through a double layer of wet cheesecloth. Cool to room temperature. Refrigerate for up to 1 week or freeze for up to 6 months.

SMOKED PORK BROTH

MAKES ABOUT 8 CUPS

Smoked ham hocks, shinbones, or knuckles
about 3 pounds

Chicken stock (previous recipe)
10 cups

---

1. Put the smoked pork bones in an 8-quart stockpot and cover with water. Bring to a boil over high heat and boil for 3 minutes. Strain the bones and discard the liquid. Rinse the bones under running water.

2. Return the bones to the pot and add the chicken stock. Set the pot over high heat and bring to a boil. Cut the heat down so that the liquid simmers very gently; you only want a few bubbles coming up now and then. Using a ladle, skim and discard any foam and fat from the pot. Simmer the stock very gently for 2 hours, skimming now and then. Pull the pot from the heat and let cool for 1 hour.

3. Using tongs, remove and discard the bones. (You can shred the meat from the pork bones and reserve it for another use.) Strain the stock through a fine-mesh strainer and then through a double layer of wet cheesecloth to remove any sediment. Cool to room temperature. Refrigerate for up to 1 week or freeze for up to 6 months.

CONCENTRATED FLAVOR / **You can simmer the finished chicken stock or the pork broth until the liquid reduces in volume. Simmering evaporates water and concentrates flavors. It also raises the ratio of gelatin to water and makes the stock more viscous. If freezer space is an issue, the concentrated stock takes up less space, and you can always add water back to the stock later on when ready to use it.**

COMPOUND BUTTER

Don't be scared off by the name. It's just a fancy way of saying you take a bunch of stuff and mix it with butter. The stuff can be anything you want, from salt and pepper to herbs and citrus zest. The beauty of compound butter is that you can keep it on hand and use it to flavor dozens of different dishes over the course of several weeks. To store compound butter, you roll it into a 2-inch-thick log on plastic wrap or parchment paper, seal the log in the plastic or parchment, and refrigerate it for up a week or freeze it for up to a month. Then you slice off little coins as needed and melt them on steak, toss them with green beans, or stir them into ragu. It's a nice way to preserve the fresh flavor of chopped herbs, which oxidize quickly when left out in the open air. But if you chop herbs and mix them with butter, they get coated in a protective layer of fat and retain their delicate aromas. Please, please, please experiment with different flavors. These are just a few of the flavor combos I use throughout the recipes in this book.

GARLIC-HERB BUTTER

MAKES ABOUT 2 CUPS

Fresh herbs
½ cup minced assorted

Garlic
1 monster clove, minced

Lemon zest
1½ teaspoons

Salt
½ teaspoon

Butter
1 cup, at room temperature

---

1. Wrap the minced herbs in a paper towel and squeeze tightly. This will remove some of the bitter juices and dry the herbs so your butter doesn't turn green. Stir the herbs, garlic, lemon zest, and salt into the softened butter. This compound butter is excellent spread on bread, dolloped on steak, or just stirred into steamed or sautéed vegetables.

LEMON-DILL BUTTER

MAKES ABOUT 1⅓ CUPS

Fresh dill
½ cup finely chopped

Lemon
1 plump

Butter
1 cup, at room temperature

Honey
1 tablespoon (optional, for honey-dill butter)

---

1. Wrap the minced dill in a paper towel and squeeze tightly to remove the liquid that could turn your butter green. Stir the dill, ½ teaspoon lemon zest, and ½ teaspoon lemon juice into the softened butter.

2. For honey-dill butter, stir the honey into the lemon zest and juice before adding to the dill and softened butter.

JALAPEÑO-LIME BUTTER

MAKES ABOUT ½ CUP

Jalapeño chile pepper
1 fat one

Cilantro
1 bunch

Lime
1 plump

Garlic
1 teaspoon minced

Salt
1 teaspoon

Butter
½ cup, at room temperature

---

1. Remove the ribs and seeds from the chile and finely dice the flesh.

2. Pick the cilantro from the stems, discard the stems, and mince the leaves. Wrap the minced cilantro in a paper towel and squeeze tightly to remove the liquid that could turn your butter green. Unroll the cilantro and measure out ¼ cup. Wrap any remaining cilantro in another paper towel and store in a zip-top bag in the refrigerator for another use.

3. Using a fork, stir the chile, cilantro, ½ teaspoon lime zest, ¼ teaspoon lime juice, the garlic, and salt into the softened butter.

TOP TO BOTTOM: Tarragon Aioli,
Homemade Mayonnaise,
Spicy Pickle Mayonnaise

MAYONNAISE

Mayonnaise is more technique than recipe. It's an emulsification of oil and water with egg yolks and lemon juice. All that means is you take ingredients that don't normally mix—oil and water—and force them to stay together, or "emulsify" them. Mayonnaise is a fundamental building block for preparing cold dishes in French cuisine and many other cuisines. Think of a tuna fish sandwich. It would be nothing without the mayo. For cold preparations, I always use homemade mayonnaise. It's so easy to make. All you do is blend the ingredients together in a food processor. You have to blend them gradually and in a certain order, but that's all there is to it. The taste of homemade mayonnaise beats the bottled stuff by a mile. Just be sure to follow the directions carefully and start with high-quality ingredients like pasture-raised eggs, plump juicy lemons, and very good grapeseed oil. From there, the sky's the limit with flavor combinations. You can add herbs, garlic, or pickles; swap out some of the oil for bacon fat; or substitute the lemon juice with lime juice or vinegar. Keep the ratio of egg yolk, fat, and acidic ingredients constant, then let your imagination run wild. Note that these mayonnaise recipes do contain raw egg yolks. If you're concerned about the safety of your eggs, buy better eggs—preferably from a farmer you know and trust.

HOMEMADE MAYONNAISE

MAKES ABOUT 2½ CUPS

Egg yolks
4

Water
up to ⅓ cup to thin, if necessary

Salt
2 teaspoons

Lemons
2

Grapeseed oil
2 cups, give or take

1. Slip the egg yolks into the bowl of food processor fitted with the metal blade. Add 2 tablespoons of the water and the salt and process until the yolks are fluffy and pale yellow, about 30 seconds. Add ¼ cup lemon juice and process for another 30 seconds. Scrape down the sides of the bowl with a rubber spatula and process the mixture until it almost doubles in volume, about a minute more. With the processor running, gradually add 1 tablespoon of the oil, drop by drop, to establish the base for the emulsion (the blend of water and fat). Continue to very slowly drizzle in the oil until the processor makes a gurgling sound and then a quieter, choppy sound as the oil becomes incorporated and the mixture thickens. The amount of oil you need to add will vary; it's more important to listen, watch, and judge the mixture as it blends to determine how much oil it needs. When the quieter, choppy sound starts, you've added enough oil. Turn off the processor, remove the top, and scrape down the sides. Cover the processor and process for a final 10 seconds to blend in what you scraped down. If the mixture is too thick, drizzle in a little more water, 1 tablespoon at a time. Refrigerate for at least 1 hour before serving. To store, cover and refrigerate for up to 1 week.

TARRAGON AIOLI

MAKES ABOUT 2 1/2 CUPS

**Homemade mayonnaise
(previous recipe)**
about 2 1/2 cups

Garlic
*2 cloves, peeled and cut
into quarters*

Fresh tarragon leaves
3 tablespoons

1. Make the mayonnaise as directed but add in the garlic when you add the lemon juice. Carry on with the rest of the recipe. After you add all the oil, sprinkle the tarragon leaves over the top of the mixture. Cover the processor, and process for another 10 seconds to incorporate the tarragon. Turn the processor off, remove the top, and scrape down the sides. Cover the processor and process for a final 10 seconds. Refrigerate for at least 1 hour before serving. To store, cover and refrigerate for up to 1 week.

SAUCE GRIBICHE

MAKES ABOUT 1/3 CUP

Olive oil
1 tablespoon + 1 teaspoon

Capers
1 tablespoon chopped

Cornichons
1 tablespoon finely chopped

**Homemade mayonnaise
(previous recipe)**
1 tablespoon

Egg
*2 teaspoons beaten and passed
through a sieve*

Champagne vinegar
1 teaspoon

Shallot
1 teaspoon

Dijon mustard
1/2 teaspoon

Fresh chives
1/4 teaspoon finely chopped

Fresh flat-leaf parsley
1/4 teaspoon finely chopped

Fresh tarragon
1/4 teaspoon finely chopped

Salt and ground black pepper

1. In a small bowl, whisk all of the ingredients until well blended. Season to taste with salt and pepper. Don't worry if it looks lumpy and slightly broken. That's normal for this sauce.

BACON-BASIL MALONNAISE

MAKES 1½ CUPS

Bacon
2 thick slices

Egg yolks
2

Water
1 tablespoon

Lemon
1 plump

Dry mustard
¼ teaspoon

Salt
¼ teaspoon

Grapeseed oil
1 cup

Fresh basil leaves
1 tablespoon, cut into thin strips

1. Heat a sauté pan over medium-high heat and cook the bacon until crisp on the bottom side, about 4 minutes. Cut the heat down to medium, flip the bacon over, and cook until crisp on that side, another 4 to 5 minutes. Transfer the bacon to a paper towel to drain. Reserve the bacon and fat.

2. Slip the egg yolks into the bowl of a small food processor fitted with the metal blade (a mini processor is perfect for this). Add the water and process until the mixture looks fluffy and pale yellow, about 30 seconds. Add 2 tablespoons lemon juice, the dry mustard, salt, and bacon pieces and process until the bacon is finely ground. With the food processor running, gradually add 1 tablespoon of the oil, drop by drop, to establish the base for the emulsion. Continue to very slowly drizzle in the oil until the processor makes a gurgling sound, then process for another 5 seconds. Drizzle in 1 tablespoon of the reserved bacon fat and process until incorporated. Turn off the processor, taste the mayo, and adjust the seasonings with salt and lemon juice as needed; you can also adjust the thickness by adding a little more water to thin it out. Cover the processor and process for a final 10 seconds. Spoon the mayo out of the processor into a bowl and stir in the basil. To store, cover and refrigerate for up to 1 week.

SPICY PICKLE MALONNAISE

MAKES ABOUT 1½ CUPS

Egg yolks
2

Garlic
1 clove, peeled

Frank's RedHot Xtra Hot cayenne pepper sauce
¼ cup

Salt
¼ teaspoon

Dill pickle chips
½ cup patted dry and firmly packed

Grapeseed oil
about 1½ cups

1. Slip the egg yolks into the bowl of a small food processor fitted with the metal blade. Add the garlic and hot sauce, and process until the mixture looks fluffy, about 30 seconds. Add the salt and all but 2 tablespoons of the pickles and process for another 30 seconds. With the processor running, gradually add 1 tablespoon of the oil, drop by drop, to establish the base for the emulsion. Continue to very slowly drizzle in the oil until the processor makes a gurgling sound and then a quieter, choppy sound as the oil becomes incorporated and the mixture thickens. Turn off the processor and add the rest of the pickles; pulse just to combine. Taste the mayonnaise and adjust the flavor with more salt or hot sauce; you can also adjust the thickness by adding a little water to thin it out. If you add ingredients, cover the processor and process for a final 10 seconds. To store, cover and refrigerate for up to 1 week.

My Favorite Roots

The roots of a plant have two basic functions: (1) anchoring the plant to the ground, and (2) store energy for the plant. Some roots store energy as starch (think starchy potatoes), and some store energy as sugar (think sweet carrots). With the exception of potatoes, the root vegetables I use most often taste sweet inside.

CARROTS. Not everyone thinks of carrots as root vegetables, but they should. Carrots can be roasted and pureed just like potatoes. Just be sure to buy good ones. I encourage anyone who shops at a local farmer's market to buy carrots there. Carrots have an extended season in most temperate climates, and farmer's market varieties tend to taste sweeter than what you'll find in the supermarket. Small young ones have the sweetest flavor. As with all root vegetables, carrots get firmer, drier, more fibrous, and less sweet as they age. Look for small ones with the green tops still attached. Heirloom varieties come in all shades from orange and yellow to white and purple. They might look misshapen, but the flavor will be much more intense than big, old, dry carrots from the grocery store.

TURNIPS. The lowly turnip has become one of my all-time favorite vegetables. Maybe it's because they are wildly underappreciated. Or maybe because I fell in love with them the first time I tried turnips raw. When you cook a turnip in water, it soaks up a lot of water, which makes it taste watery and bland. But if you roast a turnip, sauté it, or shave it raw into a salad, it displays a beautifully concentrated blend of sweetness and pungency. You get a subtle whiff of horseradish. I absolutely adore Hakurei turnips. It's a white Japanese crossbreed that ranges in size from a Ping-Pong ball to a golf ball. They have almost no skin and taste outrageously good raw. I also use purple-top turnips but avoid the oversized ones. A little golf ball–size turnip will taste exponentially better than a softball-size one.

RUTABAGAS. Talk about an underappreciated vegetable. Not a lot of people rank rutabagas at the top of their list of favorite things. I, on the other hand, think they're spectacular. They're like turnips but more intense, both sweeter and spicier. But the big, old ones can be impossible to cut. A rutabaga that's been hanging out for too long can be just this side of a rock. If you go to make one of my rutabaga recipes and the only rutabaga you can find is covered in wax, do me a favor and leave the grocery store. You'll need a hydraulic log splitter to get through it, and you won't taste the flavors I was trying to convey in the recipe. On the other hand, a small rutabaga is so tender you can eat the skin.

CELERY ROOT. This is not the root structure of the celery stalks that you see in the grocery store. It comes from a similar plant that's grown primarily for its root. Celery root (celeriac) is also best when it's really young and small. But it's not because the root gets too tough when it ages; it's because it gets soft and spongy. When you cut into a really old celery root, the dead center feels like a loaf of bread. Look for ones with the upper stalk still attached. If the stalk is crisp, green, and leafy, that's a good sign that the root hasn't dried out. Here's one vegetable you'll definitely want to peel.

BEETS. I use three main types of beets: Red Ace, golden, and Chioggia. Red Ace is the standard. It is the sweetest and tastes best roasted. To peel them, I roast the beets whole, let them rest until warm, then rub off the skins with a clean towel. The towel will get stained, so use a towel you don't mind throwing away. Golden beets fall in the middle of the sweetness spectrum. Unlike Red Ace, their color doesn't bleed, so they make a good multipurpose choice for cooking and salads. Chioggias are candy striped . . . When you cut them crosswise, you see red and white rings like peppermint candy. But that color fades when you cook them, so Chioggias are best used raw in salads or marinated.

SUNCHOKE. This is the root clod of a relative of the North American sunflower, the big bright yellow plant everyone knows. Sunchokes come from a similar plant, but one that looks more like a tall grass because the flower isn't as massive. The root grows knobby like ginger and is sold broken up into pieces based on wherever the knobs break easily. Sunchokes are generally cooked skin-on. Skin-off is reserved for days when you feel you need something senseless to do for hours on end. The alternate name, Jerusalem artichoke, comes from the sunchoke's very subtle artichoke-like flavor. It actually tastes like a cross between a waxy potato and an artichoke. Sunchokes are often shaved into salads, but I think they're at their best when roasted. High, dry heat emphasizes their potato-like quality, as the skin crisps up and the interior turns creamy. When I serve roasted sunchokes, people sometimes say, "Oh my god, this is the best-tasting potato I've ever had!"

POTATOES. I use russets, Yukon golds, fingerlings, and about a dozen other potato varieties on a regular basis. Russet Burbanks or "Idaho" potatoes are my go-to for French fries. They have the perfect blend of starch that gets crispy on the outside and fluffy on the inside. Russets also make a luxurious puree. For most other applications, especially when I want the potato to retain its shape after cooking, I use a waxy, thin-skinned type. That could be anything from a common red-skinned potato to a fingerling. The waxy varieties are lower in starch, but Yukon golds occupy the middle ground. They have less starch than a russet but more than a red-skinned potato. I use them almost exclusively for purees and creamy soups because they have such a creamy texture and golden, buttery color.

VEGETABLE PUREES

When I'm pureeing vegetables, I like to cook them in cream instead of water. I often puree the cooked vegetables with cream anyway, so why not cook them in cream right out of the gate? There is some logic behind it. When you cook water-based foods like vegetables in water, a lot of the water and water-soluble flavor compounds leak out from the vegetable into the cooking water. But when you cook the same food in something more viscous, like cream, less water and flavor leak out of the vegetable. Cooking a vegetable in cream retains more of its flavor and moisture, and the puree tastes more intense. Plus, when you use cream as the cooking liquid, the cream itself starts to turn light golden brown, which adds delicious caramel flavors. Another bonus: The puree is less likely to separate when it's kept warm for long periods of time. If you're making Thanksgiving dinner or entertaining guests, you can make these vegetable purees hours ahead of time and keep them warm. I use the purees throughout the recipes in this book, often as a smear of sauce beneath a piece of cooked protein like haggis (page 53), scallops (page 133), or pork shoulder (page 97). Or you could make a creamy vegetable soup by thinning out any one of these purees with a little stock.

CAULIFLOWER PUREE

MAKES ABOUT 1 CUP

Cauliflower
½ head, coarsely cut into large florets

Thyme
6 sprigs, tied together with kitchen twine

Whole milk
¾ cup

Heavy cream
about 2 cups

Lemon
1

Salt
about ½ teaspoon

1. Combine the cauliflower and thyme in a 2½-quart heavy saucepan. Add the milk and enough of the cream to completely cover the cauliflower. Cook over medium-high heat just until bubbles start forming around the edge of the pan, about 3 minutes. Cut the heat down to low and simmer until the cauliflower is very tender, about 20 minutes, stirring now and then. Watch the pot, as it will tend to boil over.

2. Using a slotted spoon, transfer the cauliflower to a blender and add just enough of the cooking liquid to cover the cauliflower, about ½ cup. Discard the bundle of thyme and reserve the cooking liquid. Add ½ teaspoon lemon juice and the salt to the blender and puree until the mixture is smooth and velvety, about 1 minute; add a little more cooking liquid if the mixture is too thick to puree.

3. Using a rubber spatula, press the puree through a fine-mesh strainer and discard the solids. This extra step ensures you have a smooth, velvety puree. The mixture will be about the texture of a thick custard.

CARAMELIZED TURNIP
AND POTATO PUREE

MAKES ABOUT 3 CUPS

Russet potato
1 fist-size, about 8 ounces, peeled and cut into 1-inch cubes, about 2 cups

Turnips
2 baseball-size, peeled and cut into 1-inch cubes, about 2 cups

Heavy cream
about 2 cups

Salt
1 teaspoon

1. Combine the potatoes and turnips in a 2½-quart heavy saucepan and add just enough of the cream to cover the vegetables. Stir in the salt. Cover and bring the mixture to a boil over high heat. Watch carefully because once it starts bubbling, it will boil over lightning fast! Remove the lid and cut the heat down to low. Simmer, without stirring, until the mixture starts to separate and looks like it is curdling, about 1½ hours. The milk solids will sink to the bottom of the pan and form a thick coating, and the vegetables will start to caramelize. I realize it's hard not to stir, and it seems like a crazy long time, but you have to cook the mixture this long without stirring for it to caramelize and develop a really rich flavor; you want the cream to reduce down in volume and thicken so the finished puree has a silky texture.

2. Pull the pan from the heat and use a wooden spoon to scrape all the browned bits from the bottom of the pan into the mixture. Spoon the vegetables into an upright blender and add just enough of the cooking cream to cover the vegetables. Blend to a smooth and velvety puree, about 2 minutes. Using a rubber spatula, press the puree through a fine-mesh strainer for an even more velvety texture. Your puree will be about the consistency of a thick custard.

RUTABAGA AND TURNIP PUREE

MAKES ABOUT 1½ CUPS

Rutabaga
1 baseball-size, peeled and cut into ½-inch dice, about 1 cup

Turnip
1 baseball-size, peeled and cut into 1-inch dice, about ½ cup

Heavy cream
about 1½ cups

Salt
¾ teaspoon

1. Combine the rutabaga and turnip in a 2½-quart heavy saucepan and add enough of the cream to cover by about 1 inch. Stir in the salt. Cover and bring the mixture to a boil over high heat. Watch carefully because once it starts to bubble, it will boil over lickety-split! Remove the lid and cut the heat down to low. Simmer until the vegetables are so tender you can easily smash a piece of the rutabaga between your fingers with light pressure, about 1 hour.

2. Pull the pan from the heat and let the mixture cool for 20 to 30 minutes. Spoon the vegetables into a blender and add just enough of the cooking cream so the mixture will puree and become smooth and velvety. Using a rubber spatula, press the puree through a fine-mesh strainer for an even more velvety texture. Your puree will be about the consistency of a thick custard.

HOLLANDAISE SAUCE

I learned this recipe on day three of culinary school. It's one of the French mother sauces along with mayonnaise (page 297), béchamel (milk thickened with flour and butter), velouté (chicken, veal, or fish stock thickened with flour and butter), and espagnole (veal stock flavored with various seasonings and thickened with browned butter and flour). In the world of packets and highly processed food, people forget that there is a clearly defined historical origin for hollandaise. I didn't invent it, but I do advocate that you make the sauce properly. This is my best translation of classic hollandaise made on the stovetop. Béarnaise is very similar (you boil down vinegar with shallots and garlic and add herbs), but in that recipe I use a more contemporary food processor method. You can use either method with each sauce. Either way, the recipes are meant to be building blocks. If you think a couple flavors would go well together, try them together in hollandaise.

MAKES ABOUT 1¼ CUPS

Egg yolks
3

Water
1 tablespoon + 2 teaspoons

Clarified butter
1 cup, warm

Lemon juice
2 teaspoons

Salt
1 teaspoon

Cayenne pepper
⅛ teaspoon

1. Pour 2 cups water into a 2-quart saucepan and bring to a boil over high heat. Cut the heat down to medium so that the liquid maintains a low simmer.

2. In a large stainless-steel mixing bowl, whisk the egg yolks with 1 tablespoon of the water. Pull the saucepan from the hot burner and set the mixing bowl of egg yolks over the top so the steam gently heats the bowl. Whisk the egg yolks nonstop over the steaming pan until they are thick, fluffy, and lemon colored, about 2 minutes. Getting a nice thick egg yolk mixture to start is very important. Return the pan-bowl combination to the heat. Leaving the bowl on the pan, rapidly whisk the yolks while very slowly drizzling in ¼ cup of the clarified butter. Remove the bowl from the pan and, using a rubber spatula, scrape the sides down. Whisk in 1 teaspoon hot tap water and repeat the process, moving the bowl back and forth from the steaming pan, slowly whisking in the remaining clarified butter, scraping down the sides of the bowl and whisking in 1 teaspoon hot tap water each time, until all of the butter is incorporated. You'll need to move your bowl to and from the steam to maintain a sauce-like consistency. If the mixture cools down, it will thicken up too much and get clumpy; to solve the problem, just move the bowl back to the steam and whisk to warm the butter and thin the sauce. It's a lot of back and forth because too much steam will scramble the eggs but not enough will make the hollandaise too thick. You'll quickly figure out the process. When all of the butter is incorporated, finish the sauce by whisking in the lemon juice, salt, and cayenne. Serve immediately.

3. To rewarm the sauce, place it in a large stainless-steel bowl and whisk over a pan of steaming water, which will gradually warm and thin the sauce to the proper consistency.

BÉARNAISE <u>SAUCE</u>

**MAKES ABOUT
1¼ CUPS**

Shallot
1 tablespoon finely minced

Garlic
¼ teaspoon finely minced

Fresh tarragon leaves
2 tablespoons finely minced

Black peppercorns
½ teaspoon

Red wine vinegar
¼ cup

Egg yolks
3

Water
2 tablespoons

Salt
about ¾ teaspoon + a Kevin pinch

Clarified butter
1 cup, warm

Lemon juice
2 teaspoons

Cayenne pepper
⅛ teaspoon

1. Combine the shallot, garlic, 1 tablespoon of the tarragon leaves, and the peppercorns in a small sauté pan. Add the red wine vinegar and cook over medium-low heat until the shallots are very soft and the liquid reduces in volume to about 2 tablespoons, 5 minutes or so. Pull the pan from the heat and strain the liquid through a fine-mesh strainer, reserving the liquid and discarding the solids.

2. Slip the egg yolks into the bowl of a food processor fitted with a metal blade. Add 1 tablespoon of the water and a Kevin pinch of salt. Turn the processor on and allow it to whip the yolks until they are very light yellow and fluffy, about 30 seconds. With the processor still running, add the strained vinegar reduction and process for 15 seconds. Begin adding the warm clarified butter, drop by drop at first, then in a very slow, thin stream through the feed tube of the food processor. When half of the butter is added, turn the processor off and scrape down the sides. Turn the processor back on, drizzle in 1 more tablespoon water, then drizzle in the remaining butter in a slow stream. The mixture will thicken. Add the lemon juice, ¾ teaspoon salt, cayenne, and the remaining 1 tablespoon minced tarragon and process just long enough to combine everything. If you want a thinner sauce, add a little more warm water. Pour the béarnaise into a heatproof glass bowl, cover, and place over a pot of warm water to keep warm until ready to serve. Stir the sauce briskly before using.

SLOW-ROASTED PORK BELLY

Use this simple presentation for bok choy and pork belly (page 244) or breakfast füd (page 262).

MAKES ABOUT 1 POUND

Slab pork belly
about 1 pound

Salt
2 tablespoons

Apple cider vinegar
1 cup

1. Preheat the oven to 300°F. Rub both sides of the pork belly with salt. Place in a small roasting pan that just holds the slab and add the vinegar. Wrap tightly with foil and roast for 3 hours.

2. Remove from the oven and let rest wrapped in the foil until the pork cools to room temperature. Refrigerate until ready to use or up to 2 days.

SHERRY VINEGAR REDUCTION

France has *gastrique,* and Italy has *agrodolce.* They're both mixtures of vinegar and sugar boiled down until thick and syrupy. Sweet and sour is one of the world's most common flavor combinations, from Chinese sweet-and-sour sauce to American ketchup. Here, the flavors come from sherry vinegar, orange juice, and raw cane sugar. Don't be afraid to crank up the heat here. The faster you reduce (or boil down) the vinegar, the more intense the flavors will be. I use this sauce for grilled salmon with rapini (page 197), but you could use it with almost any grilled fish. Or try switching up the flavors by using balsamic vinegar, Banyuls vinegar, or champagne vinegar and palm sugar, muscovado sugar, or black sugar. Any of those flavors would be bang-on with pork.

MAKES ABOUT ½ CUP

Oranges
3 plump

Best-quality sherry vinegar
1 cup

Raw cane sugar (turbinado sugar)
½ cup

Salt
¼ teaspoon

1. Using a vegetable peeler, remove a 1-inch strip of peel from one of the oranges. Squeeze the oranges to make ¾ cup juice. Mix the orange peel, juice, vinegar, sugar, and salt in a 10-inch skillet. Bring the mixture to a boil over high heat, then cut the heat down a little and simmer aggressively until the liquid reduces in volume and thickens to a maple syrup consistency, about 10 minutes. The reduction should be thick enough to coat a spoon, which means that when you dip a spoon into the reduction and take it out and drag your finger across the back of the spoon, the reduction should be thick enough so that the line stays clean. Pull the pan from the heat and use immediately, or refrigerate the reduction in a covered container for up to 3 weeks. As the mixture cools, it will thicken. Bring to room temperature and thin with a little hot water before using.

TAHINI SAUCE

Tahini is the workhorse of Middle Eastern cuisine. It's like peanut butter but made from sesame seeds. In Lebanon, Israel, and Syria, most of the food is light and lean. Tahini adds richness and a slight bitter edge. This sauce is pretty classic, including lemon juice for acidity, garlic for pungency, and a drop of honey for sweetness. When you're making the sauce, you'll see it clump up as you stir in the lemon juice. Don't worry; just keep stirring. The sauce will eventually become smooth. If it doesn't, trickle in a little water until it gets nice and smooth. At that point, the sauce will be bulletproof. You can hold it in the refrigerator for several days without it separating. I use this sauce to balance the flavors of cast-iron skillet chicken (page 89) and as a garnish for shawarma (page 188). You could also use it on a simple grilled chicken sandwich.

MAKES ABOUT 1 CUP

Lebanese tahini
½ cup

Lemon
1 plump

Garlic
1 clove, mashed to a paste, about 1 teaspoon

Salt
1 teaspoon

Olive oil
about ⅓ cup

Honey
a drop, if needed

1. In a medium bowl, whisk the tahini, 2 tablespoons lemon juice, the garlic, and salt until the mixture is very thick or "tightened." It will get so thick that you'll have trouble stirring it. Keep stirring; your arm will get tired, but keep stirring for about 2 minutes. Slowly whisk in just enough water—2 to 3 tablespoons—to bring the tahini back to its original spoonable consistency. Slowly whisk in the olive oil until the mixture is smooth. When you taste the sauce, you should detect a dry bitterness with a touch of acidity. If the sauce tastes flat or overly bitter, add a little salt and just a drop of honey. Store tightly covered in the refrigerator for up to 3 months. Bring to room temperature before serving.

TAHINI / You can find tahini, or ground sesame paste, in most grocery stores these days; but the quality varies wildly. Some brands taste mild and nutty; others taste nasty and bitter. When adding lemon juice and salt, let your taste buds guide you. You want to add just enough to balance out any bitterness. Or look for Lebanese tahini, which is consistently less bitter than tahini from other origins (see Sources, page 327).

SALSA BRAVA

You see *patatas bravas* in almost every Spanish tapas restaurant. It's fried potatoes with spicy tomato sauce. My version of the sauce isn't traditional but embodies the spirit of brava sauce with plucky, peppery, pungent, fiery flavors. I use raw garlic for pungency, smoked chile powder for fire and smoke, sherry vinegar for acidity, and fennel pollen for floral aroma. It's good on everything, so make extra. Try it as a dip for anything fried, serve it with scrambled eggs, or spoon it over grilled fish or meat. This is absolutely one of the single-most-requested recipes at Woodfire Grill. I never bothered to write down the recipe. I just put it together whenever I need it. I like it very plucky (see page 11) because I usually serve it with fried food like crispy green beans (page 227). But if you are serving it with eggs, adjust the flavors as necessary.

MAKES ALMOST 3 CUPS

Canned whole tomatoes
14½-ounce can

Piquillo chile peppers
12-ounce jar, drained

Garlic
2 heads, about 12 cloves, peeled

Sherry vinegar
1 tablespoon + 1 teaspoon

Sweet paprika
1 tablespoon

Fennel pollen
2 teaspoons

Salt
2 teaspoons

Espelette pepper
1 teaspoon

Smoked serrano chile powder
1 teaspoon

Ground cinnamon
¼ teaspoon

Olive oil
¼ cup

1. In a food processor fitted with a metal blade, blend the tomatoes and their juice, the piquillo peppers, garlic, vinegar, paprika, fennel pollen, salt, Espelette pepper, serrano chile powder, and cinnamon, about 5 seconds. The mixture should be a little chunky and loose. With the processor running, slowly add the olive oil in a steady stream. The mixture should be fairly smooth. Transfer the mixture to a bowl and let the flavors develop for at least 30 minutes and up to 2 hours. Taste and adjust the seasoning with additional salt and vinegar as needed. Salsa brava should have an aggressive, strong flavor because it is used in small amounts to punch up the flavor of a dish.

PREP TIP / Piquillo peppers, fennel pollen, and smoked serrano chile powder are becoming more available these days, but if you can't find them, see the Sources on page 327. You can also replace the serrano chile powder with chipotle chile powder and swap out the sweet paprika for smoked paprika.

BACON JAM

This recipe became famous on *Top Chef* Season 6. They gave us an escargot challenge at Daniel Boulud's restaurant in Las Vegas. I had never cooked with snails before, but I did know from eating them dozens of times that they don't have a lot going on. Not much fat, not much flavor. I needed richness, and bacon was in our cook's pantry. I didn't want to cook strips or chunks of bacon because that would steal the show from the snails. I tried something completely off the cuff. I roasted the bacon, then braised it. After a long braising time, it developed the same viscous, intense sweetness as fruit jam. The judges liked it. Boulud thought it was a classic Southern recipe from my grandmother. I suppose there is a timeless quality to it. I created it for seafood, and it does work better on fish than on meat. Adding bacon jam to a grilled rib eye would be sickeningly rich. But on poached shrimp, snails, or a lean fillet of fish, it's perfect.

The recipe is made like risotto. You add liquid to the bacon in a pot, let it boil down until it's almost gone, then add more liquid. The deep flavor of the jam depends 100 percent on your allowing the liquid to evaporate each time. After three or four additions of liquid, the bacon should be so tender that a fork will slide in and out of it. Think of the bacon as a piece of fruit. It has to get supersoft before it can become jam.

MAKES 1½ CUPS

Bacon
8 ounces, cut into 2-inch lengths

Onion
¼ cup sliced lengthwise into ¼-inch strips

Salt

Dark brown sugar
3 tablespoons packed

Chicken stock
3 cups

Ground black pepper

Espelette pepper
½ teaspoon

Honey
1 tablespoon

Butter
1 tablespoon

1. Heat a Dutch oven over medium-high heat and add the bacon; cook for 1 minute, stirring a couple of times. Cut the heat down to medium and cook until the fat has cooked out of the bacon (rendered), about 8 minutes. Add the onion and a pinch of salt to the pot. Stir and cook until browned, an additional 5 minutes. Add the brown sugar and stir to combine. Crank the heat up to high, add 1 cup of the stock, and bring the mixture to a boil. Cut the heat down to medium and cook the mixture at an aggressive simmer until it's thick and almost all of the liquid evaporates, about 10 minutes. Add another 1 cup stock and repeat the process. When the mixture thickens to a jam-like consistency, add the remaining 1 cup stock and stir in a Kevin pinch of salt, 6 grinds of black pepper, and the Espelette pepper. Add the honey to the mixture and carefully transfer to a blender; it will be hot. Blend the mixture until smooth, then return it to the pot and cook over medium-high heat, stirring a few times, until it reduces in volume to about 1½ cups and turns brick red, about 10 minutes. Pull the pot from the heat and, using a sturdy wooden spoon, stir in the butter.

PREP AHEAD / The bacon jam can be covered and refrigerated for up to 2 weeks. Just warm it up a bit before serving.

OVEN-ROASTED TOMATO SAUCE

I make this recipe at the end of the summer, when I'm up to my elbows in "scratch and dent" tomatoes. Then I can it so I have tomato sauce all winter long. It doesn't matter what kind of tomatoes you use, as long as they are overripe. Those are the ones you want here. Follow the directions closely. It might seem strange, but you want to char the top of the tomatoes in the oven. The tomatoes should blister and caramelize; that's how you develop rich, roasty flavor. The tomatoes will look quite dry and you might think, "How the hell is this a sauce?" But don't worry—when you pass them through a food mill, the tomatoes will take on the consistency of perfectly thickened tomato sauce. I like a little punch in the sauce, so I roast Calabrian chiles and garlic along with the tomatoes. If you don't like spicy food, leave out the chiles. If you have some oregano in the garden, add that to the sauce. Tomato sauce is pretty adaptable.

1. Preheat the oven to 500°F. Spray a 16 by 12-inch roasting pan with nonstick spray.

2. Add the onion, garlic, and peppers to the pan and scatter on the brown sugar, shaking the pan to distribute everything. Quarter the tomatoes and arrange in a single layer in the pan, skin side up. Sprinkle the tomatoes evenly with the salt.

3. Transfer the roasting pan to the oven and roast until the tomatoes are evenly charred, 15 to 20 minutes. Stir the tomatoes so that the uncharred sides of the tomatoes are exposed to the air. Roast for another 15 to 20 minutes. Stir again and roast for another 15 to 20 minutes. Set aside to cool.

4. Pass the tomato mixture through a food mill fitted with the medium disk. Stir in about ¼ teaspoon lemon juice, then taste the sauce. Every tomato is different; you may need a little more salt, a little more lemon juice, a little more brown sugar, or all three.

MAKES ALMOST 3 CUPS

Vidalia onion
1 softball-size, thinly sliced

Garlic
12 cloves, halved and crushed

Pickled Calabrian chile peppers
6 plump ones, stems on

Dark brown sugar
1 teaspoon

Heirloom tomatoes
4 pounds extremely ripe

Salt
2 ½ teaspoons

Lemon
1 plump

TOMATE FRITO

This sauce is almost like tomato confit. You mix the ingredients raw, put them in a pan with a copious amount of olive oil, and let the whole mess cook undisturbed for a ridiculously long time. Within a couple of hours, the water cooks out of the tomatoes and they begin to fry. That's the *frito* part. Once that happens, the tomato flavor concentrates tremendously. It's so much more delicious than letting tomatoes stew on the stovetop. Oranges and red wine vinegar add brightness. Capers and anchovies add salty punch. Onions, garlic, and fennel bring subtle aromas, and red pepper flakes give it a spicy edge. With the concentrated tomato flavor, the sauce tastes savory, sweet, salty, and pungent all at once. It's meant to be eaten at room temperature, when the flavors are most in balance. I like it with grilled scallops (page 196) or any seafood. It's also fantastic on pasta. It can be refrigerated for weeks, so you'll have plenty of opportunities to use it.

---

1. Put the oranges, tomatoes and juice, onion, fennel, olives, capers, garlic, and tomato paste in separate piles in a deep 12-inch sauté pan. Lay the anchovies over the top, pour in the vinegar, and sprinkle with the salt and red pepper flakes. Add just enough of the olive oil to cover the ingredients. I like to leave everything in individual mounds for better caramelization.

2. Cover the pan and bring to a boil over high heat. Cut the heat down to low, cover, and cook for 15 minutes. Remove the lid and gently stir to combine the ingredients, scraping up all the caramelized bits into the sauce.

3. Continue cooking, uncovered, at a low simmer for another hour, stirring now and then just to keep the mixture from sticking to the bottom of the pan. Almost all of the water will cook out of the vegetables and the mixture will start to sizzle like it's frying. The color will also change from bright tomato red to darker, muddy brick red.

4. Remove and discard the orange pieces. Stir the mixture, again scraping up any caramelized bits into the sauce. Pull the pan from the heat and let the mixture cool to room temperature. Transfer to a covered container and store in the refrigerator, where it will keep for about a month. The oil will rise to the top as the mixture cools; skim off all but a thin layer of oil before using.

MAKES ABOUT 4 CUPS

Navel oranges
2, each cut into 8 wedges, peels on

Whole peeled canned plum tomatoes
28-ounce can

Onion
1 baseball-size, diced, about 1 ½ cups

Fennel
½ baseball-size bulb, diced, about 1 cup

Oil-cured Arbequina olives
½ cup pitted and coarsely chopped

Nonpareil capers
¼ cup (nonpareils are the smallest variety of capers)

Garlic
6 fat cloves, coarsely chopped, about 3 tablespoons

Tomato paste
3 tablespoons

Vinegar-marinated white anchovy fillets
7

Red wine vinegar
1 cup

Salt
3 tablespoons

Dried red pepper flakes
1 teaspoon

Olive oil
about 2 cups

TOMATO JAM

You probably know your way around canned tomatoes. Here's another trick to stash up your sleeve. It's basically homemade ketchup but exponentially better. You boil the tomatoes with sugar and spices until they break down and get nice and thick, then puree everything with a blender. Once you make this, you'll be slathering it on burgers, dunking fries in it, and serving it with eggs. I like it with venison kabobs (page 220). It's also surprisingly good with vanilla ice cream and a drizzle of honey.

1. Empty the can of tomatoes and juice into a heavy-duty, nonreactive 3-quart saucepan. Using your hands, squeeze and crush the tomatoes. Stir in the tomato paste, onion, sugar, vinegar, garlic, salt, and cinnamon and bring the mixture to a boil over medium-high heat. Cut the heat down to medium-low and simmer until the mixture thickens, about 45 minutes, stirring now and then. Pull the pan from the heat and use an immersion blender or upright blender to puree the mixture until smooth. Return the mixture to the heat and simmer until it has a thick, jam-like consistency, another 10 minutes. Store, covered, in the refrigerator for up to 3 months.

MAKES ABOUT 2 CUPS

Whole peeled canned plum tomatoes
28-ounce can

Tomato paste
6-ounce can

Onion
⅓ cup finely minced

Dark brown sugar
½ cup packed

Red wine vinegar
¼ cup

Garlic
3 tablespoons minced

Salt
1 teaspoon

Ground cinnamon
¼ teaspoon

FRIED CROUTONS

Croutons have a singular purpose: to add crunch. The name itself means "crusty cubes." I use them to alter the texture of a dish without turning the spotlight away from the dish's main ingredients. Look at the buttermilk-marinated fennel with satsumas and jalapeños (page 161), for instance. It has some really big flavors, but you lose a lot of texture because the ingredients are cut small. Croutons add textural contrast without altering the other flavors. Gazpacho is another good example. Drop a few croutons in there and when you're five sips in and getting tired of the soft vegetable puree, a bite of something crunchy makes the soup exciting again. For a simple variation on these, replace the olive oil with strained, rendered bacon fat.

MAKES ABOUT 1 CUP

Olive oil
about ¾ cup

Day-old rustic Italian or sourdough bread
3 slices, each about ½ inch thick

Salt
about ½ teaspoon

1. Heat a 10-inch sauté pan over medium-high heat. Add the olive oil to a ¼-inch depth in the pan and heat the oil to 325°F. The relatively low frying temperature allows the croutons to soak up a little oil, which adds flavor and keeps the croutons from being too crunchy all the way through.

2. Line a plate with a double layer of paper towels.

3. Trim and discard the crusts from the bread. Using a serrated knife, cut the bread into perfect ½-inch cubes. Add the cubes to the pan and stir for 1 minute to coat with the oil. Cook undisturbed until the croutons turn a light golden brown, about 2 more minutes. The croutons will continue cooking a little after you remove them from the pan, so keep that in mind; you don't want them too crunchy. Using a slotted spoon, transfer the croutons to the paper towels and immediately sprinkle with the salt. These croutons should be made just before using because their high oil content gives them a short shelf life of only 2 hours or so.

PEACH **BUTTER**

This is my riff on apple butter. We get a hell of a lot more peaches in Georgia than we get apples. During peach season, we're up to our eyeballs in them, and they ripen fast. I love them fresh, but they lose a lot of flavor when you cook them. I figured out a way to bring that flavor back. Peaches have a stone (pit) in the center, which is very closely related to the kernel inside an apricot and to the kernel inside an almond (which is the actual almond nut). Used in small quantities, apricot kernel oil and almond extract make cooked peaches taste more like fresh peaches. Peach butter on warm biscuits (page 62) is one of my favorite morning foods, and it's absolutely mind-blowing on pork chops. I also use it as the base for caramelized peach ice cream (page 102). It's not especially perishable, so keep some in the fridge. I've never had it on hand long enough for it to go bad.

1. Combine the peaches, brown sugar, cinnamon, allspice, cloves, nutmeg, and salt in a Dutch oven. Cover and simmer over medium-high heat for 10 minutes. Give it a stir, then cut the heat down to low, cover, and cook until the peaches are soft, about 25 minutes. Remove the lid, crank the heat up to medium, and simmer until the peaches are falling apart, another 20 minutes. Stir in the almond extract and pull the pot from the heat. Let the mixture cool for 10 minutes. Puree the peaches with a stick blender or in an upright blender until smooth.

2. Heat a 12-inch skillet over high heat until smokin' hot. If the pan isn't actually sending smoke into the air, it's not hot enough. Pour the peach puree into the hot pan and use the washing machine method (see page 12) to stir until you smell the mixture starting to caramelize, about a minute. Pull the pan from the heat and continue stirring for another minute. The mixture will be a shade darker and smell fabulous . . . peaches, caramel, yum.

3. Cool the peach butter to room temperature, then transfer to an airtight container and refrigerate until ready to use.

MAKES ABOUT 2 CUPS

Peaches
3 pounds very ripe ones, pitted and cut into ½-inch wedges (peel left on), about 8 cups

Light brown sugar
1 cup packed

Ground cinnamon
½ teaspoon

Ground allspice
a pinch

Ground cloves
a pinch

Freshly grated nutmeg
a pinch

Salt
a pinch

Almond extract
⅛ teaspoon

LEFT TO RIGHT: Horseradish,
Shallots, Beets, Rutabaga

QUICK PICKLES AND PRESERVES

Most people know pickles as cucumber dill pickles, but a pickle is more of a preservation technique than a specific food. The method is pretty straightforward. You heat up an acidic liquid like vinegar, lemon juice, or lime juice along with whatever spices you like—such as coriander, black pepper, and garlic—then submerge the food to be pickled in the liquid and let it cool. The water rushes out of the food and the pickling liquid rushes in. Make sure your pickling liquid is aggressively seasoned. A bland pickle is no more useful than a broken bucket. Pickles are supposed to be little flavor bombs. They should taste sour and salty and be crunchy at the same time. More often than not, their role in a dish is to grab your attention. When a sandwich starts to get boring, a bite of pickle makes it pop again. I use quick pickles all over the recipes in this book, from pickled beets with charred broccoli (page 22) to pickled garlic with grilled sturgeon (page 186) to pickled horseradish with Scotch eggs (page 122).

PICKLED RUTABAGA

MAKES ABOUT 1 CUP

Rutabaga
1/2 pound, peeled and cut into 1/4-inch dice, about 1 cup

Champagne vinegar
1 cup

Sugar
1 cup

Water
1/2 cup

Dry mustard
2 tablespoons

Ground turmeric
2 teaspoons

Salt
1/4 teaspoon

1. Combine the rutabaga, vinegar, sugar, water, dry mustard, turmeric, and salt in a nonreactive saucepan. Bring to a boil over high heat and then cut the heat down to medium-low so that the liquid maintains a steady simmer. Simmer the rutabagas until they are fork-tender, about 45 minutes. Pull the pan from the heat and let the rutabagas cool in the pickling liquid. Store in a glass jar with a tight-fitting lid in the refrigerator for up to 2 weeks.

PICKLED HORSERADISH

MAKES ABOUT 1/2 CUP

Horseradish root
1 thick piece, about 2 inches long

Garlic
1 clove, quartered

Champagne vinegar
1 cup

Dry mustard
1 teaspoon

Salt
1 teaspoon

1. Peel the horseradish and grate on a Microplane grater to measure 1/2 cup packed. You can make more, but your arm will get really, really tired as it's a very firm root and it's hard to grate! Combine the horseradish with the garlic in a small bowl.

2. In a small nonreactive saucepan, combine about a tablespoon of the vinegar with the dry mustard and stir to make a paste. Slowly stir in the remaining vinegar and salt and bring to a boil over high heat. Pull the pan from the heat and pour the hot liquid over the horseradish and garlic. Cool to room temperature, about an hour. Strain the horseradish and reserve 1/4 cup of the liquid. Combine the horseradish and reserved liquid in a half-pint canning jar, cover tightly, and refrigerate for up to 2 weeks.

PICKLED BEETS

MAKES 2 CUPS

Beets
3 Hacky Sack–size

Water
about ¼ cup

Cider vinegar
2 cups

Sugar
1 cup

Yellow mustard seeds
2 tablespoons

Salt
1½ teaspoons

Star anise
2 pods

Cinnamon stick
1 piece, about 4 inches

1. Preheat the oven to 375°F.

2. Rinse the beets and trim off the stem ends so the beets will sit flat. If the roots are long, trim and discard them. Pour the water into a small baking dish that will hold the beets in a single layer. Set the beets, flat end down, in the dish and cover the dish with foil. Transfer to the oven and bake until the beets are just fork-tender, about 30 minutes; the baking time really depends on how fresh your beets are. If they're freshly picked, they'll cook much quicker than if they've been held in cold storage at a grocery warehouse. You don't need the beets to be completely soft through and through but cooked just enough to absorb the pickling liquid later on.

3. While the beets are cooking, make the pickling liquid. Combine the vinegar, sugar, mustard seeds, salt, star anise, and cinnamon in a nonreactive pan and bring to a boil. Cut the heat down to low and simmer gently for 5 minutes. Pull the pan from the heat and strain and discard the solids.

4. Pull the baking dish from the oven and remove the foil. Let the beets rest just until they are cool enough to slip off the skins, 10 to 15 minutes. Rub your hands with a little oil so they won't get stained with beet juice. Using a clean but ratty towel (one you don't mind ruining), rub the skins off the beets and discard. This method is better than using a vegetable peeler because you don't lose any of the beet along with the skin.

5. At this point, you can cut the beets any way you like—slices, wedges, batons, or even with a melon baller to make tiny beet balls! The larger the piece, the longer it will take to completely absorb the pickling liquid.

6. Either way, put the cut beets into a pint jar and add enough pickling liquid to cover the beets. Cover and refrigerate for at least 2 days before using. The pickling liquid can be strained and reused, or you can boil down the pickling liquid to make a beet syrup—great for a sauce or plate garnish. The beet syrup would be great drizzled over greens, and it's perfect for potatoes and fabulous with goat cheese.

PICKLED SHALLOTS

MAKES ABOUT ¾ CUP

Sugar
½ cup

Cinnamon stick
1 piece, about 2 inches long

Red wine vinegar
½ cup

Allspice berries
3

Star anise
1 pod

Shallots
6, thinly sliced on a mandoline

1. Combine the sugar, red wine vinegar, star anise, cinnamon, and allspice in a medium saucepan and bring to a boil over a high heat. Using a slotted spoon, fish out the whole spices and discard them. Add the shallots and blanch in the pickling liquid for 1 minute. Fish out the shallots and spread them in a single layer on a baking sheet; let cool to room temperature. Pour about half of the pickling liquid into an 8-ounce jar and cool to room temperature. Add the shallots to the pickling liquid in the jar, cover, and store in the refrigerator for up to 3 weeks.

PICKLED GARLIC

MAKES A LITTLE MORE THAN ¼ CUP

Garlic
6 cloves, coarsely chopped, about ½ cup

Champagne vinegar
3 tablespoons

1. Combine the garlic and vinegar in an 8-ounce jar and secure the lid. Shake to combine and let sit until the flavors blend, at least 30 minutes and up to 3 days. For a different look, you can also slice the garlic.

CANDIED GARLIC SYRUP

MAKES ABOUT ½ CUP CANDIED GARLIC CLOVES AND 1¼ CUPS CANDIED GARLIC SYRUP

Sugar
1 cup

Cider vinegar
1 cup

Garlic
3 whole heads, each clove peeled and trimmed of its woody end, about 30 cloves total

1. In a small nonreactive saucepan, stir together the sugar and vinegar and bring to a boil over medium-high heat. Add the garlic and cut the heat down to low; cook until the garlic is golden brown and soft, about 30 minutes. Store the garlic in the syrup mixture, covered, in the refrigerator.

CONFIT GARLIC

MAKES ABOUT ½ CUP CLOVES AND 2 CUPS GARLIC OIL

Garlic
3 whole heads, each clove peeled and trimmed of its woody end, about 30 cloves total

Olive oil
2 cups

1. Put the garlic cloves and olive oil in a small saucepan. Bring the oil almost to a simmer over medium heat, but don't let it boil. Cut the heat down to low and cook until the garlic is golden brown and soft, 20 to 25 minutes. Pull the pan from the heat and let the garlic cool in the oil. Store covered in the refrigerator for up to 2 weeks.

SOURCES

When I started cooking at Woodfire Grill, it hit home that sourcing ingredients is equally as important as cooking skills and cooking techniques. The restaurant's first chef, Michael Tuohy, dedicated a remarkable amount of time to finding the best products. Most cooks would say, "I need to buy some free-range chicken; where is the closest place?" Michael took a different approach. He would get samples of 10 free-range birds, salt and cook each one the same way, and then taste them. He placed the labels underneath the plates and we would try each chicken and pick the best. Only then would Michael flip over the plate to reveal where the chicken came from. We did this time after time with every ingredient. It was an exhaustive process, but it taught me to be more discerning about what ingredients I choose. It teaches you that not every ingredient is the same even though it has the same name or the same label or comes from the same region. Ingredients can be vastly different from one another, depending on breed, genetics, soil and climate, farming and ranching techniques, and processing techniques. Take olive oil, for example. You can buy olive oil at the grocery store that costs $3 or $33. If you're not wildly educated about the subtleties between different types of olive oil, you say, "What the hell is the difference? Why should I spend $30 more for a bottle of oil?" But caring about quality begins a lifelong process of decoding product labels, understanding how various ingredients are processed, and asking food producers the right questions.

We could write an entire book on this subject, but here are some basic questions to ask about any product.

Caring about quality begins a lifelong process of decoding product labels, understanding how various ingredients are processed, and asking food producers the right questions.

← WES SWANCY FROM RIVERVIEW FARM

What is the ingredient's origin? Knowing where food comes from helps you determine its quality. For instance, smoked paprika is a particular product that originated in the rural farmland of Spain. If you know that that's where it's from, you know that buying a brand from that place will more than likely give you a good product. If you know that saffron grows in North Africa and France, buying saffron from those areas will give you a good product. Or look at tahini. I prefer tahini from Lebanon. The Lebanese are crazy about tahini, so they have more discerning quality control than some other countries. You can always buy ground-up sesame seeds from America, but knowing the Lebanese obsession with tahini, you'll get better quality if you buy Lebanese. In the case of produce, look for produce that advertises its origin, whether at a farmer's market or in a grocery store. If the purveyor is proud enough of the origin to advertise where the produce came from, it's a fair sign that the

quality is good. It's not about bragging rights that you bought from such and such a farm. It's about accountability, so you have some assurance that you're buying good-quality ingredients.

How has the ingredient been grown or raised? There are a lot of ingredient labels and buzzwords like *organic, natural, biodynamic, grass-fed, pasture-raised, cage-free,* and so forth. Most people know loosely what *organic* and *sustainable* mean. But learning about them on a deeper level is something you could spend a lifetime doing. What's often neglected is that every farmer has a different set of priorities about what's most important in terms of growing practices. Some favor local over organic. Others vice versa. As a chef, I believe that buying locally is more important than buying organically. For one, organic is not just a methodology. It's a label and a sales pitch. A vast number of growers support practices that are as good as, or in many cases better than, what's required to get

The absolute best way to source any ingredient is to have a conversation with the person who grew it. That's why farmer's markets are so great. The farmers stand across the table from you, and if you pick up a pepper, you can ask the farmer about it. And that's exactly what you should do. Farmers appreciate you taking an interest in their food. Ask them, "How do you like this variety?"

↗ CHARLOTTE SWANCY FROM RIVERVIEW FARM

← NICHOLAS DONCK FROM CRYSTAL ORGANIC FARM

produce certified and labeled organic. But many of these growers operate farms that are too small to spend $10,000 on getting certified organic, especially if they only produce $20,000 of product a year. That's why talking to farmers at farmer's markets is so important. Ask them about what they do, how they grow their produce or raise their animals. Actual farming practices are much more important than labels.

Is the ingredient in its original state? Or has it been highly modified? Going back to the olive oil example, one of the big differences among olive oils is purity. Paying $33 for a bottle of olive oil usually gets you oil from a specific farm that uses a specific variety of olive and extracts the oil using traditional methods that yield the purest possible extra-virgin oil. For $3 a bottle, you might get the dregs from a mix of olives from a mix of farms. It pays to ask yourself, "How pure is it?" It's almost always best to buy ingredients in their most original state rather than buying those that are heavily modified or processed. Even if you don't know the exact processing steps, buying foods in their original state allows you to do the processing yourself as a cook. You make the decisions. I'd much rather buy carrots intact, covered in dirt, than carrots washed and trimmed down and bagged. You might think, "Why would I want to buy something that requires more work and doesn't look as nice?" Because the look of ingredients can be deceiving. If the producer cuts off the bad parts during processing, the consumer doesn't know there were bad parts of the produce to begin with. Plus, when produce comes completely scrubbed and washed, its shelf life is shorter. Generally speaking, it's better to buy something in its most natural form.

The absolute best way to source any ingredient is to have a conversation with the person who grew it. That's why farmer's markets are so great. The farmers stand across the table from you, and if you pick up a pepper, you can ask the farmer about it. And that's exactly what you should do. Farmers appreciate you taking an interest in their food. Ask them, "How do you like this variety?" They'll be candid and tell you: "The eggplants didn't come in so great this year. It was a dry season." No matter what the response is, you'll learn something about the ingredient you're about to buy and eat. The same goes for farmers who sell meat. They will share with you every tiny detail about how they raise and process the animals. You just have to ask them.

I've spent a lot of time nurturing relationships with farmers so that I can get the best possible ingredients. Only when the ingredients come in do I start planning and writing the menus for Wood-fire Grill. The recipes in this book encourage you to do the same thing—to get out and see food in its raw state, buy the best ingredients, and only then flip through the recipes to see what dishes the food can be used in. The whole point is of this book, and my cooking in general, is to showcase great ingredients.

Most of my recipes are approachable and down to earth. There are only half a dozen things in this entire book you have to mail-order, but I've specified those ingredients because they are worth the effort. I don't encourage you to mail-order asparagus from Peru. But AOC-certified Espelette pepper direct from France might just lead to a food epiphany. When you taste a product that is the pinnacle of its kind, one that you just can't get anywhere else, you often have this taste awakening, this experience where you say, "Oh my god, this is delicious!" And that could be the very ingredient that makes the entire dish successful.

Look at a football team, for example. You could have an amazing team, great coaching, great offense, killer defense, and a very cohesive game. But your team could be a failure if you forget the little things. If you haven't bothered to get a good kicker, you can lose game after game after game. It's a tiny piece of the puzzle, like salt or olive oil in cooking, and it seems like you might be able to get away with something that's just average instead of excellent. But you can't. If you buy great produce, great meat, high-quality vinegar, and the best olive oil but then put those ingredients in a cheap, thin aluminum pan on your stovetop and burn the shit out of everything, what is the point? This doesn't mean that everything in your kitchen has to be expensive. Quality comes at every price level. It just means that good cooking starts with good ingredients and good equipment. Buy the best that you can, and that one simple move will improve the taste of your cooking.

Local, Sustainable Products Nationwide

www.localharvest.org
Type in a zip code and find farms and farmer's markets in your area.

www.eatwild.com
A map of natural, grass-fed, and pastured pork, beef, lamb, poultry, eggs, and milk produced in your area. Click on your state and find a farmer close to you.

www.seafoodwatch.com
Download a Pocket Guide that shows you the best choices for sustainable seafood in your area.

Ingredients

PRODUCE

Fresh wild mushrooms

Earthy Delights
1161 East Clark Road, Suite 260
DeWitt, Michigan 48820
800-367-4709
www.earthy.com

MEAT, POULTRY, AND SEAFOOD

Beef

Painted Hills Natural Beef
P.O. Box 245
Fossil, Oregon 97830
877-763-2333
www.paintedhillsnaturalbeef.com

White Oak Pastures
P.O. Box 98
Bluffton, GA 39824
229-641-2081
www.whiteoakpastures.com

Canadian bacon

The Real Canadian Bacon Company
55 East Long Lake Road
Troy, Michigan 48085
866-BACON-01 (866-222-6601)
www.realcanadianbacon.com

Country ham, smoked ham hocks, and American bacon

Benton's Smoky Mountain Country Hams
2603 Highway 411 North
Madisonville, Tennessee 37354
423-442-5003
www.bentonscountryhams2.com

Nueske's
203 North Genesee Street
Wittenberg, Wisconsin 54499
800-392-2266
www.nueskes.com

Georgia white shrimp

Walter's Caviar & Seafood
P.O. Box 263
Darien, Georgia 31305
912-437-6560
www.georgiaseafood.com

Hog casings and curing salt

The Sausage Maker, Inc.
1500 Clinton Street, Building 123
Buffalo, New York 14206
888-490-8525
www.sausagemaker.com

Poulet Rouge

Joyce Foods
4787 Kinnamon Road
Winston-Salem,
North Carolina 27103
336-766-9900
www.joycefoods.com

Pickles, Grains, and Grocery

Green peanuts

Hardy Farms Peanuts
Route 2, P.O. Box 2120
Hawkinsville, Georgia 31036
888-368-NUTS (888-368-6887)
www.hardyfarmspeanuts.com

Grits, farro, Carolina Gold rice, and stone-cut oats

Anson Mills
1922-C Gervais Street
Columbia, South Carolina 2920
803-467-4122
www.ansonmills.com

Indian green chile pickles and turmeric pickles

Anything Indian
5500 Friendship Boulevard
Chevy Chase, Maryland 20815
240-245-0891
www.anythingindian.com

Marcona almonds and piquillo peppers

La Tienda
3601 La Grange Parkway
Toano, Virginia 23168
800-710-4304
www.tienda.com

Tutto Calabria pickled chiles and King's Hawaiian Buns

www.amazon.com

Grandma Utz chips

Utz Quality Foods, Inc.
900 High Street
Hanover, Pennsylvania 17331
800-367-7629
www.utzsnacks.com

Oil, Vinegar, Chiles, and Spices

Espelette pepper

La Cucina Rustica
1800 West Hawthorne Lane
Suite 203
West Chicago, Illinois 60185
800-796-0116
www.cybercucina.com

Fennel pollen

Pollen Ranch
P.O. Box 44090
Lemon Cove, California 93291
800-821-5989
www.pollenranch.com

Finishing-quality olive oil, herb oil, lemon olive oil, pumpkin seed oil, Calogiuri lemon olive oil, Arbequina olive oil from chile, and citrus vinegar

Atlanta Foods International
255 Spring St. SW
Atlanta, Georgia 30303
800-966-6172
www.atlantafoods.com

Hatch chiles, New Mexico green and red chile powder

Hatch Chile Express
P.O. Box 350
Hatch, New Mexico 87937
800-292-4454
www.hatch-chile.com

Noble XO vinegar, sturgeon, Pacific halibut, and salmon

Mikuni Wild Harvest
866-862-9866
www.mikuni.myshopify.com

Smoked serrano chile powder

Williams-Sonoma
877-812-6235
www.williams-sonoma.com

Za'atar

Penzeys Spices
12001 West Capitol Drive
Wauwatosa, Wisconsin 53222
800-741-7787
www.penzeys.com

SAUCES AND SYRUPS

Arthur Bryant's Barbeque Sauce

Arthur Bryant's Barbeque
Brooklyn Barbeque Corporation
1727 Brooklyn
Kansas City, Missouri 64127
913-788-7500
www.arthurbryantsbbq.com

BLiS maple syrups

BLiS
3759 Broadmoor Avenue SE
Grand Rapids, Michigan 49512
616-942-7545
www.blisgourmet.com

Ghost pepper sauce

Dave's Gourmet, Inc.
2000 McKinnon Avenue
Building 428, #5
San Francisco, California 94124
800-758-0372
www.davesgourmet.com

Lebanese tahini and pomegranate molasses

Bakkal International Foods
5690 Roswell Road NE #100,
Sandy Springs, Georgia 30342
404-847-9942
www.bakkalinternational.com

Sauer's mustard and Duke's mayonnaise

The C.F. Sauer Company
2000 West Broad Street
Richmond, Virginia 23220
800-688-5676
www.cfsauer.com
www.dukesmayo.com

Sriracha and sambal olek

Hotsauce.com
P.O. Box 801933
Miami, Florida 33280
877-999-7282
www.hotsauce.com

Veal demi-glace

Bonewerks Culinarte
808 Packerland Drive
Green Bay, Wisconsin 54303
800-542-3032
www.bonewerksculinarte.com

White soy sauce

Dean & Deluca
4115 East Harry
Wichita, Kansas 67218
800-221-7714
www.deandeluca.com

Equipment

All-Clad cookware, Le Creuset cookware, mandolines, Microplane zesters, sieves, sizzle plates, stand mixers, waffle irons, Y-peelers, and more

The Cook's Warehouse
1544 Piedmont Road, Suite 403-R
Atlanta, Georgia 30324
866-890-5962
www.cookswarehouse.com

Lodge cast-iron cookware

Lodge Manufacturing Company
423-837-7181
www.lodgemfg.com

Sausage-making equipment and supplies

The Sausage Maker, Inc.
1500 Clinton Street
Building 123
Buffalo, New York 14206
888-490-8525
www.sausagemaker.com

Seasonal Recipe Index

I was nervous the first time I cooked dinner at the James Beard House in New York City. Should I buy everything in New York? Or bring all my ingredients with me? I settled in the middle and decided to buy the really perishable ingredients in New York but bring everything else with me. I wrote the dinner menu like I always write menus—based on seasonal ingredients. It was the end of June, and we had beautiful field peas in Atlanta that I planned to serve with fried pigs' head. The beets were coming up nice and big at that time, and I resolved to serve chunky slabs of them with roasted venison. But when I got to New York to buy the perishable ingredients, there weren't any field peas at the farmer's markets. It was too early in the season. Plus, the beets were tiny instead of big because it was early in the beet season in New York. I didn't freak out. I used what they had. I served green beans in place of field peas with the pigs' head and changed the look of the venison dish to use New York's smaller beets instead of Atlanta's big ones.

That's the thing to remember about seasonality: My late spring and a New York late spring and a Washington State late spring all occur at different times. The idea of eating seasonally is 100 percent dependent on eating local. Seasons don't neatly arrange themselves around the earth into four distinct categories of winter, spring, summer, and fall with clear start and end times. I've had Decembers in Atlanta with temperatures in the high sixties one week and the low thirties the next. That drastically changes what ingredients become available in markets. Some plants do well in changing weather; others don't. Turnips, for instance, are pretty hardy and grow in lots of weather conditions. Here in the South, I get turnips in the spring and then again in the fall. The marinated turnip salad (page 162) is perfect in both of those seasons. That salad is not just a "spring" dish or a "fall" dish.

Sure, some plants, like asparagus and strawberries, have a well-defined season. They grow best in the spring and early summer in the South. But other plants can grow two, three, or four times a year. You can't always say, "This is a winter fruit" or "That's a summer vegetable." When you're planning menus and buying and cooking ingredients, keep in mind that seasons blend together. There will be seasonal crossover. There will be multiple seasons for some ingredients. Cooking with the seasons means paying attention to what's coming up when. That's part of the fun of cooking and eating in the first place. When sweet corn comes around in the summer, it's exciting every single year. It gives you something to look forward to in the spring and something to reflect back on in the winter. That kind of pleasure is hard to get when you shop at a supermarket that makes every ingredient available all year long. Do you really crave strawberries in December? When you shop at farmer's markets, your mouth starts watering in late spring just thinking about the first plump, juicy strawberries of the season. If you really want to understand seasonality and cook with the seasons, shop at farmer's markets. If it's at the farmer's market, it's in season.

I developed all of the recipes in this book over the course of a year using seasonal ingredients that were available during any given month. That's just the way I cook. The list that follows shows you what recipes were developed in what season of the year. To cook seasonally, choose recipes within each season at different times of year. The big caveat is that the list is based on seasons I experience in the Southern United States. Late spring may come three to four weeks later in your neck of the woods and might coincide with my early summer. Or you might find that carrots come up in both the spring and fall in your part of the world. Don't take this list as gospel. It's just a general guide. The most important thing is to eat and cook with the seasons by buying ingredients that are growing well near you at any given time of year.

The idea of eating seasonally is 100 percent dependent on eating local.

Metric Conversions and Equivalents

Metric Conversion Formulas

To Convert	Multiply
Ounces to grams	Ounces by 28.35
Pounds to kilograms	Pounds by .454
Teaspoons to milliliters	Teaspoons by 4.93
Tablespoons to milliliters	Tablespoons by 14.79
Fluid ounces to milliliters	Fluid ounces by 29.57
Cups to milliliters	Cups by 236.59
Cups to liters	Cups by .236
Pints to liters	Pints by .473
Quarts to liters	Quarts by .946
Gallons to liters	Gallons by 3.785
Inches to centimeters	Inches by 2.54

Approximate Metric Equivalents

Volume

¼ teaspoon	1 milliliter
½ teaspoon	2.5 milliliters
¾ teaspoon	4 milliliters
1 teaspoon	5 milliliters
1¼ teaspoons	6 milliliters
1½ teaspoons	7.5 milliliters
1¾ teaspoons	8.5 milliliters
2 teaspoons	10 milliliters
1 tablespoon (½ fluid ounce)	15 milliliters
2 tablespoons (1 fluid ounce)	30 milliliters
¼ cup	60 milliliters
⅓ cup	80 milliliters
½ cup (4 fluid ounces)	120 milliliters
⅔ cup	160 milliliters
¾ cup	180 milliliters
1 cup (8 fluid ounces)	240 milliliters
1¼ cups	300 milliliters
1½ cups (12 fluid ounces)	360 milliliters
1⅔ cups	400 milliliters
2 cups (1 pint)	460 milliliters
3 cups	700 milliliters
4 cups (1 quart)	0.95 liter
1 quart plus ¼ cup	1 liter
4 quarts (1 gallon)	3.8 liters

Approximate Metric Equivalents continued

Weight

¼ ounce	7 grams
½ ounce	14 grams
¾ ounce	21 grams
1 ounce	28 grams
1¼ ounces	35 grams
1½ ounces	42.5 grams
1⅔ ounces	45 grams
2 ounces	57 grams
3 ounces	85 grams
4 ounces (¼ pound)	113 grams
5 ounces	142 grams
6 ounces	170 grams
7 ounces	198 grams
8 ounces (½ pound)	227 grams
16 ounces (1 pound)	454 grams
35.25 ounces (2.2 pounds)	1 kilogram

Length

⅛ inch	3 millimeters
¼ inch	6 millimeters
½ inch	1¼ centimeters
1 inch	2½ centimeters
2 inches	5 centimeters
2½ inches	6 centimeters
4 inches	10 centimeters
5 inches	13 centimeters
6 inches	15¼ centimeters
12 inches (1 foot)	30 centimeters

Oven Temperatures

To convert Fahrenheit to Celsius, subtract 32 from Fahrenheit, multiply the result by 5, then divide by 9.

DESCRIPTION	FAHRENHEIT	CELSIUS	BRITISH GAS MARK
Very cool	200°	95°	0
Very cool	225°	110°	¼
Very cool	250°	120°	½
Cool	275°	135°	1
Cool	300°	150°	2
Warm	325°	165°	3
Moderate	350°	175°	4
Moderately hot	375°	190°	5
Fairly hot	400°	200°	6
Hot	425°	220°	7
Very hot	450°	230°	8
Very hot	475°	245°	9

Common Ingredients and Their Approximate Equivalents

1 cup uncooked white rice = 185 grams

1 cup all-purpose flour = 140 grams

1 stick butter (4 ounces • ½ cup • 8 tablespoons) = 110 grams

1 cup butter (8 ounces • 2 sticks • 16 tablespoons) = 220 grams

1 cup brown sugar, firmly packed = 225 grams

1 cup granulated sugar = 200 grams

Information compiled from a variety of sources, including *Recipes into Type* by Joan Whitman and Dolores Simon (Newton, MA: Biscuit Books, 2000); *The New Food Lover's Companion* by Sharon Tyler Herbst (Hauppauge, NY: Barron's, 1995); and *Rosemary Brown's Big Kitchen Instruction Book* (Kansas City, MO: Andrews McMeel, 1998).

ACKNOWLEDGMENTS

Valerie Combs, the light of my life, the greatest gift that has ever been given to me, the one who in her virtue makes me believe that I can become a better man. She inspires me every day and this book is the fruit of that inspiration.

E.J. Hodgkinson, my chef de cuisine at Woodfire Grill and general right hand man. He woke up every morning way before dawn to come in and help me make this book what it is. Some of the recipes belong to him, but all of them were made possible because of his unending dedication and loyalty. I couldn't do it without him.

Cathy and Kevin Gillespie, my parents and longtime Chef Kevin devotees. They have always stood behind me and believed that my dreams would all one day come true. Without your support, none of this would have ever become a reality.

Geneva Gillespie and Coylene Higgins, my grandmothers, and still the best cooks I know. Many of these recipes are simply my version of something I learned from them. They taught me to love food and to believe in the power food possessed. It always brought our family together and my hope is that that tradition can continue from these pages.

Gena Berry, for being the one who spent endless hours documenting my dishes and then turning them into something that everyone could understand and reproduce. If it had been left up to me alone I fear this book would probably have been completely unusable. Thankfully, now it won't be.

Nicolas Quiñones, Bernard Moussa, Steve McConnell, and the staff of Woodfire Grill—without my business partners, sous chef, and dedicated staff this book could never have come to life. They kept the restaurant along its course many nights when I was exhausted and needed a break. Thank you for believing in this dream with me.

Dave Joachim was tasked with making all of my insane ramblings and general musings on life into a book that people would want to read, and not prompt them to commit me to an asylum. As impossible as this may have seemed at times, it was obviously a success. For this I am most grateful.

Angie Mosier is the genius behind all of the breathtaking photography in this book. As a fellow Southerner, I knew that she was the only person who could capture the story that existed on the other side of the lens. I believe that the beauty of both the world I live in and the food that I love leapt out from every page, and it's Angie's talent that makes that the case.

Rodrigo Corral, Noah Armstrong, and the crew at Rodrigo Corral Designs deserve a tremendous amount of credit for creating such a beautiful book. I wanted so badly to know that this work was designed with the same love and care as the recipes that appear within it; obviously my dream has come true. Thank you.

To Kirsty Melville, Jean Lucas, and the extensive team at Andrews McMeel. These amazing individuals have worked a very long time to make my dream of writing a book possible. They have believed in this project from the start, and even in times of madness, allowed me to make this the book that I wanted it to be. These words can never sum up the debt of gratitude I owe them. Thank you.

Lisa Ekus and all the staff at the Lisa Ekus group, these gals . . . and guy, are responsible for helping find our wonderful publishing company, Andrews McMeel, and being the catalyst to get this book into the works. These guys keep me busy and make it possible for me to spend time doing all the things I really love. Thank you.

Melissa Libby and the staff at Melissa Libby and Associates. Melissa began as my publicist and has grown over time into a role that combines part PR person, part Kevin wrangler, part therapist, and so much more. If she were not here I would lose all semblance of sanity I still have. Thank you for keeping me grounded.

To anyone whose name is not here, you all have known me long enough to know that I tend to be a bit spacey at times, but also that I never forget those who have supported me. I love you all.

INDEX